BODYSCAPE

Western art has long sought to find a perfect method of representing the body. With the loss of faith in the modernist profect, the perfect, straight, white body of modernism is now seen as fiction. But what sort of body will take its place? In *Bodyscape*, Nicholas Mirzoeff explores body images in visual culture, from revolutionary France to contemporary New York.

Mirzoeff's illuminating study engages with artists' use of different kinds of body images in painting, sculpture, photography and film. He shows the centrality of the body in the work of artists from da Vinci to Manet, from Paul Strand to Kiki Smith. Mirzoeff traces the many ways in which concerns about race, gender, sexuality, nation and technology are reflected in representations of the body and the body politic, from the paintings of David to the Vietnam Veterans memorial. He also considers figures of the Madonna, from Ingres to Picasso to Madonna the performer, and inscriptions of race on to the visual body, from documentary photography of the colonial Belgian Congo to the art of Jean Michel Basquiat.

Nicholas Mirzocff is Assistant Professor of Art History at the University of Wisconsin-Madison. He is the author of *Silent Poetry: Deafness, Sign and Visual Culture in Modern France*.

VISUAL CULTURES
Series Editor: Anthea Callen,
University of Warwick

BODYSCAPE

Art, modernity and the ideal figure

Nicholas Mirzoeff

London and New York

For Dan and Sacha

First published 1995
by Routledge
11 New Fetter Lane, London EC4P 4EE

Simultaneously published in the USA and Canada
by Routledge
29 West 35th Street, New York, NY 10001

© 1995 Nicholas Mirzoeff

Typeset in Goudy Old Style by
J&L Composition Ltd, Filey, North Yorkshire
Printed and bound in Great Britain by
Biddles Ltd, Guildford and King's Lynn.

British Library Cataloguing in Publication Data
Mirzoeff, Nicholas
Bodyscape. – (Visual Cultures Series)
I. Title II. Series
704.942

Library of Congress Cataloguing in Publication Data
A catalogue record for this book has been requested

ISBN 0–415–09800–9 (hbk)
ISBN 0–415–09801–7 (pbk)

CONTENTS

FIGURES

ACKNOWLEDGEMENTS

This book was written in dialogue with my students over the past seven years, so I'd like to thank all my classes at the University of Warwick, the University of California, Irvine and the University of Wisconsin, Madison. Special thanks to Anthea Callen who first suggested that I teach a course on the body and later commissioned this book for her series. Both actions are typical of her intellectual and personal generosity, rare qualities indeed in the modern academy. Rebecca Barden was a model editor, ably assisted by Tamsin Meddings and Sophie Powell. Thanks to Moira Taylor and Bill MacKeith for handling the production process with efficiency and skill. Anita Duquette of the Whitney Museum of American Art was generous in assisting me to locate photographs. It is a cliché of acknowledgements to end by saying that without one's spouse the book never would have been written. In this case, it happens to be true. Kathleen Wilson provided a model of engaged scholarship in her own right, continually urged me to continue with this project when I lost enthusiasm for it and, most importantly, gives me a reason to do all this and more.

INTRODUCTION

Your body is not itself. Nor, I should add, is mine. It is under siege from the pharmaceutical, aerobic, dietetic, liposuctive, calorie-controlled, cybernetic world of postmodernism. The body has become a central concern both in academia and the wider culture, providing one of the few points of direct contact between these often divorced spheres. After the scandal over Robert Mapplethorpe's 1988 exhibition, the rise of new techniques of medical imaging of the body, and the dissolution of many of the norms of sexualized identity, the body question continues to gain urgency. Indeed, at all times of social uncertainty in the West, the representation of the body has been a key concern. The current moment is an amplification of the experience Walter Benjamin perceived in the generation who lived through the First World War: 'A generation that had gone to school on a horse-drawn street car now stood under the open sky in a countryside in which nothing remained unchanged but the clouds, and beneath those clouds, in a field of force of destructive torrents and explosions, was the tiny, fragile, human body' (Benjamin 1968: 84). Today the sky itself has changed, as a result of pollution, global warming and deforestation. Rapid and dramatic shifts in technology occur every year, not once a generation. In a world where change has become the norm, it seems inevitable that the body must change as well. Yet there is a sense, articulated by Benjamin, that if the body changes, then everything has been transformed. The body is at once the final point of resistance to the global imperatives of postmodernism and the first to be affected by them.

In recent years, there has been a rush to claim that such transformations have already occurred. Critical theorists have proclaimed the appearance of the 'body without organs', while technology enthusiasts have hailed computer environments as a new form of communication beyond the limits of the individual body. But it may be premature to announce such an epochal shift. The early Christian prophet Origen convinced his followers in the

1

second century AD that the human body was about to be destroyed by God, and ever since messianics have waited on hilltops for such dawns, only to be disappointed time and again. It is thus more than coincidence that announcements of the radical transformation of the body as we know it have the flavour of Christian eschatology. In the early excitement over postmodernism, it seemed that some such millennial moment was at hand. Now the postmodern seems rather less dazzling, and rather more prob-lematic. As the divisions between the developed and underdeveloped world sharpen, and as racism and nationalism grow daily, the philosopher Jean-François Lyotard's gnomic comment that 'there is a certain sorrow in the *zeitgeist*' once again appears closer to the spirit of the postmodern. In this sense, the postmodern is not so much beyond the modern as a crisis of the modern. The goals and methods of the modern period seem open to question as never before, causing some to seem transcended, others newly contemporary, and others simply beside the point. These tensions are exacerbated by the divide between the relatively few 'Western' nations which might be considered postmodern and the much larger group of nations for which modernism and modernizing are still key issues. The purpose of this book is to pursue a series of historical investigations into the visual representation of the body to see how much it has really changed.

For the body has been the principal subject of Western art since the Renaissance. At the same time, the body is also a central locus and meta-phor for understanding and exploring political change, in the broadest sense, whether as the body politic, in debates over the nature of sexuality, or sociobiology's claims to explain personality by heredity. The modern period may be characterized in this regard as having an awareness that the body is mutable, incomplete and altogether human. This alarming feeling of instability has led to numerous efforts to control the development of the physical body by promoting certain physical characteristics at the expense of others. The postmodern sense of the body is a realization of the costs and weaknesses of such Utopian projects. These related and interactive ideas explain both why the body has been such a focus of recent academic, popular and political attention, and why these discussions are of such importance. The experience of modernity in Western societies – that is to say, the development of mass industrial society – led artists, critics and intellectuals to form a critique of their own time that has come to be known as modernism. Within art history the identification of modernism with abstract techniques of representation seemed to characterize figura-tion as inherently conservative, bypassing and evading this sense of corporal dis-ease. In the 1980s, the repressed body returned as a central artistic question, for artists as diverse as the German Neo-Expressionists, feminists like Barbara Kruger, Kiki Smith and Cindy Sherman, and graffiti artists, such as Keith Haring and Jean-Michel Basquiat.

The body in art must be distinguished from the flesh and blood it seeks to imitate. In representation the body appears not as itself, but as a sign. It cannot but represent both itself and a range of metaphorical meanings, which the artist cannot fully control, but only seeks to limit by the use of context, framing and style. This complex of signs is what I shall call the bodyscape. At the same time, the corporal sign has very real effects upon the physical body, especially in regard to determining what is held to be 'normal'. Furthermore, each physical body forms an individual whole, but it may represent many bodies and have a role in many different technologies. From Leonardo da Vinci's *Mona Lisa* (1503–6) to Marcel Duchamp's *Nude Descending a Staircase* (1912), Western art has sought to find one perfect method of representing the human body, in order to overcome the weaknesses of the physical body. The failure of visual culture to achieve this task has engendered a palpable sense of dis-ease about the bodyscape.

In an effort to deny this failure of representation, Western visual culture has evolved several icons to represent the perfect body, whether spiritual or political, which can only be known as visual representations. The body politic of the early modern absolutist monarchies and the modern state has achieved plenitude only as visual representation, from the portrait of the king to the Vietnam Veterans Memorial. Equally, the mother of Jesus, an obscure figure who rated only four mentions in the Gospels, became the Virgin Mary through the transmission and dissemination of the Madonna icon. This process, in which the imperfect body is made whole in its representation, has been extended so that certain bodies have become the subject of a discursive inscription so thorough that they are invisible in any other way. This overwriting has rendered the body of the Jew, the African and others as 'visibly' different, confirming the perfection of the Western subject by this 'self-evident' difference of race. These themes form the subject of this book, which contributes to the genealogy of the (post)-modern body image from the Enlightenment to the present.

In these dog-days of postmodernism, it is questionable not only whether the body may serve as a representation of wider ideals, but whether any representation can be more than narrowly effective. It has become a commonplace to assert that there is a clear divide between the modern, single body and the postmodern fragmented body. I shall argue, however, that this opposition depends on a restricted interpretation of modernism in order to render an equally restricted view of the postmodern. In place of a linear narrative which opposes a unitary, universal, Enlightenment body to its supposed recent fragmentation under the duress of late capitalism, it may be more fruitful to pursue the idea that the modern body of the Enlightenment was both fragmented and universal. The seeming continuity of this formal opposition was none the less attended by a range of cultural and political meanings in different times and places. The tension between these different but co-existing modes of representing the body was a central element in the transformation of modern culture. This is not to suggest, however, that a dialectic in the Marxist sense operated within the body, which has now come to a synthesis in the postmodern period. Rather, it is to perceive the postmodern as in the first instance a revaluation of the modern. When 'postmodern' ideas or practices are observed in the modern or early modern periods, this is not an indication that, like the poor, the postmodern has always been with us, but that the postmodern reading of the modern is now sufficiently flexible to incorporate such elements into its story, which would previously have been repressed or ignored. Some of the most favoured sources for contemporary historians and critics, such as the travel narrative, the medical textbook, the photograph, or the courtesy manual, were simply not regarded as worthy of study until recent times. As the interpretation of the modern becomes more complex, nuanced and hybrid, many of the old interpretive certainties have disappeared – the rise of the proletariat, the triumph of abstraction, the apogee of the modernist novel, and so on. It may be that, despite its deceptively fashionable clothing, the rise and fall of the modern body is simply among the last of these grand narratives to wither away.

THE BODY BATTLE

While it is clear that, in the words of Barbara Kruger's powerful photomontage, *Your body is a battleground* (Figure 1), the stakes and outcome of the struggle are not as straightforward as they are often presented. This picture has become widely known through its use on book covers and as a political poster. Kruger's work makes a profound impact through its combination of dramatic black and white photography, with text spelt out in white on red, using her distinctive signature fonts. Perhaps this very effectiveness has led to the subtlety of her work often being overlooked. Who is fighting over the body? And what are the stakes? The meaning of this work has appeared clear, since Kruger redesigned it to serve as a poster for an

Figure 1 Barbara Kruger, *Your body is a battleground* (1989), Eli Broad Family Foundation, Santa Monica. Courtesy of Mary Boone Gallery, New York.

abortion rights rally in Washington in 1989. The body in question was thus revealed to be female, and the battle was over reproductive rights. This reading of the poster is certainly correct, but it is not so clearly true of the original picture, which, on closer attention, is visibly designed to elude definitive interpretation. The assumption that the person addressed by the slogan 'Your Body is a Battleground' is female runs against the usual grain of Kruger's work. In such pieces as *Your Gaze Hits the Side of My Face*, the second person is taken to refer to a man. Kruger's play with her own previous work creates a sense of ambiguity as to the identity of the person addressed by her text. For the prevailing political culture in which Kruger works has suggested a female–female address on reproductive rights, while

5

her own work suggests a female–male conversation. Neither possibility can be excluded, but neither can be entirely correct.

The photograph behind the text gives rise to still further ambivalence. It is split down the middle, with a woman's face being shown in traditional, positive form on the left, but in negative on the right. The two halves seem to form one face, but there is nothing in the image to prove that both halves of the face were taken from the same woman. The alternating negative and positive images could have a number of meanings. It may be a play with the possibilities of the photographic image, a refusal of the objectivity that black and white photography presents. Or it may be an X-ray image of the woman's face. Or, more ominously still, it may refer to the flash of radiation that follows a nuclear explosion, a possibility enhanced by the battleground referred to in the text. The woman's appearance is far more typical of the 1950s than of 1980s New York, with her lipstick and carefully plucked eyebrows. The echo of nuclear nightmare equally seems to refer us back to the curious confluence of the Cold War and Abstract Expressionism. Kruger's deliberate intervention in superimposing her coloured text over the photographs makes it clear that the opposition between the two halves is not natural, but a photomontage. She disrupts all the predictable binary oppositions that might be made around her work, such as male/female, art/photography, Self/Other, modern/post-modern, and so on.

Kruger has assembled the face from fragments, making the intervention of the artist very clear. Her work can be contrasted with that of Robert Mapplethorpe, ironically enough, given the scandals that have been caused by his work. At the Cincinnati obscenity trial concerning the 1988 exhibition of Mapplethorpe's work entitled *The Perfect Moment*, numerous critics attested to the formal quality of his art, his use of conventions such as the Golden Mean, and his resolutely orthodox means of representation. At the time, many believed that this was simply a strategy to fool the jury into accepting his work as art. This attitude not only condescends to the jurors, who, as unqualified members of the general public, are presumed to be incapable of judging the value of a work of art, but misses an important insight into Mapplethorpe's work. Whereas Kruger sees the body as a contested and divided field, Mapplethorpe asserted the right of the male, black, gay body to stand for the Universal. Both deployed a self-conscious and disruptive strategy in their art practice, which has become a staple of interpretations of postmodernism. Their very different modes of address are in themselves symptomatic of the crisis in representation that has become a cliché of modern and postmodern times.

6

For there is always a history, even for our sense of dislocation from history. As the practice of quotation in postmodern photography has become transformed from a strategy to a style, the sense of these quotations can become lost (Solomon-Godeau 1991: 106). Kruger's use of citation is much more precisely motivated. The body is involved in struggles that are political but are also inescapably issues of representation. How can the body be shown? Whose body should be shown? What corporal practices are 'normal', hence fit to be seen, and which are 'deviant', and must be kept out of sight, off the scene, that is, *obscene* (Nead 1992). In these questions, the past insistently returns, asking similar questions, but in different form. A famous short story by Jorge-Luis Borges presented itself as a scholarly article evaluating the work of a fictional writer called Pierre Menard. His greatest achievement was held to be his word-for-word rewriting of Miguel Cervantes' *Don Quixote*, which Borges reinterprets to show that identical passages could have a very different meaning if written in the twentieth rather than the sixteenth century. Even seemingly identical works may not actually be the same in different places or at different times. Through the practice of citation, postmodern art questions the basis of a formalist interpretation of visual culture, dependent on concepts of the evolving pictorial tradition, and a constant, linear progression of styles.

THE BODY IN THEORY

The remarkable resurgence of art history in the last twenty years – associated with such figures as Svetlana Alpers, Mieke Bal, John Barell, Ann Bermingham, Norman Bryson, Anthea Callen, T.J. Clark, Tamar Garb, Rosalind Krauss, Stephen Melville, Lynda Nead, Fred Orton, Craig Owens, Marcia Pointon, Griselda Pollock, Irit Rogoff and many others – has marked a concerted attempt to place art history in dialogue with contemporary critical thought in the humanities and social sciences. The spread of interest in the visual representation of the body in particular has been spurred by feminist analyses of the female nude and the representation of sexuality (Pointon 1990 and Nead 1988). The sheer size of the subject is intimidating and, despite some important collections of essays (Adler and Pointon 1993), there has not yet been a survey of the representation of the modern body. This book, which undertakes that task, is none the less also in the essayistic tradition, as defined by the nineteenth-century poet and art critic Charles Baudelaire in 1846: 'Criticism should be partial, passionate, and political, that is to say done from an exclusive point of view, but from a point of view which opens the widest horizons' (Baudelaire 1990: 101). I aim to survey current debates, illuminate their development and possibilities and, in pursuing specific case studies, provide a basis for further investigations. Inevitably there are gaps in such an endeavour which does not claim or hope to be comprehensive. The visual material studied ranges from the canonical masterpieces of Poussin, Delacroix and Manet; to unknown archives of visual material, such as Herbert Lang's photographs from the Congo; and the work of contemporary artists such as Jean-Michel Basquiat, Lorna Simpson, and Cindy Sherman.

If there is less attention than is traditional to the canonical works of high modernism – although Gauguin, Picasso and Robert Morris are all discussed – that is partly because my intent is to envisage a history of visual culture which is not dominated by these over-familiar totems. Indeed, it may seem less than entirely coincidental that at the very moment that the white, heterosexual male body ceased to hold the standard of the Universal Ideal, the very question of the body's image was discarded by avant-garde art. The eclipse of figuration by abstraction in the aftermath of the Second World War may come to be seen as one episode among many, rather than as a definitive new direction. My purpose is not to denigrate modernism. But it is important that one particular form of representation, such as abstraction, should not continue to hold the mantle of being considered more 'radical' in both artistic and political terms than any other. While the partisans of abstraction have been loud in their denunciations of what they see as the reductiveness of social art history, they have been less quick to refute their own assumption that abstraction is inherently better than figuration. I will instead pursue the idea, encapsulated by Paul Gilroy, that 'much of what is identified as postmodern may have been foreshadowed, or prefigured, in the lineaments of modernity itself' (Gilroy 1993: 42). However, in order to perceive these interactions, it will be necessary to move away from the accustomed periodization, narrative and landmarks of modernism to create a far more fluid sense of modernity, one which dispenses with the notions of centres and margins, or avant-gardes and Classics, and instead creates chains of connection and interconnection. The narratives contained in the following chapters are improvisations on this theme.

There is no established history of representations of the body to be followed. Even if the subject were to be limited to the female nude, very different approaches have recently been taken to this now controversial topic. In part, this uncertainty marks the entry of art history into cultural studies. Cultural studies, the historical and theoretical approach to the culture of a particular period or society, has come a long way since its inception at the Birmingham Centre for Contemporary Cultural Studies in the 1970s. Divorced from its national context as an oppositional response to Thatcherism, cultural studies has become an international shorthand for the deliberately eclectic and hybrid intellectual practice of the present moment. Furthermore, intellectuals and academics have rallied to cultural studies as a place in which the politics of culture can still be addressed, in response to a resurgent formalism in both traditional and theoretical garb. Rather than offer overarching solutions to eternal questions, cultural studies takes particular problems within our own time and examines their history and genealogy.

The body has become a central topic in cultural studies for two reasons. First the Anglo-American academy has become strongly influenced by the work of Michel Foucault. Foucault reconceptualized the modern period in terms of the relation between institutions, individuals and discourse, that is to say, the possible conceptual range of a set of ideas. In this way, Foucault ineluctably connected power to knowledge, reversing many preconceptions along the way. *Discipline and Punish: The Birth of the Prison* (1977) showed that the abolition of public torture and execution was motivated less by increased humanity than by the aspirations of legislators and jurists to produce a more effective form of punishment. The discipline of the prison was closely related to that of the school, the barracks and the factory. All these institutions sought to produce what Foucault called the 'docile body'. In his *History of Sexuality* (1981), he extended this argument to the disciplining of sexuality, demonstrating that the Victorians did not repress sex and sexuality, as many had previously argued, but in fact made them the subject of an obsessive and extensive literature and practice. Together these texts describe the rise in the eighteenth century of a new notion of the subject, under the discipline of surveillance techniques, which Foucault termed 'a political technology of the body in which might be read a common history of power relations and object relations'. In a striking image, Foucault depicted this power as the panopticon devised by the English utilitarian Jeremy Bentham (1748–1832). The panopticon was a building constructed so that numerous inhabitants could be kept under surveillance by a few guardians, who were invisible to the inmates. Although no true panopticon was ever built, Foucault interpreted the panopticon as the model for that dense layer of discourse, which mediates and links the poles of subject and body. Later he was to call this force 'bio-power', as a testament to the centrality of the body in modern power networks. His work was both profoundly insightful and meticulously researched, and has caused a fundamental reconsideration of the evolution of modern society, which has led to the renewed scholarly interest in the history of the body.

His colleague Gilles Deleuze has, however, consistently emphasized that Foucault's intellectual achievement was possible precisely because the societies of discipline were coming to a close: 'The disciplines underwent a crisis to the benefit of new forces that were gradually instituted and which accelerated after World War II: a disciplinary society was what we no longer were, what we had ceased to be' (Deleuze 1992: 3). We are able to analyse the panopticon because we are no longer securely contained within it, or more precisely, because the panopticon is no longer the model of power. The result is not, however, a brave new world. Surveillance has changed its character, but it has scarcely disappeared. Many of the tasks in industry and commerce that formerly required a disciplinary control of the entire body are increasingly being performed by computers and robots. This change can be understood as the distance between Charlie Chaplin's physical struggle with the production line in his film *Modern Times* (1936) and the supremely efficient and superhuman androids in the *Terminator* (1984), *Alien* (1979), and *Star Trek: The Next Generation* (1993). Whereas Chaplin's body becomes so attuned to the rhythm of the assembly line that he wrenches everything he meets, the android renders the close discipline of the factory unnecessary by its remarkable adaptability and capacity for labour. The car manufacturers, who gave the name Fordism to the disciplined modern production line, have now found that it is more profitable to give the remaining human workers a greater degree of autonomy in the workplace. This freedom has, of course, very strictly controlled limits, but it marks the shift from a society of surveillance to what Deleuze calls the societies of control. Now, rather than being observed from without, we monitor and control our own bodies. We check each others' body fluids for possible contamination, measure our blood sugar count, and worry about our cholesterol levels.

Perhaps even more importantly, the world is no longer divided by secure geographical frontiers, demarcating the developed from the underdeveloped, the 'Free World' from the 'Communist Bloc', Europe from its Others, and so on. The geopolitics of the Cold War have been replaced by a fluid and indeterminate field of power relations, in which the nation state no longer plays the dominant role. Furthermore, the postcolonial world is no longer directly under the sway of the Western powers, producing a marked sense of dislocation among Western political elites and electorates alike. In the words of filmmaker Trinh Minh-ha: 'There is a

Third World in every First World, and a First World in every Third World'. In significant measure, this erosion of borders has been caused by the growing Brazilianization of the developed economies, separating a rich elite from an increasingly impoverished permanent underclass. As the world is no longer regulated by the treaties of Versailles, Trianon and Bretton Woods, it often seems to resemble earlier incarnations of history, were it not for the very significant difference that there are no colonies and no vast tracts of land 'out there' to be claimed and exploited.

The societies of control are less costly to administer and more effective than the repressive panopticon. But, as Foucault repeatedly emphasized, power is never simply repressive. It is exercised, not owned. That is not to say that there are no directions to power, nor that it is uncontrollable, but that each mode of power brings with it both new forms of resistance and new modes of possibility. It is possible for genuine gains in individual or social freedom to occur within a system of power. It is difficult to generalize about power in its different modes, but one observation seems worth venturing here. Systems of power are most susceptible to subversion and modulation in their earliest days of existence before it has become fully clear what changes have occured. If it is true that the present moment marks one such change, it is not surprising that the body, the prime subject of the society of discipline, should again be a central concern of governments, corporations and intellectuals. The body was and is a key site of that resistance provoked by any exercise of power. In this sense, the body can be seen as a point of resistance between Enlightenment modernism and postmodernism belonging wholly to neither and preventing the complete realization of any regime of power.

These analytical considerations have been thrown into sharp relief by the global crisis resulting from Acquired Immuno-Deficiency Syndrome, better known as AIDS. In June 1993, the World Health Organisation estimated that 14 million people worldwide have been infected with HIV, the virus which causes the conditions lumped together under the title AIDS. WHO predicts that between 30 and 40 million people will be infected by the year 2000. Indeed, by 1994 another 3 million people had been infected, bringing the total to 17 million. AIDS has so far resisted all efforts to find a cure. The spread of the epidemic has shaken Western faith in medicine, which until recently had seemed on the verge of conquering disease with the development of vaccinations and antibiotics. AIDS has often been compared to syphilis, which was widespread in Europe from the fifteenth century until the development of penicillin during the Second World War. In the nineteenth century, fears of syphilis were a major factor in the organization of bio-power recorded by Foucault. The peculiarities of HIV make it unlikely that any single cure for AIDS can be found to parallel the triumph of antibiotics over syphilis. Its long latency period has brought on an uneasy acceptance of the fact that, in the epidemiological universe, we are all connected. AIDS has eroded our trust in medicine, modern society's shining achievement. It has constructed new forms of imagining the body, in terms of T-cell counts and CD–4 clusters. In 1981, when the disease was identified, most of us were not aware that we had such a thing as an immune system. Now we are all only too conscious of our body as a defence mechanism against a hostile outside world, afraid that the worm may already be in the bud, and newly struck by the notion that a person is the sum of their experience. Above all, hundreds of thousands of people have died from the consequences of AIDS, including Michel Foucault.

My use of historical references and contexts, far from being a simple alternative to formalist approaches, raises new problems of framing, of discursivity, and of causality. For if it is evident that the representation of the body raises historical questions, it is far from obvious how those questions might be resolved. Art historians cannot simply continue to refer to historical sources as 'context' or 'background'. For the influence of theorists such as Hayden White, Joan Scott and Michel Foucault has led to a widespread revaluation of the practice of history writing, in which distinctions such as that between the subject of a work (for example, a series of paintings) and its context (information about contemporary events, pertinent either to the artist's life or the subject-matter of the works themselves) can only be seen as rhetorical strategies designed to ensure the continuation of a certain form of reading. These choices need to be reconsidered and directly addressed. A history of visual culture needs to organize its subject-matter around themes, rather than individuals; periods, rather than nation states; and to reconsider who and what should receive the focus of our attention. This entails a re-evaluation of the history of the discipline itself and it requires a new approach to art history writing. Such a history should not privilege any one form, medium, practioner or style. Instead, it seeks to understand the constitutive parameters of any discourse of visual representation, what is included and what must be excluded. It abandons once and for all the teleological histories that have dogged the history of visual culture for so long, under titles such as *The Rise of Modernism*, *The Triumph of the West* or *The Waking Dream of Photography*. It will, in short, strive to be a decentred history, that must work towards an understanding of the essential interconnectedness of culture. Rather than pursue the nation state model of art history that remains the basis for most art historical employment and curricula, it is time to study what Edward Said has called 'the map of interactions, the actual and often productive traffic occurring on a day-by-day, and even minute by minute basis among states, societies, groups, identities' (Said 1993: 20). Rather than presuppose an opposition between art, history and theory leading to a series of intellectual compromises, the artwork should be seen as the meeting place for all three, requiring a fluid and diverse approach to its interpretation that cannot be limited to formal, historical or theoretical methodologies but should seek to use them all as required.

WRESTLING WITH THE ANGELS

These tasks are often daunting. In a striking phrase, Stuart Hall has described the labour of working within cultural studies as 'wrestling with the angels' (Hall 1991: 280). His unusually poetic image is presumably based upon the Old Testament story of Jacob's all-night wrestling match with the archangel Gabriel. The Biblical account tells the story as follows:

> And when he saw that he prevailed not against him, he touched the hollow of his thigh; and the hollow of Jacob's thigh was out of joint, as he wrestled with him.
> And he said, Let me go, for the day breaketh. And he said, I will not let thee go, except thou bless me.
> And he said unto him, What is thy name? And he said, Jacob.
> And he said, Thy name shall be called no more Jacob, but Israel: for as a prince hast thou power with God and with men, and hast prevailed.

Curiously, the fresco, *Jacob Wrestling with the Angel* (1853–61) (Figure 2) by Eugène Delacroix (1798 1863), was the first representation of this scene in the long history of Western religious painting. On one wall of the Parisian chapel of St Sulpice he was commissioned to decorate, Delacroix created an image of the Biblical story to very modern ends. Delacroix's representation of the body in this work is a metonym for the interpretations pursued in this book. Obviously, the subject is a fight, giving another resonance to the phrase 'Your Body is a Battleground'. However, this a different battle from that envisaged by Barbara Kruger. What does it mean to fight an angel? Contemporary critics saw a number of possible meanings. For the pseudonymous Pharès, the *Jacob* was 'the combat of matter against the spirit' (Johnson 1989: 166). Others saw it as an allegory of social conflict, of man against his fate, or of Delacroix's own life. In all of these interpretations, the angel represents something more than just another body, and we

13

Figure 2 Eugène Delacroix, *Jacob Wrestling with the Angel* (1853–61),
Saint Sulplice, Paris. Lauros-Giraudon/Bridgeman Art Library.

are left with Jacob's struggle with himself, interpreted in various ways. The fight was long and damaging, for the wound inflicted by the angel is permanent, and Jacob thereafter walked with a limp. For all the taut musculature of Jacob's Classical frame, the angel prevails.

If we follow the story of Jacob and the angel, Hall's engagement with theory seems to produce a different and disabled mode of being. However, the encounter with the angel is also the beginning of Jacob's authority. He has become disabled in the sense that he is aware of the limits achievable by his body. In the first chapter of this book, I examine how this awareness has recently been denied by certain conservative critics in favour of a revival of the Classical body of the nineteenth century centred upon an exaltation of Greece at the expense of other ancient cultures, such as that of Egypt. Following Martin Bernal's critique of classical learning in *Black Athena* (1987), I demonstrate that the myth of the Corinthian Maid inventing painting in ancient Greece was deployed in the late eighteenth and nineteenth centuries as a means of excluding any other Mediterranean or African peoples from the history of art. This same myth has recently been re-examined by the philosopher Jacques Derrida, who has perceived a moment of blindness at the heart of drawing. Blindness has been a privileged figure in modern art criticism and I seek to ground this metaphor, and Derrida's interpretation of it, by interacting medical concepts of blindness with pictorial depictions of the blind from Nicolas Poussin to Robert Morris. Whereas *ancien régime* writers and artists were interested in the blind as different examples of the limited sensory capacities of the human being, modern medicine created a distinction between the normal sighted person and the pathological blind. However, the absolute distinction between the normal and the pathological was nuanced by distinctions created within the overarching categories. As a result, blindness came to be perceived as less damaging than other sensory deprivations, such as deafness. In the nineteenth century, blindness became associated with moral insight in a strikingly gendered fashion. Blindness was represented as natural and feminine, intimately connected with, and opposed to, the masculine quality of cultural insight. Derrida failed to question this modern construction of blindness. The perfect body envisaged by the Classical revival and the poststructuralist concatenation of blindness and insight thus depend upon essentialist concepts of the body, of race and gender resepectively. Such reliance upon essentialized corporal characteristics, despite the knowledge of the mutability of the body, generates the current sense of dis-ease relating to the bodyscape.

In order to compensate for the deficiencies of the actual body artists imagined various manifestations of the perfect body, which could only be fully known in visual representation. Delacroix devised *Jacob Wrestling with the Angel* during France's Second Republic (1848–52), which had overthrown the monarchy by popular insurrection in February 1848, only then bloodily to repress an uprising by the Parisian working-classes in June. In this unstable and unprecedented political situation, much artistic attention was paid to the question of representing the state (Clark 1973). Jacob and the angel represent two aspects of power, secular and divine. They are clearly distinguished from the ordinary mortals, such as Jacob's servants who are shown departing on the right. In the course of the struggle, Jacob ceases to be himself but becomes a doubled being, Jacob known as Israel. As a prince, Jacob now has two bodies, his own natural body and the body politic. Here the angel represents the undying body politic, whereas Jacob/Israel represents the natural body, which must eventually die and is already disabled. This mystical cohabitation of two bodies in the one person of the prince has a long history in the West, which is distinct from that of other civilizations. In the second chapter, I examine this history of this cohabitation from the absolutist monarchies of the seventeenth and eighteenth centuries to its transformation and reconceptualization during the French Revolution and Napoleon's Empire (1789–1815). The Neo-Classical figure of the Republic sought to engage its audience as part of its formal properties. This political and gendered notion of the witness to the monument, as opposed to the silent spectator, sets the Republican monument apart from later Classical representations of the body politic, despite their superficial similarities. In a brief excursus, I examine the use of the body politic in the Nazi sculpture of Arno Breker and the competing representations at the Vietnam Veterans Memorial to suggest that such tensions are still very much in force. None the less, the body politic is no longer a key issue due to the decline of the nation state.

In the third chapter, I examine the perfect body in the different context of the spiritually perfect form. This chapter analyses the redeployment of the Madonna icon, first developed in the Middle Ages and Renaissance, in the nineteenth and twentieth centuries. Like the angel, whose body was neither wholly human nor wholly divine, the figure of the Madonna was a pictorial icon representing a body that was both real and unreal. For Mary was both the human mother of Jesus and the divine Virgin Mary, whose perfection was declared by the Catholic Church in 1854. Ingres adapted Raphael's Madonna in order to create a typology of woman that was to influence both Picasso and the Hollywood screen goddesses. The body of the Madonna stood above the normal female body, which in turn was superior to that of the fallen woman. Thus the Madonna was not simply opposed to the prostitute in the nineteenth-century imagination, as Freud and his followers have claimed, but constituted two parts of a series in which race and class played central roles. Recent times have seen the Madonna turned on her head both by the singer Madonna in mass culture and by photographer Cindy Sherman in art spaces, only to return in the latest generation of emaciated supermodels. I have chosen to emphasize the Madonna and her angels as a corrective to the seeming obsession in nineteenth-century studies with prostitutes and commercial sex, not as an exercise in religious observance. This history demonstrates that even the Immaculate body of the Madonna was neither simply opposed to her Other, the fallen woman, nor beyond comparison to the everyday person. Even the bodies of angels and saints could not fully attain the standard of the Ideal, but contained elements of the hybrid, the interconnected and the fragmented.

The Western tradition represented by the Madonna and the body politic has been defined by nothing so much as its strenuous efforts to repel alien outsiders from membership of its club. The definition of the Other as wholly different from the Self was, of course, haunted by anxiety that difference was more apparent than real. It was therefore crucial that difference should not only be known but visible. In the modern period (1750–1945), the pseudo-science of 'race' dominated such efforts to visualize difference. It is important to say from the outset that biological 'race' is nothing more than a cultural construct, a discourse sustained by power, no matter what evidence can or cannot be found to support it (Gould 1981). In the final chapter, I consider two related aspects of the inscription of race on to the body. First I describe the 1909–15 expedition of the American Museum of Natural History to the Belgian Congo, the heart of darkness itself. The expedition leader Herbert Lang was an enthusiastic photographer, who sought to use the evidence of his camera to bolster his support for the notoriously brutal colonial regime in the Congo and to supply anthropological data in the search for scientific racism. Instead, his photographs were the ambivalent product of colonial mimicry, showing not the truth of imperialism, but an intersection between the colonizer and the colonized. By contrast, Jean-Michel Basquiat undertook to redeploy his art from the streets and clubs of 1980s New York to painting at the heart of whiteness, the art scene. He sought to explore the dependence of modern art upon a notion of racial difference in order for its works to signify. He further endeavoured to imagine ways of representing the body without signifying race. Basquiat looked for a new sense of identity in the culture of diaspora, even as the art world rewrote his story as the traditional rise and fall of an outsider. Both histories show at once the importance of race in the visual culture of the West and the ways in which, despite the strenuous efforts of many to the contrary, the result has been a hybrid creolization. Indeed, it is now necessary to refuse arbitrary distinctions between 'Western' and 'non-Western' culture and to focus instead on the manifold points of intersection and interaction between and among peoples and states.

The book thus pursues a form of historical narrative in which the first chapter takes an overview of the representation of the body and is followed by chapters which focus on specific instances of that discourse in the eighteenth, nineteenth, and twentieth centuries respectively. Each chapter is to a certain extent independent, with the intention that they might be used for teaching purposes, but the whole combines to form one possible narrative of the body's representation in the modern and postmodern period. In an epilogue, I discuss the postmodern revival of the Neo-Classical theory of 'the pregnant moment', the decisive incident in a narrative which was considered particularly suitable for history painting. The pregnant moment in a story – from the Bible, Classical or modern history – was that which best expressed both the dilemma involved for the actors and its resolution. The pregnant moment has now been reincarnated as the perfect moment. This phrase was of course the title of Robert Mapplethorpe's controversial posthumous exhibition, which was first accepted and then rejected by the Corcoran Gallery in Washington DC, and was later the subject of an obscenity trial in Cincinnati. I discuss the claim to universality made by Mapplethorpe's work. Race, sexuality and political engagement dominate these works, which, it is often argued, thus excludes them from being considered art in the proper sense. Even if Mapplethorpe's perfect moment can be excluded from the category of high art, it is by no means clear that the perfect moment is possible in more traditional media. The dis-ease caused by the bodyscape can now only be assuaged in a perfect moment encapsulated by a fleeting glimpse of bodily perfection, shown in slow motion replay. The representation of the body can now only be achieved in the replay of a split-second gesture or moment. In this moment, it is time finally to give a place to those who look at art, not as passive observers, but as active witnesses. The true crisis of the body is as much in its representation and the understanding of that representation, as in its substance, providing the motive force behind a transformation of representation which can as yet only be imagined.

1

BODYSCAPES

The discipline of art history rests on certain key assumptions, which are indispensable to its normal operations. One of these, presented to every student who ever takes an art history survey course, is the specific concern of this book, namely the thesis of the perfectly expressive human form. It is exemplified by the drawing of *Vitruvian Man* by Leonardo da Vinci (Figure 3), which has become one of the most reproduced and well-known images in Western art. The male figure is represented twice, once standing, the other with arms and legs extended. In this way, the proportions of this ideal body represent the dimensions of two perfect forms, the circle and the square. *Vitruvian Man* has become the expression of a belief in the perfect form of the human body that art enacts. In this image, the body and its image are not separate but uniquely together. The body functions, like the circle and the square, as a signifier that exactly expresses its signified. There is no excess, no unexplained dimension or activity, an idea which has recently gained a new currency in certain conservative circles within art history.

However, I shall work from the assumption that the tension between the imperfection of the body in itself and the idealized body in representation is a condition of its representation. The sense of dis-ease which results from such awareness has motivated both art practice and criticism of representations of the body; or bodyscapes, as I shall call them. In his late work, *Civilization and Its Discontents*, Sigmund Freud argued that all the sources of unhappiness originate outside the sphere of the ego, which believes itself to be secure and distinct from the 'outside'. The first point of that outside, and the first cause of unhappiness, is the body: 'We shall never completely master nature; and our bodily organism, itself a part of that nature, will always remain a transient structure with a limited capacity for adaptation and achievement' (Freud 1961: 33). The first source of

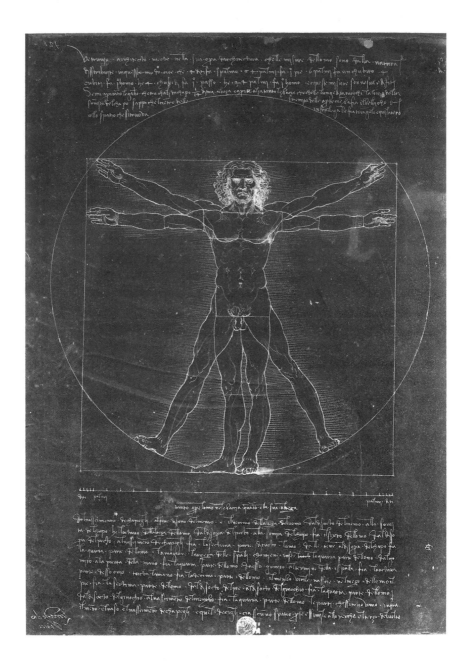

Figure 3 Leonardo da Vinci, *Vitruvian Man*, Galleria dell'Accademia, Venice/
Bridgeman Art Library.

bodily dis-ease is its inevitable insufficiency. In her definition of the body, Elizabeth Grosz expands upon Freud's notion:

> By *body* I understand a concrete, material, animate organization of flesh, organs, nerves, muscles, and skeletal structure which are given a unity, cohesiveness, and organization only through their physical and social inscription as the surface and raw materials of an integrated and cohesive totality. The body is, so to speak, organically/biologically/naturally 'incomplete'; it is indeterminate, amorphous, a series of unco-ordinated potentialities which require social triggering, ordering, and long term 'administration.'
>
> (Grosz 1992: 243)

Representations of the body are one means of seeking to complete this inevitably disjunctured entity. The coherence of the represented body is, however, constantly undermined by the very incompleteness these images seek to overcome. The body is the object of whose materiality we are most certain, but the undefinable potential of that inevitably incomplete materiality remains a constant source of unease. In this sense, the body is conceived less as an object than as an area, which gives us a strong sense both of location and dislocation, as the philosopher Jean-Luc Nancy observes:

> Bodies are not 'full', of filled space (space is always full): they are *open* space, that is to say in one sense, space that is properly *spacious* rather than spatial, or that which one could perhaps call *place*. Bodies are places of existence, and there is no existence without place, without *there*, without a 'here', a 'here it is' [*voici*] for the *this* [*ceci*]. The body-space is neither full, nor empty, there is no outside nor inside, any more than there are no parts, no totality, no functions, no finality.
>
> (Nancy 1992: 16)

The impulse to represent the body in visual culture is located within these contradictions. The dimensions, sources and history of this compulsion to represent the body form the ground for this book.

BODY FRAGMENTS VERSUS UNIVERSAL FORMS

Leonardo himself did not believe that one body alone could signify perfectly without outside assistance, and knew that his natural figure of Man needed to be completed and supplemented with artificial techniques of the body. For example, in describing how to represent gesture, he advised artists to imitate the sign language of the deaf:

> The forms of men must have attitudes appropriate to the activities that they engage in, so that when you see them you will understand what they think or say.

21

> This can be done by copying the motions of the dumb, who speak with movements of their hands and eyes and eyebrows and their whole person, in their desire to express that which is in their minds. Do not laugh at me because I propose a teacher without speech to you, who is to teach you an art which he does not know himself, for he will teach you better through facts than will all the other masters through words.[1]
>
> (Leonardo 1956: 105)

Leonardo knew that the visual arts of his day were inevitably silent, and that the forms of the body he depicted in his work did not necessarily create an intelligible story on their own. He thus used the technique of sign language in order to overcome the insufficiency of his representations of the body. It requires, in other words, an assembly of various fragments of bodily attributes to create one functioning bodyscape – even Vitruvian Man has a double. He might even be deaf.

In the last ten years, however, there has been a return in art history and criticism towards a Classical ideal of the body. Undoubtedly, part of the motivation of this move has been a desire to escape the seeming cynicism of the contemporary moment, a belief that everything has been done before. Rather than attend to the irony inherent in the postmodern practice of citation, conservative critics have taken this parodic and humorous strategy as the literal expression of a culture without ideas. In the words of British critic Peter Fuller, founding editor of the influential journal *Modern Painters*, there is 'a prevailing tendency towards general anaesthesia'. Needless to say, Fuller and his fellow travellers are exempt from this charge, and are alone able to perceive the damage being done by the philistines. *Modern Painters* under Fuller was well designed and presented, with an acute sense for publicity, and combined a certain 'common sense' hostility to contemporary art with a voguish British triumphalism. Unlike many conservative critiques of contemporary art, however, Fuller was not simply against art, but stood for a clear and increasingly influential position. Until his early death in 1992, Fuller embodied the art historical direction of what Stuart Hall has called 'The Great Moving Right Show', incarnated by the Thatcher government. In the late 1970s Fuller challenged John Berger for the role of leading Marxist art critic, only at once to undergo a crisis of committment and to reemerge, like his model John Ruskin, as a Tory of the old school. He now believed that conservatism meant an opposition to all things modern, whether political or artistic, and a defence of tradition. Fuller was as opposed to Margaret Thatcher, whom he saw as a radical, as he was to his one-time colleagues on the Left. He uniquely compared the Marxist John Berger and Tory cabinet minister Norman Tebbit as similarly anaesthetic critics. Fuller equated Tebbit's comparison of tabloid newspaper pin-ups with old master painting and Berger's discussion of the nude in *Ways of Seeing* (1972).[2]

Fuller pursued a very English and very corporeal line in his conversion to what he called moral criticism. In an earlier flirtation with pyschoanalysis, Fuller rediscovered the human figure as a means of reviving the arts. He approvingly quoted the nineteenth-century art historian Walter Copland Perry on the *Venus de Milo*: 'The figure is ideal in the highest sense of the word: it is a form which transcends all our experience, which has no prototype or equal in the actual world, and beyond which no effort of the imagination can rise' (Fuller 1988a: 15). Although this Platonic reading of the human figure had long been a staple of aesthetics, it struck Fuller as having remarkable potential: 'Since men and women at all times and in all places . . . possess *roughly* the same physical and sensory potentialities, it may be possible to identify a necessary (though not a sufficient) component common to all 'good' sculpture which is not subject to significant historical determination or cultural variation' (Fuller 1988a: 20). This idealist position overlooks the fact that it is precisely through the differences between our roughly similar constitutions from which culture gains its meaning. In the modern period in particular, those differences have been more observed and more instrumental than ever before and cannot be wished away.

For in the nineteenth century, biologists such as Lamarck and later Darwin reversed traditional notions of divine creation in favour of an evolutionary schema of the development of human, animal and plant species. Rather than being considered an unchanging copy of divine perfection, the human body now had to be considered as one evolving species among many. As long as human superiority was considered divinely ordained, there was no need to insist upon the perfection of human corporality, but now such idealism had to refute or evade evolutionism. Initially, the destabilizing effects of evolutionism were offset by the older thesis of polygenism, that is, the notion that the human species was not one, but composed of several distinct and incommensurable races. Darwin's 1859 treatise, *The Origin of Species*, insisted instead that evolution had taken place within one unitary human race over a span of time that far exceeded the Biblical chronology. The inference was both that Linnaeus' eighteenth-century division of humanity into European, African, Asian and American races was incorrect and that the human body had not ceased to change, nor would it in the future. Statistical reseach confirmed that the individual body is not a constant but changes rapidly in response to social conditions. The average height of French military conscripts was 1.65m in

1880, 1.68 by 1940, 1.70 by 1960 and 1.72 by 1974 (Dagognet 1992: 169)
The modern body is not universal or divine but regularly changes. This
average conceals a much wider range of difference between social classes.
Indeed, Social Darwinists such as Herbert Spencer used such ideas to
restore traditional notions of essential differences between races and
classes, whose origin was not now simply biological, but the biological
reflected through the social. In 1886, Lord Brabazon informed his readers
of another world beyond that of the middle class:

> Let the reader walk through the wretched streets . . . of the Eastern or
> Southern districts of London. . . . [S]hould he be of average height, he will
> find himself a head taller than those around him; he will see on all sides pale
> faces, stunted figures, debilitated forms and narrow chests. Surely this ought
> not to be.
>
> (Steadman Jones 1971: 308)

Brabazon's proposed solution to the problem was biological imperialism
via the relocation of the diseased masses in the colonies. His guiding
principle was that the body not only changes but can be changed. Whereas
Darwin had left the engine of evolution to nature, Spencer and the other
Social Darwinists believed that they could direct evolution to their own
desired ends. The consequences of these beliefs were both dramatic and
tragic, leading to eugenics and extermination camps on the one hand; and
the genuine achievement of modern medicine in preventing and curing
disease on the other.

Fuller's aesthetics depended upon the latest variant of such cross-ferti-
lization between biology and social policy, the sociobiology espoused by
E.O. Wilson. Sociobiology argues that social inequalities, such as the
differences between men and women in modern societies, are the consequence of irrefutable biological differences and are thus natural. In this
view, evolution takes place only within strictly contained parameters,
rather than affecting the entire species, returning sociobiologists to the
theories of Linnaeus. Despite the widespread condemnation of these ideas
as scientifically unsound, sociobiologists hold that human behaviour can
only be understood as a response to inherited genetic dictates. In the words
of Richard Dawkins, a biologist whose writings have achieved considerable
popular success, 'the genes are the immortals . . . individuals and groups
are like clouds in the sky or dust-storms in the desert' (Shilling 1993: 48–
53). Fuller adapted this position into an new aesthetic which held that
modernity was not simply ugly but contrary to our biology. He quoted
Wilson: 'Is the mind predisposed to life on the savanna, such that beauty in
some fashion can be said to lie in the genes of the beholder?' Fuller's

answer was in the affirmative, leading him to assert that modern architecture was antipathetical to our 'natural' desire for the curved form: 'the anger in the human soul rises up against the tower blocks' (Fuller 1988b: 233). It is similarly clear that this biological sense of the aesthetic is felt more profoundly by some than others. Ironically enough, given its assertion of humanity's African origins, a sociobiological aesthetic is the return of white supremacism in disguise.

Fuller's position was symptomatic of a new direction among conservative groups in contemporary art and politics in both the United States and the United Kingdom. The ultra-conservative political position Fuller occupied has now crystallized into a die-hard block on the right wing of the Conservative party in the British House of Commons, united by a hatred for foreigners in general and Europe in particular. In the United States, Senator Jesse Helms led an assault on the National Endowment for the Arts, which articulated a sense of rage in conservative circles that the human body was being 'violated' by artists. Under the Reagan/Bush administration sociobiology gained respectability in government. One Bush appointee, Frederick K. Goodwin, instigated a furore in February 1992, when he advised a meeting of the National Health Advisory Council that inner city violence could well be understood with reference to the behaviour of primates: 'Now one could say that if some of the loss of social structure in this society, and particularly within the high impact inner city areas, has removed some of the civilizing evolutionary things that we have built up and that maybe it isn't just the careless use of the word when people call certain areas of certain cities jungles, that maybe we have gone back to what might be more natural, without all of the social controls that we have imposed upon ourselves as a civilization over the thousands of years in our own evolution.' Goodwin was evidently referring to those parts of American cities in which African-Americans or Latinos are in the majority, rather than the white suburbs. His argument blends a Freudian sense of civilization as a restriction on instinctual behaviour, with the eugenic belief that in the unnatural environment created by humanity, evolution no longer functions 'correctly', that is to say, by promoting the survival of the fittest. These arguments have not been heard in the political mainstream since the active eugenic policy of sterilization and extermination of the 'unfit' in Hitler's Third Reich.

Those opposed to such ideas have often stressed that the postmodern body is not an ideal whole but an assemblage of fragments. In the contemporary world, such arguments run, the fragmentation of the body has become a fact of everyday life. If you have enough money, your face and

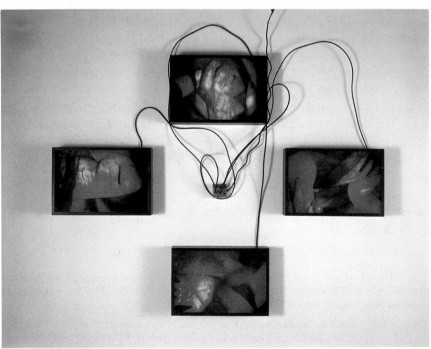

body can be remoulded to any suitable shape. With the appropriate contact lenses, eye colour can be changed to match your clothes. Medical techniques allow thousands of people to live with someone else's vital organs replacing their own malfunctioning parts. In less radical fashion, it is common throughout the West for people to control and change the shape of their bodies by dieting, exercise and body building.

A number of contemporary artists have made the fragmented body the subject of their work, most notably the American sculptor Kiki Smith. Her work has recently been branded 'controversial', after the National Endowment for the Arts withdrew funding from an exhibition in Boston, entitled *Corporal Politics*, which featured her work. In exemplary postmodern fashion, the rock band Aerosmith stepped in and made up the shortfall. Yet Smith's work is more meditative, even elegiac, than confrontational. Her 'Projects: Kiki Smith' (1990–2) (Figure 4) is a row of water containers labelled in Gothic script with the names of various bodily fluids. The macabre overtones prompted by this touch of Hammer horror suggest that the jars may have been used in a Frankenstein-style rehydration of a dried body. But, on reflection, the more profound horror is that our collective fluids once mingled in passion and now their meeting contains the possibility of death. Our bodies, far from presenting a defensive wall to the outside world are all too open and vulnerable. In an earlier collaboration with the late David Wojnarowicz, Smith created a group of four photographer's light boxes overlaid with photographs of sections of the two artists' bodies, covered in blood (1982–91) (Figure 5). The boxes are connected to each other with cables, and collectively to a plaster model of the human body in fetal position. The cables suggest the umbilical cord, linking child to mother, and the internal lymphatic and circulatory systems. The sculpted body and its means of vital support intersect across the light boxes, in the form of the photographs. It is the hands which make the strongest impression in these pictures, but it is unclear in what activity they are engaged. On one level, hands suggest communication, touching and healing, but they are covered in blood, evoking surgery or even torture. Smith forces our attention to the fragile, interconnected biospheres in which we live.

Figure 4 (opposite, top) Kiki Smith, installation view of the exhibition 'Projects: Kiki Smith', 10 November 1990–2 January 1991, MoMA, © 1995 The Museum of Modern Art, New York.

Figure 5 (opposite, bottom) Kiki Smith with David Wojnarowicz, *Untitled* (1982–91), four photographic light boxes, photograph courtesy Pace Wildenstein, New York.

This sense of the body is widely understood to be its 'postmodern condition'. However, the fragmented body is not a recent creation, but has been indispensable to the representation of the body throughout the modern era. In the eighteenth century, men and women wore wigs, makeup and beauty patches to transform their appearance on a daily basis. One popular form of entertainment was the masked ball or masquerade, in which masked participants could indulge their sexual proclivities at will, with little respect for the social conventions of marriage. For the French writer Marivaux writing in the *Spectateur Français*, this tendency to hide the true self behind a mask extended even to the unadorned body, for we are all '[w]earers of faces, men and women' (Marivaux 1969: 123–7). As he moved through the crowd outside the theatre, Marivaux mused on what makes up a face and concluded that they can be put together at will, so that an ugly woman with '[a] face composed by vanity' could compete success-fully with a beautiful woman. The external value of appearance was now dependent on our actions. The face itself became a mask, no guide to what might transpire. In this performative sense of identity, the body was not a natural, changeless resource but a malleable tool, which responded to individual desires for self-fashioning. The historian Michel de Certeau has described one strategy for the resistance of governmental power in similar terms. He uses the term *la perruque*, the French for wig or masquer-ade, to refer to the everyday resistance of individuals behind a screen of conformity. The fragmented body, assembled from various modes of iden-tity and completed with a range of prosthetic devices, has been a staple component of Western modernity.

The current sense of the fragmented body as new and different is not simply mistaken, however, but a response to the collapse of the nineteenth-century discourse of the ideal body in representation. The notion of the Classical body, which Fuller adopted from nineteenth-century criticism and gave a modern spin with sociobiology, was from the very outset designed to demonstrate the superiority of the Northern, white 'races' and to justify their imperial policies. The Classical heritage of the West, upon which so many claims of cultural superiority have been based, has recently been shown to have been drastically distorted by the nineteenth-century Classical ideal, which depended above all on the notion that the ancient Greeks were Aryans, and thus the 'races' of Northern Europe were their legitimate descendants. In his emerging trilogy *Black Athena*, the Classical scholar Martin Bernal has painted a very different history of the reception of Antiquity in the eighteenth and nineteenth centuries to that which is usually presented by art historians. Strongly influenced by the work of the African historian Cheik Anta Diop, Bernal argues that the ancient Greeks themselves believed that the most significant portions of their culture were derived from Egypt and the Near East. Bernal's thesis is two-fold. First, he describes the creation of what he terms the Aryan model of Greek history in late eighteenth- and early nineteenth-century Europe. Until this time, historians had accepted the version of Greek history given by Herodotus in the sixth century BC – referred to as the Ancient Model by Bernal – which held that Greece owed much of its culture and civilization to ancient Egypt and Phoenicia. But in the modern period, the Ancient Model was replaced with the thesis that a Dark Age intervened in Greece between the Mycenean civilization, which flourished on Crete in the third millenium BC, and the Classical civilization of Greece from 1200 BC. This Dark Age was ended, according to what Bernal calls the Aryan Model, by the arrival of white peoples from the North, known as the Dorians, who colonized Greece, introducing Indo-European language and the other qualities necessary for the flowering of Greek culture. This version denied any Egyptian or Phoenician influence whatsoever on the Greeks, and thus overthrew the received wisdom of two thousand years. Bernal departs from the now traditional reading of the history of Classical scholarship by seeking motivations other than the pursuit of disinterested knowledge behind this change. He amasses a convincing array of evidence to suggest that the development of race science in nineteenth-century Europe, which held whites to be superior and blacks to be inferior, made it impossible to conceive of the glory that was Greece being derived from the ideas of black Africans and semitic Phoenicians. Bernal's second thesis asserts that the Ancient Model was in fact broadly speaking correct. Using his formidable linguistic skills, Bernal claims to have traced large numbers of Egyptian and Phoenician words in the ancient Greek vocabulary, which had previously resisted the efforts of etymologists. Furthermore, in a recently published second volume, Bernal deploys a range of archaeological evidence in claiming that Greece was colonized by Egyptians and Phoenicians in the late eighteenth century BC and that there was no Dark Age (Bernal 1991). Thus ancient Greek culture and civilization developed from the culture of Egypt and Phoenicia brought by the successful colonizers.

While Bernal's scheme for the actual history of the ancient Mediterranean is still hotly disputed, Classicists have conceded that modern Classical scholarship was indeed founded by men who were profoundly and openly racist. In the same breath, many Classicists add that these failings of their intellectual forebears are well known and have long been discounted in modern scholarship and that, in any event, the factual discoveries of nineteenth-century scholars still stand regardless of their prejudices. Bernal and his supporters reply that what is important is not so much the facts that these scholars emphasized, but those they distorted or suppressed. Nor is this a simple question of Classical historiography. As Bernal writes, if he is right it will be necessary to

> recognize the penetration of racism and continental chauvinism into all our historiography, or philosophy of writing history. The Ancient Model had no major 'internal' deficiencies, or weaknesses in explanatory power. It was overthrown for external reasons. For 18th and 19th-century Romantics and racists it was simply intolerable for Greece, which was seen not merely as the epitome of Europe but also as its pure childhood, to have been the result of the mixture of native Europeans and colonizing Africans and Semites. Therefore the Ancient Model had to be overthrown and replaced by something more acceptable.
>
> (Bernal 1987: 2)

His thesis has profound implications for art history and especially for the revival of the Classical body as a standard for art. If Greek art has achieved the prominence it enjoys in Western culture not because of its inherent merit, or embodiment of the spirit of democracy, but as an illustration of race science, then it is obviously invalidated as a universal measure of quality. Both the work itself and its reception will need to be looked at again.

For it is clear that the history of modern Western aesthetics can be tracked following Bernal's thesis that Hellenization depended upon the exclusion of all semitic and African influences from European culture. As early as 1720, the French writer Dubos argued that the Jews did not make visual representations of their God because 'the impression made thereby was too great for a people naturally inclinable to grow passionately fond of all objects capable of moving them' (Dubos 1748: 30). Dubos' comment was codified into a racialized system by the founder of art history Johann Winckelmann in his *History of Ancient Art* (1764). Winckelmann believed that Greek art, inspired by the love of liberty and dedicated to the pursuit of the beautiful, could not have any connection with the Egyptians, whose art he found repulsive:

> How can one find even a hint of beauty in their figures, when all or almost all of the originals on which they were based had the form of the African? That is they had, like them, pouting lips, receding and small chins, sunken and flattened profiles. And not only like the Africans but also like the Ethiopians, they often had flattened noses and a dark cast of skin.
>
> (quoted in Bernal 1987: 244)

For Winckelmann, it was literally inconceivable that such an 'inferior' racial type could produce the art he so admired. This distinction was not simply

30

a question of aesthetics or of intellectual history, but was an important justification for both slavery and imperialism. In his 1774 *History of Jamaica*, written to justify the practice of colonial slavery, Edward Long made an explicit parallel between eighteenth-century enslaved Africans and the ancient Egyptians, who were:

> a people without taste, without genius, or discernment; who had ideas only of grandeur, ill understood: knavish, crafty, soft, lazy, cowardly, and servile, superstitious in excess, and extravagantly besotted with an absurd and monstrous theology; without any skill in eloquence, poetry, music, architecture, sculpture, or painting, navigation, commerce, or the art military. . . .In these acquisitions, however imperfect, they appear far superior to the Negroes, who, perhaps in their turn, as far transcend the Ægyptians in the superlative perfection of their worst qualities.
>
> (Long 1774: II 356)

The inadequacies of the Egyptians explained and justified the bondage of slavery. In turn, Long's caricature of the capacities of eighteenth-century Africans was taken as evidence of the inferiority of Egyptian art, which he would not even classify as painting or sculpture, much less as the origin of Western culture.

This radical, racialized distinction between Africans, Semites and Europeans became a staple of nineteenth-century art history, and was certainly shared by Fuller's model, Walter Copland Perry. Perry accepted a similarity between Egyptian sculpture and early Greek work, but was dismissive of any possibility that Greek art was derived from Egypt:

> There is no future in the Egyptian statue; the artisan who produced it is not working by his own lights, and striving to do his very best in his own way, but the skilful bondman working in fetters for a task-master, and producing eternal repetitions of an unchanging type – the lifeless monsters of hieractic prescription.
>
> (Perry 1882: 57)

Although political oppression played its part in this failure, its root cause was

> the dark and gloomy caverns and the secret and ghostly chambers of the Oriental mind. During the earlier part of their history, both Greeks and Romans looked with mingled contempt and dread on the gloomy superstitions of Egypt and Assyria, as only fitted for barbarians and slaves.
>
> (Perry 1882: 667)

Perry did not believe for one moment in the unity of the human race, as expressed through the body. On the contrary, as a good nineteenth-century Classical scholar, he believed that Greek sculpture was concrete evidence of the superiority of the Aryan race over all others, especially the Africans and Orientals. It was no accident that the history of 'Man' was illustrated in the nineteenth century as a progression from the monkey via the black to the Greek statue. Far from being divorced from the particular predilections of its day, Classical art had scientific status as evidence of white superiority. Of course, such readings are not the fault of the works themselves, but it makes any revival of such criticism unpalatable, to say the least.

BLINDNESS AND INSIGHT

The transition between Bernal's Ancient and Aryan Models requires a more detailed demonstration, and I shall pursue it by an examination of the Enlightenment debate concerning the origin of painting. Today this question is more likely to be posed in psychological fashion, as to what psychic or primal need is requited by art, than by historical inquiry, but in the Enlightenment an entirely serious debate was held as to the historical origin of painting and sculpture. By the end of the eighteenth century the legend of Dibutade, or the Corinthian Maid, had become accepted as the most convincing response to this question. By placing the origin of art in ancient Greece, the new discipline of art history downgraded all earlier art, especially Egyptian art. In tracking the rise of Dibutade, we can thus observe the change in Classical history described by Bernal. This confluence of modernism and race was not a coincidence but a constituent part of the uneasy relationship between the perfect and fragmented body in the modern period, which could not be Universal but was both historically and culturally situated.

Furthermore, the French philosopher Jacques Derrida has recently made use of the legend of the Corinthian Maid to examine the relationship between blindness, insight and visual representations of the body. Blindness, Derrida argues, is not a metaphor but is actually inherent in the process of representation as mythically enshrined by the Corinthian Maid. However, Derrida's own argument is shaped by modern, gendered notions of blindness as both a disease and a moral condition. In what follows, I examine the central paradox of blindness and insight to illuminate the impossibility of creating an image of the perfect body. The seemingly neutral physiological condition of blindness became gendered in the nineteenth century so as to contrast masculine insight with feminine blindness. In order to understand the power of the relationship between blindness and insight, it is essential to understand how both sighted and blind people have represented the condition in medical, psychical and intellectual terms. Modern figure drawing in its broadest sense cannot be abstracted from the complex and fissured processes by which modern individuals vest their individual corporal experience with meanings and identity.

The source for the legend of the Corinthian Maid is the Roman historian Pliny, who tells the story of the Maid's father, Budades of Sikyon, a potter who invented clay modelling. Pliny continues to relate that she

> was in love with a youth, and when he was leaving the country, she traced the outline of the shadow which his face cast on the wall by lamplight. Her father filled in the outline with clay and made a model; this he dried and baked with the rest of his pottery.

The story is somewhat confused and at different times, it has been claimed as the origin of painting (Dibutade's outline) and sculpture (Budades' figure). Seeking to prove his story, Pliny also claimed that the figure was preserved at Corinth for many years. Despite the later prominence given to this myth, it occupies only two lines of Pliny's *Natural History* and was not highlighted by Pliny as of especial importance. The first translation of Pliny's section on art into French in 1725 (which was subscribed to by Isaac Newton and the painter François Boucher) observed in a note: 'Whatever the truth of it, here is the essential thing: he [Budades] believed that one must consult nature, and seek perfection by the choice of the most beautiful things which She offers us' (D..D..1725: 53). At this time, the anonymous translator did not even perceive the story as referring to Dibutade.

In 1728, Henry Bell published *An Historical Essay on the Original of Painting*, which investigated the origins of the visual arts. Bell made no mention of the Dibutade story, and described the history of Egyptian art at considerable length. He was respectful towards the Greeks, but not overly so. He recorded that the famous painter Apelles, who was believed to have painted Alexander the Great, used only white, yellow, red and black paint. But he questioned how he could have been truly the greatest artist without blue, which would have prevented him from depicting the sky and sea, as well as denying him the use of all colours created by blending with blue (Bell 1728: 79). When Joshua Reynolds came to give his famous lectures at the newly founded Royal Academy in London from 1769, he also made no reference to the myth of Dibutade. He did make a series of distinctions as to the nature of art, which opened a wide gap between the civilized West and its Others. In describing the task of painting, he opined in 1786:

Perhaps it ought to be as far removed from the vulgar idea of imitation, as the refined civilised state in which we live, is removed from a gross state of nature; and those who have not cultivated their imaginations, which the majority of mankind certainly have not, may be said, in regard to arts, to continue in this state of nature. Such men will always prefer imitation to that excellence which is addressed to another faculty that they do not possess; but these are not the persons to whom a Painter is to look, any more than a judge of morals and manners ought to refer to controverted points upon those subjects to the opinions of people taken from the banks of the Ohio, or from New Holland.

(Reynolds 1975: 233)

Reynolds perceived a ladder of civilization, stretching from the most primitive to the most civilized, exemplified by the contrast between the civilized Europeans and the 'primitive' peoples they were now encountering on their voyages of exploration and colonization. Reynolds painted a portrait of the Tahitian known to the British as Omai, who returned to England with Captain Cook. Reynolds dressed Omai in elegant Classical robes and painted him full-length, the highest quality of portraiture. However, he emphasized the corporal distinctions between this 'primitive' man and the Western audience looking at the work, by making the tattoos on Omai's body clearly visible (Guest 1992). Difference in the modern era does not just exist, it has to be visible. In Reynolds' view, one of the functions of art was to make the distinction between the civilized and the primitive apparent: 'The untaught mind finds a vast gulph between its own powers, and those works of complicated art, which it is utterly unable to fathom; and it supposes that such a void can only be passed by supernatural powers' (Reynolds 1975: 94). The very existence of Omai's portrait was a testament to the cultural divide between Europeans and the Tahitians.

For fifty years after Reynolds' *Discourses*, the measure of that gulf was the leap taken by Dibutade in creating painting, as Ann Bermingham has recently emphasized: 'With the founding of the Royal Academy, the popularly understood role and purpose of the visual arts were recast. For this reason, the Corinthian Maid occupied a central yet ambivalent place in the period's construction of painting' (Bermingham 1992: 141). This conceptual breakthrough was held to be inherently impossible for the 'primitive' mind, such as that of the Egyptians. The growing popularity of the story led late eighteenth-century painters in England and France, such as Joseph Wright of Derby, Jean-Baptiste Regnault and Jean-Baptiste Suvée, to depict the Maid drawing her lover's outline on numerous occasions (Figure 6). By

Figure 6 Joseph Wright of Derby, *The Corinthian Maid* (1783–4), Paul Mellon Collection, © 1994 Board of Trustees, National Gallery of Art, Washington.

1801, Henry Fuseli could say in the Royal Academy, where Reynolds had ignored the entire story only thirty years before, that:

> If ever legend deserved our belief, the amourous tale of the Corinthian maid, who traced the shade of her departing lover by the secret lamp deserves our sympathy, to grant it; and leads us at the same time to some observations on the first mechanical essays of painting, and that *linear method* which, though passed nearly unnoticed by Winckelmann, seems to have continued as the basis of execution, even when the instrument for which it was chiefly adapted had long been laid aside.
>
> (Fuseli 1801: 8)

Fuseli used the legend to argue not just for the Greek origins of art, but for the original importance of line over colour, the watchword of the Neo-Classicists. Dibutade retained a prominent place in academic discourse throughout the nineteenth century, remaining a subject for painters until the difference and superiority of the Greeks was plain to all. In 1821, Shelley exclaimed:

> We are all Greeks. But for Greece we might still have been savages and idolators. The human form and the human mind attained to a perfection

in Greece which has impressed its images on those faultless productions whose very fragments are the despair of modern art, and has propagated impulses which can never cease, through a thousand channels of manifest or imperceptible operation, to enable and delight mankind until the extinction of the race.

(Bernal 1987: 290)

Shelley may have been thinking of Fuseli's drawing, *The Artist Overwhelmed by the Grandeur of Ancient Ruins*, depicting the artist in despair next to the surviving hand and foot of the Colossus of Constantine in Rome. The surviving fragments contributed to a myth of the previous, perfect whole to which Western art must again aspire. The Dibutade story played its part in constructing a Neo-Classical theory of art which was Western, the work of genius not merely imitation, and based upon the depiction of the perfect, Greek body. As late as the Salon of 1865, famous for Manet's *Olympia*, the French state chose instead to purchase Louis Lamothe's *L'Origine du dessin*, a classic rendition of the Dibutade legend (Clark 1985: 119).

Dibutade's story served Neo-Classicism very well, but it has its own peculiarities that tend to undermine the notion of the perfect body. In an exhibition he curated at the Louvre in 1990, the philosopher Jacques Derrida, best known for his concept of deconstruction, turned his attention to the question of blindness in art. In so doing, he considered the representations of Dibutade and made an important observation. In many of the images of Dibutade, she is in fact not looking at her lover at all but only at his shadow, rather than copying directly from nature as the Neo-Classical theorists asserted. This detail is especially true of the French versions of the theme by Suvée and Regnault. In Regnault's painting *Dibutade ou l'Origine du dessin*, (Château de Versailles) Dibutade conveniently turns so that her Classic profile is revealed, and looks away from her lover to trace his outline on the pedestal of a Doric column. He is absolutely indifferent to her activity and looks directly out of the frame at the viewer. The question of who looks at whom, and who is seen by whom is thus central to this picture. Given the mythological importance of the subject, Derrida argues that this

> shadow-writing in each case inaugurates an art of blindness. From the outset, perception belongs to recollection. Butades writes, and thus already loves in nostalgia. Detached from the present of perception, fallen from the thing itself – which is thus divided – a shadow is a simultaneous memory, and Butades' stick is a staff of the blind.

In other words, Derrida continues, there is a relationship between the visible and the invisible that is always threatening to break down. This

36

argument is indebted to the earlier work of phenomenologist Maurice Merleau-Ponty, *The Visible and the Invisible*, quoted here by Derrida:

> When I say that everything visible is invisible, that perception is impercep-tion, that consciousness has a 'blind spot', that to see is always to see more than one sees – this must not be understood in the sense of a *contradiction* – it must not be imagined that I add to the visible . . . a non-visible. – One has to understand that it is visiblity itself that involves a non-visibility.
>
> (Derrida 1993: 51)

The anatomical feature of the blind-spot, where the optic nerve joins the retina, is that which permits physiological vision. So too, insists Derrida, is a blind-spot essential to visual representation, not as its opposite, but as an integral and constitutive feature of representation as a process of memory. As long as Dibutade has her lover with her, she has no need to draw him. As long as she looks directly at him, she cannot draw him, for she cannot see the outline to trace. She must look away from the object she is depicting in order to depict it. Dibutade is an inhabitant of Plato's cave, that imaginary realm where mortals attempt to see the essence of things from their shadows cast on the cave's wall by the fire. But the cave-dwellers neither can nor wish to leave. In the full light, they can see nothing at all. So too the artist, in Derrida's view, cannot perceive the act of representation:

> The staring eye always resembles an eye of the blind, sometimes the eye of the dead, at that precise moment when mourning begins. . . . Looking at itself seeing, it also sees itself disappear right at the moment when the drawing desparately tries to recapture it. For this cyclops eye sees nothing, nothing but an eye that it thus prevents from seeing anything at all. Seeing the seeing and not the visible, it sees nothing.
>
> (Derrida 1993: 57)

THE CANON OF BLINDNESS

Derrida's philosophical investigation leaves many questions to be answered by art historians. Blindness was and remains a central metaphor in Western art, representing and permitting insight and understanding for the artist, gendered male, over his 'female' subject-matter. Here it now seems to suggest that visual representation is the outcome of an interplay between the metaphor of insight and the physiological structures of sight. Following Derrida's provocative comments, I shall now re-examine the canon of the blind and blindness from Poussin via David, Ingres and

Delacroix to Paul Strand and Robert Morris. Given the force attached by Merleau-Ponty and Derrida to the physiology of seeing, I shall consider blindness not just as a metaphor but as a condition. For Derrida himself stands within a historical construction of blindness as insight, which is not natural but is less than two hundred years old. How did depictions of blindness change in accord with changing notions of sight and blindness? In what ways is the metaphor of blindness affected by these changes? And what becomes of the Classical body that is known not through insight metaphorized as blindness but through insight enabled by blindness?

In France the modern period is held to begin with the reign of Louis XIV (1648–1715). For art history, this period marks the foundation of the Academy of Painting and Sculpture and the beginnings of public debate over the nature and accomplishments of art. One central moment in this history came in 1666 when Louis ordered that the Academy should hold conferences on works of art for the edification of an audience composed of their peers, students and, occasionally, government ministers. The Seventh conference was given by the artist Sébastien Bourdon, who chose a painting by Nicolas Poussin (1593–1665), *Christ Healing the Blind at Jericho* (1651), as the springboard for his discussion of light, for Poussin was regarded as the greatest artist of the French school (Figure 7). He emphasized that Poussin had chosen to represent an early morning scene, which cast a strong blue light from the left side of the canvas. Bourdon elaborated upon the advantages of such morning light, which later became so conventional that only the angled fall of light from the left was retained. Bourdon, however, read Poussin's painting as a treatise on luminosity:

> For though all the Parts retain their true Teints, yet the Shade which passes above them, is as it were a Veil to extinguish their Vivacity, and hinder their having so much strength as to fill the View, and thrust out other Objects more considerable, and on which the Painter has laid greater Stress. But in return, he has not failed to fill those Places with Light where he saw it would not hurt the beauty of the Figures.
>
> (Bourdon 1740: 132)

His audience, however, were not satisfied with such subtleties and demanded to know where the multitude of witnesses described in the New Testament had gone in Poussin's painting. Bourdon replied that

> We cannot suppose that all the Multitude who followed Christ could be about him at once, and being some steps from him, they were concealed by the Buildings. That there are Witnesses enough of the Action, since by that person cloathed in Red, who appears surprised, the Painter has represented the Astonishment of the *Jews*; and by him who is looking very near, he shews the desire that Nation had to see Miracles wrought. A greater Number of

Figure 7 Nicolas Poussin, *Christ Healing the Blind at Jericho* (1651), Louvre, photograph courtesy of Photo R.M.N. – R.G. Ojeda.

Figures would only have occasioned Confusion, and hindered those of Christ and the blind Men from being seen so distinctly.

(145)

This literal reading of the painting belied what now seem to be the obvious metaphorical connotations of the painting, connecting the blindness of the figures to the light being spread by Christ. Just as the king could heal by his touch, one might argue, so could artists bring vision into being by their brushstrokes. In this view, the royal artists of the Academy could then claim connection to the sacred person of the king and imbibe something of his divine essence from his aura. Bourdon, however, also insisted on a literal interpretation of blindness:

By the Action of the first blind Man, his Faith and Confidence in him who is touching him is expressed; in the second, the Favour he is asking is likewise shown. It is common for Persons who are deprived of any one of the five Senses to have the rest better and more subtle; because the Spirits which move in them, to make them known what they want, move with greater force having fewer Offices to perform; thus they who have lost their Sight, have a more acute Hearing, and a more sensible Touch. This is what Mr Poussin has intended to express in the last blind Man, and in which he has wonderfully succeeded. For by his Face and his Arms one may know he is all Attention to the Voice of the Saviour, and endeavouring to find him out. This attentive Hearkening appears in his Forehead, which is not quite smooth; the Skin and

39

all the other Parts of which are drawn up. He likewise discovers it, by suspending all the Motions of his Countenance, which continue in that Posture to give time to his Ear to listen more attentively, and that he may not be diverted.

(164)

Bourdon thus used the new insights of Cartesian science to explain that the blind have sharper hearing than the average person, a myth that has long outlasted the medical theory of the spirits from which it was devised (as the body has a finite number of spirits to enable the senses, the loss of one sense leaves more spirits available for the others and they are thus enhanced). In fact, the blindness which is on the verge of being cured in Poussin's image calls attention, then, not to insight but to the human voice. Bourdon read the rhetoric of Poussin's painting through physical blindness and found it the key to the expression of the 'Voice of the Saviour'. He envisaged blindness as a means of intensifying the tactile and auditory response to the painting, rather than as a signifier of incapacity. Light had to be arranged by the painter in such a way as to prevent illegibility, creating a balanced visual economy, which Bourdon described as 'a fine Oeconomy of Colours and Lights . . . which makes an agreeable Concert and Charming Sweetness that never cloys the Sight' (170).

The mute painter's achievement was like that of the blind in calling a sensible world into being, while deprived of certain sensory tools. For just as there is a moment of blindness inherent in the act of visual representation, the resulting image was inevitably silent. Throughout the *ancien régime*, artists turned to the gestural sign language of the deaf as a means of overcoming this deficiency for, as the French writer du Fresnoy put it:

Mutes have no other way of speaking (or expressing their thoughts) but only by their gesture and their actions, 'tis certain that they do it in a manner more expressive than those who have the use of Speech, for which reason the Picture, which is mute ought to imitate them, so as to make itself understood.
(Dryden 1695 [1648]: 129)

The mute picture required the assistance of the deaf in order to signify. For in the early modern period, the simple binary opposition between the able-bodied and the disabled did not exist. Instead, the human body was perceived as inevitably imperfect, each person having certain skills that others might not possess. Even Louis XIV had regular bleedings and purgatives before any unusual or tiring activity to purify his body. If the sacred body of the Sun King could be considered imperfect, then his subjects were even more vulnerable. The artists of the period were quick to figure blindness and deafness as complex metaphors in their work, in ways which have been insufficiently recognized.

In the eighteenth century, the sensualist philosophy of the Enlightenment continued this relativist concept of the body, but gave it a moral connotation. Sensualism held that the mind was formed directly from sensory experience and that those with differing senses had different minds. In his *Letter on the Blind*, the philosopher and critic Denis Diderot (1713–1784) reflected at length on the distinctions between the blind and the sighted, pursuing his conviction that: 'I doubt that anything at all can be explained without the body' (Josephs 1969: 50). He first mused on the morality of the blind, which he found wanting:

> I suspect them of inhumanity. What difference would there be for a blind man between a man who urinates and a man who, without complaining, was spilling blood? . . . All our virtues depend upon our manner of sensing, and the degree to which things affect us! Ah! Madame, how different the morality of the blind is from our own. How that of a deaf man would differ again from that of the blind, and how a being which had one sense more than us would find our morality imperfect, to say the least.
>
> (Diderot 1975 – ; vol. 4 (1978): 27)

Diderot found the blind different to the sighted but did not pretend that the sighted were perfect. Indeed, he went on to reflect on ways in which the lack of sight could even be an advantage. He argued that the blind have a tactile memory in the same way that the sighted have a visual memory. The sensation of a mouth on the hand of a blind man and the drawing of it amounted to the same thing, as both were secondary representations of the original. But the blind person had an advantage when it came to abstract thought: 'The person born blind perceives things in a far more abstract manner than us, and in questions of pure speculation, he is perhaps less subject to making mistakes' (32). Diderot's example was the blind English mathematician Nicholas Saunderson:

> Those who have written about his life say that he was prolific in fortunate expressions . . . But what do you mean by fortunate expressions, you may perhaps ask? I would reply, Madame, that they are those which are proper to a sense, to touch for example, and which are metaphorical at the same time to another sense, like sight; there was thus a double light for those who spoke to him, the true and direct light of the expression, and the reflected light of the metaphor.
>
> (Diderot 1978: 41)

Paradoxically, therefore, the sighted person gained a greater illumination by discussing a topic with a blind person.

The paradox was a central concept in Diderot's thought. In the *Paradox on the Actor* (1773–8), Diderot examined this question at length. Discussing the actress Mlle Clairon, he observed:

> If you were with her while she studied her part, how many times would you cry out: 'That is just right!' and how many times would she answer: 'You are wrong!' Just so a friend of Le Quesnoy's once cried catching him by the arm: 'Stop! you will make it worse by bettering it – you will spoil the whole thing!' 'What I have done', replied the artist, panting with exertion, 'you have seen; what I have got hold of and what I mean to carry out to the end you cannot see.'
>
> (Lacoue-Labarthe 1989: 262)

The artist's vision was doubled, like that of the *philosophe* conversing with the blind man, seeing what is present, what is implied and what is yet to come. The true blindness was not that of the visually impaired but of those who believed they could see like the artist but could not. Diderot disliked the 'false mimetician or abortive genius who simply *mimes the mimetician*'. The paradox in question stemmed from Diderot's notion that actors 'are fit to play all characters because they have none'. In the process, actors step outside their characters: 'He must have in himself an unmoved and disinterested onlooker. He must have, consequently, penetration and no sensibility, the art of imitating everything, or, which comes to the same thing, the same aptitude for every sort of character and part' (257). For actors to accurately represent the widest range of emotions, it was essential that they themselves have no emotions. Actors constantly observed their work in order to make it appear natural and unforced. For this reason, the British artist John Opie (1761–1807) refused to paint actors at all. Acting was to be no one in order to be everyone, just as it is the blind spot which permits seeing.

In Jacques-Louis David's *Bélisaire, reconnu par un soldat qui avait servi sous lui au moment qu'une femme lui fait aumône* (Lille: Musée Wicar, 1781), blindness was again used by the artist to express a sense of paradox. Belisarius was a Roman general who, after many successes, lost the confidence of the Emperor Justinian and was blinded by him. David (1748–1825) showed the now blind general begging for alms, at a moment when he is recognized by one of his former soldiers. Belisarius' blindness thus comes to have a metaphorical meaning, suggestive of his indifference not merely to his fate but to the potential spectator. This painting of the blinded Roman general has recently been hailed by art historian Michael Fried as the first truly modern painting, in which David can be seen 'reinventing the art of painting' (Fried 1983: 160). Fried in effect proposes that the picture itself postulates a certain blindness in that it is constructed

42

without the needs of a spectator in mind. He argues that David followed Diderot's remark in his *Salon of 1767*: 'A scene represented on a canvas or on stage does not suppose witnesses' (Fried 1983: 97). Fried discerns a central distinction between such absorption, which is praised, and vulgar theatricality, which is to be condemned. He argues that David constructed an image which refused theatricality, and instead opted to create a pictorial space in which the characters are wholly absorbed and unaware of the possibility of spectatorship.

Such analyses run counter to the notion of the paradox, developed above, and indeed Fried noted that the late publication of the *Paradox* renders it less relevant for eighteenth-century art history. However, this argument cannot apply to the central example of the *Belisarius*, which was exhibited in the Salon of 1781. Fried applies Diderot's comments of 1762 to David's work:

> If, when one makes a painting, one supposes beholders, everything is lost. The painter leaves his canvas, just as the actor who speaks to the audience [*parterre*] steps down from the stage. In supposing that there is no-one else in the world except the personnages of the painting, Van Dyck's painting is sublime.
>
> (Fried 1983: 149)

Certainly the actor addressing the audience destroys the illusion of the performance but the paradox remains that they know the audience is there. Diderot was not afraid that the actor might communicate with the audience in general but that he might speak to the *parterre*, the popular audience standing in front of the stage. This group was never envisaged in the eighteenth century as being equivalent to the entire audience, as Fried translates it, but were disparaged as a rowdy, disruptive group of pleasure seekers. In the eighteenth century the *parterre* were able to disrupt plays to such an extent that one new production by the Comédie Française had to be cut from five acts to only one and a half. It was a cliché of eighteenth-century French aesthetics that, while the public could form accurate judgements of artistic works, the *parterre* and its socially mixed clientele could not be equated with that public.[3]

Fried's analysis of David's painting concentrates upon the use of architecture to create a sense of space, focusing on the plane created by the Arch of Triumph, which makes it plain that the *Belisarius* was 'a painting not made to be beheld' (158). Although this architecture did not appear in the Van Dyck print upon which Fried considers it 'virtually certain' that David modelled his work, it was not an original motif. The Arch was in fact borrowed from the illustrations to Jean-François Marmontel's wildly successful novel *Belisarius* (1767) (Boime 1987: 175). Many of the other details of David's painting were taken directly from Gravelot's engravings, including the horrified Roman officer, the block of stone upon which Belisarius' cane rests, and the general's outstretched gesture. The original features of David's work were, then, the woman giving alms and the use of an inscription. The inscription reads 'Date obolum Belisario' (Give an obol to Belisarius). In the first version of the painting, it is slightly obscured by Belisarius' staff, but it is prominent in the later copy now in the Louvre. This tag does not feature in Marmontel's text, or any of the other painted versions of the Belisarius story before and after David's work. In itself, it requires a beholder, for only a spectator of the image would be in a position to read it. Furthermore, only an outside beholder would need such an inscription for all the figures painted by David are only too aware of the identity of the general. It would be stretching credulity to suggest that the wandering, blind general carved the sign himself to attract alms. The inscription is an interpellation by David which addresses the outside spectator and calls attention to the political message of the painting. In English political satire, Belisarius had been a symbol of government ingratitude and incompetence since 1710, when a pamphlet compared the then disgraced Duke of Marlborough to the Roman general.[4] Ever since, plays and pamphlets had hearkened to Belisarius as a metaphor for the failings of government.[5] In 1768, the leading radical journal the *Political Register*, published a print decrying the 'tyrannical' British policy towards the American colonies, in which the dismembered figure of Britannia is captioned 'Date obolum Belisario' (Wilson 1995). The *Political Register* was well known in Paris and ties between British and French radicals were sufficiently close in the period for Jean-Paul Marat, the future revolutionary leader, to campaign in Newcastle and publish his first book – *The Chains of Slavery* (1774) – in English translation. The caption places David's work as one of his first political statements, and it was no coincidence that he made it more legible in the later version.[6]

David did not simply add a political label to an illustration in Marmontel's novel, but changed the dynamics of the scene with the addition of the woman giving alms. Her presence allows the soldier to drop back and recognize his former leader from a safe distance, but more importantly it gives a gendered dynamic to the painting. Gender roles were similarly important in the British print, contrasting Britannia's virtue with the effeminacy of the British political elite. The horror of the soldier is caused as much by the reduced circumstances of the general, indicated by the woman's act of charity, as by his blindness. The paradox of the *Belisarius* is precisely this opposition of gender roles. In the *Paradox*, Diderot advised his readers to '[t]hink of women, again. They are miles beyond us in sensibility; there is no sort of comparison between their passion and ours. But as much as we are below them in action, so much are they below us in imitation' (Lacoue-Labarthe 1989: 263). The unknown woman who acts out of pity for the fallen general is the counterpoint to the masculine sensibility of the soldier. She is also the inspiration for David's exercise in artistic imitation and it is inspiration that, for Diderot, sets the true artist apart from the crowd. 'The beauty of inspiration' was what the artist Le Quesnoy could see and his visitor could not. It is what gives a work its force and enthusiasm. But that moment must be contained and controlled in conscious reflection, the masculine quality which women are held to lack. This paradox is contained in the epigram Diderot wrote for the *Belisarius*: 'Every day I see it, and always I believe I am seeing it for the first time.' The doubled insight of the witness to the blind is given force and freshness by the differing reactions of the spectators within the frame, according to their gender stereotypes. Only the spectator outside, whether it was the artist observing himself, the Salon spectator or the critic, could fully appreciate and meditate upon these different reactions and insights.

Blindness in *ancien régime* art, then, called attention to the relativism and vulnerability of human sensory perception, and the paradoxical nature of artistic creation. The blind were not used as metaphors beyond the specific limitations of their condition, but constituted an important point of reference for sensualist philosophy, as it strove to understand understanding itself. As Ménuret de Chambaud, a principal contributor to the great *Encylopedia* of Diderot and d'Alembert, opined: 'Perhaps it is true that in order to be a good moralist, one must be an excellent doctor' (Rey 1993: 25). However, not long after these words were written, philosophy took a turn away from sensualism to the more abstracted pursuit of epistemology, and medicine became inseparable from morality. In the second half of the eighteenth century, medical science began to rely on a distinction between the normal states of the body and its pathology, that is, its diseases and abnormalities. Disease, abnormality and immorality became linked in a powerful trinity which is still in force today. Georges Canguilhem has analyzed the spread of a distinction between the normal and the pathological from the first appearance of the terms in the mid-eighteenth century to their widespread acceptance in the nineteenth century:

> In the course of the nineteenth century, the real identity of normal and pathological vital phenomena, apparently so different, and given opposing values by human experience, became a kind of scientifically guaranteed

dogma, whose extension into the realms of philosophy and psychology appeared to be dictated by the authority biologists and physicians granted it.

(Canguilhem 1991 [1966]: 43)

Sensualist philosophy, which depended upon the authority of sense impressions, was among the first areas to be so affected.

Blindness was at once categorized as a pathological state of the body, in distinction to the normal condition of sight. During the French Revolution the state appropriated the wealth of the Quinze-Vingts, the charitable hospital for the blind in Paris, due to the tradition that patients said prayers for the Church and the King. Moreover, those blind persons who had formerly been in the nobility or clergy received a higher pension than others and there were suspicions of immoral conduct in the hospital. In its place, the revolutionaries proposed to create a national network of 'residential assistance for all the blind, public asylums for those who have neither habitation to shelter them, nor family to care for them' (*Observations* An II: 37). In place of royal charity, the Revolution hoped to construct a national, moral and egalitarian system of assistance for the blind, which did not entail any change in the medical care of the blind.

Although there was a seemingly absolute distinction between the pathological blind and the normal sighted, it was soon blurred by further classification among the ranks of the pathological. As the nineteenth century progessed, it became clear that, despite the physical limitations of blindness, it was regarded as less morally debilitating than other sensory loss. In particular, the blind came to be seen as superior to the deaf – in the minds of the hearing and seeing – and to be endowed with special moral qualities. The blind and deaf pupils of the state were initially housed together during the French Revolution, until political discord among their educators forced a separation in 1793. At this time, both the deaf and the blind were seen as pre-civilized beings who required the assistance of the state to render them human. In a pamphlet published in 1793, Perier, a deputy administrator at the Institute for the Deaf, adamantly insisted on the need for such an institution: 'The Deaf-Mute is always a savage, always close to ferocity, and always on the point of becoming a monster.' Even after birth, the 'savage' Deaf could mutate into monstrous forms without the restraining hand of the disciplinary Institute. The language used to describe the deaf was also applied to the blind, as here by one administrator of the blind school in 1817: 'The moral world does not exist for this child of nature; most of our ideas are without reality for him: he lives as if he was alone; he relates everything to himself' (Paulson 1987: 95). The initial breakthrough in the education of the blind was the invention of a raised typeface by Valentin Haüy, condensed by Louis Braille (1809–1852) into the code of dots with which we are familiar. As discussions of the old chestnut regarding the preferability of blindness or deafness continued, the issue was decisively resolved (by those who could see and hear) in favour of blindness. For the loss of hearing was held to entail the loss of voice and hence of thought. When the blind read Braille, they converted the dots into the pure medium of sound, which more than compensated for its non-alphabetic character, whereas the deaf used sign language, and thought without sound. By late century, official French government manuals on the care of the abnormal advised that Braille was 'an intermediary system between the manuscript and the printed text', but in sign language, 'all spiritual ideas will be unhappily materialized' (Couètoux and de Fougeray 1886: 131 and 19). Thomas Arnold (1823–1900), who founded a small school for the deaf in Northampton in 1868, believed that the blind: 'mentally, morally and spiritually [are] in a more advantageous condition than the deaf'. If the blind could create 'a mental language of vibrations and motions' from touch, the deaf were restricted to 'a language of mimic gestures . . . which is destitute of all that phonetic language provides of antecedent progress in thought and knowledge' (Arnold 1894: 9–15). In 1840, Braille was considered arbitrary and deaf sign language had won a certain acceptance, but by 1890 it was Braille that had become acceptable and the deaf were considered pre-civilized. Nothing essential had changed in the nature of sign language and Braille in the intervening fifty years. In Arnold's widely accepted viewpoint, the decisive factor in this change of opinion was the blind's ability to hear. Sight was 'much inferior in providing us with available mental images and an organ of expression', indicating that hearing alone was now considered a 'pure' sense. Arnold's privileged point of reference was the French neurologist Jean-Martin Charcot (1825–1893), as the 'abnormal' became the province of what was termed medico-psychology. By way of contrast, French officials considered that deafness rendered even the sense of sight pathological: '[the deaf person] knows that what he does not see does not exist for him; he does not look, he *devours*' (Denis 1895: 23–6). Medico-psychology thus considered the loss of sight to be far less grievous a blow than deafness. This sense that the blind are more 'human' than the deaf has persisted to the present and accounts for the greater sympathy and funding that is available for the blind.

The rise of this perceived morality of blindness from the nineteenth to the early twentieth century can also be traced in the cultural representation of blindness. In Paul De Man's famous essay, *The Rhetoric of Blindness*, he advances the case that a writer only gains a certain insight because of his or her blindness to other aspects of the problem:

> Insight could only be gained because the critics were in the grip of this peculiar blindness: their language could grope toward a certain degree of insight only because their method remained oblivious to the perception of this insight. The insight exists only for a reader in the privileged position of being able to observe the blindness as a phenomenon in its own right – the question of his own blindness being one which he is by definition incompetent to ask – and so being able to distinguish between statement and meaning.
>
> (De Man 1983: 106)

De Man's argument is central to the modern canon of blindness as outlined in this chapter. In the pursuit of clarity, insight and self-expression, successive modernist artists have deployed blindness as a key figure for their work. De Man does not, however, clarify that this relationship of blindness and insight is both historically specific – as opposed to a universal truth about criticism – and gendered. The gendered dimension of the Dibutade myth and David's *Belisarius* came to be transferred to this critical relationship valorizing insight as inevitably and uniquely masculine.

In both Romantic and Neo-Classical painting, blindness was used as a figure for insight and morality. Jean-Auguste-Dominique Ingres (1780– 1867) was the leader of the French Neo-Classical school from the collapse of Napoleon's Empire in 1815 until his death. Ingres created a series of painted manifestos, setting out the influences and beliefs of a Neo-Classicism which sought to reclaim the French Classical tradition, stemming from Poussin, while bypassing the images of the French Revolution. As a leading student of David, Ingres was well placed to carry out this artistic revision of history painting, in accord with the wider rewriting of history during the Restoration (1816–30). In his vast ceiling painting, *The Apotheosis of Homer*, Ingres reinvented French Neo-Classicism after the Revolution (Figure 8). This painting, installed in the Louvre in 1827, literally put the lid on what can be called the French cultural revolution (Bianchi 1982). It is a history painting, the most important genre of painting in the period, which became the precondition of all French history painting, depicting the appropriate sources and inspirations for this art. At the centre of the painting is the figure of Homer being crowned by the Muses, surrounded by those who have followed in his wake. Ingres depicted an artistic lineage which passed from the ancient Greek artists Apelles and Zeuxis, via the Renaissance masters Raphael and Poussin, ending by inference with Ingres himself. At the heart of this artistic pedigree sits the blind poet Homer, author of the *Iliad* and the *Odyssey*. Blindness was thus for Ingres quite

Figure 8 J.A.D. Ingres, *The Apotheosis of Homer* (1827), Louvre, Paris/Bridgeman Art Library.

literally the origin of representation. Clearly, Homer's blindness cannot be understood in the relativizing sensory tradition of the Enlightenment, for Ingres sought to deify Homer, not to place his work in relation to that of others. His blindness, symbolized by his closed eyes, is metaphorical and suggests instead that, in order to achieve the degree of insight attained by Homer, some sacrifice is necessary. Despite his success, Ingres believed that he too had suffered in his artistic career. His *Jupiter and Thetis* had been a dramatic failure at the Salon of 1811 and after his *Saint Symphorien* suffered a similar fate in 1834, Ingres refused to show his work at the Salon. It is hard not to take the metaphor of blindness a little farther. Ingres excluded his own master David and the other leading French Neo-Classicists, such as Gros, Gérard and Girodet from his vision of painting. Homer's blindness was matched by Ingres' own metaphorical blind spot concerning his own artistic formation in the Neo-Classical school of David, overlooked in his painting in favour of the eternal verities of Homer.

Ingres was haunted by the symbolism of blindness. In 1816, he completed the first of many versions of the theme *Oedipus and the Sphinx*, in which Oedipus is shown answering the Sphinx's riddle. His successful response ensured that the second part of his oracle would be enacted, for having already unwittingly killed his father, Oedipus was now to marry his mother. Oedipus is finally the agent of his own destruction, when he seeks to uncover the causes of a plague and discovers the truth of his own actions. By way of self-punishment, Oedipus blinds himself. The Freudian overtones of this story are only too apparent. For Freud, the Oedipus myth was a representation of the most fundamental masculine desires to kill the father and sleep with the mother, as well as of its most potent fear, namely Oedipus' blindness, equated to the fear of castration. It is in fact arguable that without the nineteenth century construct of blindness as moral sacrifice, Freud would not have been able to use the Oedipus myth as he did. Blindness appears at the centre of Ingres' history paintings precisely because of these new resonances it acquired in the period. The meanings conveyed by blindness as metaphor were, however, complex and irreducible to a single message. It was a short step from the moral insight of Homer to the castrated gaze of Oedipus. Blindness became a complex figure in Ingres' work, standing for representation, for morality and for the construction of the masculine ego itself, always haunted by the fear of castration, itself envisaged as blindness.[7]

For Ingres' depiction of history painting is a striking example of what Donna Harraway has called the patriline. His *Homer* is a homosocial world in which women appear only in non-human form as Muses. The transmission and reproduction of cultural value was envisaged as a purely masculine affair, eliminating the fear of castration and the blind(ed) gaze. A central theme of eighteenth-century painting had been the 'fallen father', to use Carol Duncan's insightful phrase. History and genre painting had sought to construct an authoritative father figure in a society widely believed to be unusually susceptible to feminine influence. For many revolutionary leaders, this feminizing of the French state was to blame for the political weaknesses and corruption of the *ancien régime*. Even avowed supporters of the monarchy agreed that, in the words of the painter Elizabeth Vigée Lebrun, 'the women reigned then. The Revolution dethroned them' (Vigée Lebrun 1989: 49). Rather than return to this charged political controversy, Ingres elided it by creating an idea of culture as the exclusive province of the white male. From its foundation in 1648, the French Academy of Painting had permitted women to become members in theory, although few in practice were able to gain the necessary training. But in 1776, it was felt to be necessary to limit the number of potential women members to four. Even then, the admission of Vigée Lebrun in 1783 required considerable politicking to evade the censure of the leading Academician Pierre (Vigée Lebrun 1989: 34–5). The reformed nineteenth-century Academy excluded women altogether. In Ingres' representation of civilization, there was no place for women.

Eugène Delacroix (1798–1863), the leader of the Romantic school of painting, also represented blindness as the origin of representation, even though he is usually considered as being directly opposed to Ingres' Neo-Classicism. Delacroix chose as a subject *The Poet Milton Dictating to His Daughters* (1826). For the Romantics, the blind poet Milton occupied the same position of authority as Homer for the Neo-Classicists. The subject had been treated by Henry Fuseli in 1799, but he was so anxious to represent Milton's blindness that the poet has ashen skin and sunken eyes, looking more like Boris Karloff's Frankenstein than an inspired poet. Delacroix represented the scene in quieter but altogether more effective fashion. Just as David used the woman giving alms to give meaning to his *Belisarius*, so did Delacroix highlight the contrast between the active women and their passive father. Milton becomes the supreme embodiment of the superiority of the voice and hearing over sight, as his powers of creativity are constrasted with the women, who although sighted, are fit only to copy down their father's words. The poet's insight is such that it overcomes his physical blindness. Milton retains his patriarchal authority, despite having suffered the loss of his sight, and his potency is doubly attested to by the presence of his daughters. Delacroix's confident embrace of blindness as a gendered metaphor for creativity and morality was to gain ascendancy over Ingres' homosocial vision. While the Neo-Classical Ingres saw blindness as both the origin and the potential annihilation of representation, the modern Romantics bestowed creativity on the individual male and were unconcerned to construct secure artistic genealogies. Indeed the Oedipal gesture of revolt became *de rigueur* for any aspiring young artist.

The high point of this moralizing trajectory came with Paul Strand's (1890–1976) photograph *Blind Woman* (1916) (Figure 9). Taken as a manifesto for Strand's departure from the gradated tones of the Photo-Secession movement, his representation of blindness thus embodied revolt and coming of age. The photograph has long been hailed as a modernist masterpiece:

> The portrait conveys *qualities*: endurance, isolation, the curious alertness of the blind or nearly blind, and a surprising beauty in the strong, possibly Slavic, head. The whole concept of blindness is aimed like a weapon at those whose privilege of sight permits them to experience the picture, much like the 'dramatic irony' in which an all-knowing audience observes a doomed protagonist onstage. Although he excluded bystanders from the picture, Strand

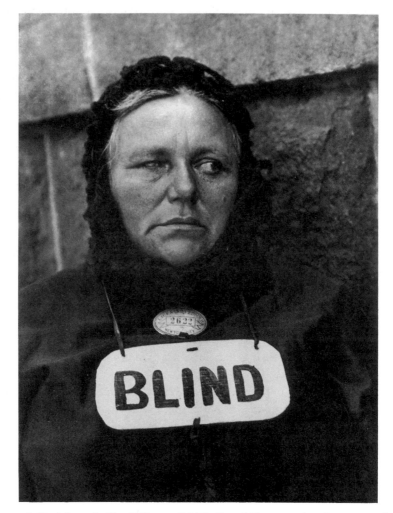

Figure 9 Paul Strand, *Blind Woman* (1917), Royal Photographic Society, Bath.

included everyone who sees it. This extraordinary device gives the photo-graph its particular edge, adding new meaning to a simple portrait.

(Haworth-Booth 1987: 5)

In this view, Strand's photograph of the blind woman functions as an abstract, moral discourse on perception. The weapon of blindness belonged not to the blind woman but to the photographer. It was no coincidence that Strand photographed a blind woman. In so doing, he collapsed the moral exchange created by David and Delacroix between the blind man and the sighted woman into one figure. Strand's deployment of gender constituted the originality of his work, for photographers had long considered the blind as an intriguing subject. As early as 1858, the photographic journal *La Lumière* reported the placard of a Parisian male beggar: 'Give to the poor blind man, he will not see you' (*La Lumière* 1858: 99). In Strand's work, the woman represents the modernist quandry as to the nature of perception, but it is the photographer who has the key to representation rather than the figure within the image. In his quest to deny the woman any specificity, Strand erased her name and any details about her in order to make blindness a more effective symbol. If blindness is to be fully effective as a moral lesson, it cannot be dogged by such trivial details. None the less, the history of the blind, as opposed to the abstract idea of blindness, is present in this photograph. The blind woman wears a brass badge, bearing the legend 'Licensed Peddler. New York. 2622'. The badge, together with the crudely painted sign reading BLIND, attests to the state's intervention in controlling the 'degenerate' population. In order to sell items on the street, the woman has to be registered and classified, involving tests to ensure that she is 'really' blind and not simply 'idle'. These policies were the culmination of over a century of designating the blind as pathological and hence a problem for the body politic. Strand's abstract moral lesson was enabled and given meaning by the classification and labelling of the blind by that nexus of medical and political authority which Michel Foucault has named bio-power. As a meditation on representation, the photograph takes blindness to be the origin of representation, but denies the woman any participation in this process, except as its object.

This interpretation of the role of blindness in representation received ironic confirmation when the American Minimalist artist Robert Morris (b. 1931) set about his series entitled *Blind Time* in 1973. Morris had pursued a critique of the prevalent modes of art practice, criticism and display in a variety of media since the early 1960s. Now, seeking to move on from his site-specific earth pieces of the early 1970s, Morris undertook a series of works in which he was unable to see. He assigned himself a specific task and a length of time in which to complete it, drawing on paper with his fingers. By so doing, Morris sought to disrupt the modernist obsession with sight and its representation, as Maurice Berger has noted:

> Like being lost in a labyrinth, such drawing processes radically altered the artist's sense of control of his own actions. By undoing the compositional claims of the artist over his work, the *Blind Time* series distanced the artist from the modernist conceits of ego and temperament. Because the artist's

masterful control of his process was now rendered irrelevant, such works travestied the obsession of formalist abstraction with compositional balance and harmony.

(Berger 1989: 151)

Morris soon decided to take this process one step farther. In 1976, he commenced the series *Blind Time II*, in which he used a woman who had been blind from birth as what he termed an 'assistant'. The woman, known only as A.A., was recruited from the American Association for the Blind and was asked to carry out similar tasks to those Morris himself had previously performed. The experience was not a success. A.A. quickly became sceptical of the project and confused as to its intentions. Here, for example, Morris commented:

> She had no idea of illusionistic drawing. I described perspective to her and she thought that was absolutely ridiculous, that things got smaller in the distance. She had no conception of that. She kept asking me about criteria, got very involved in what is the right kind of criteria for a thing. And there was no way that she could find any and finally that sort of conflict became very dramatic. She was operating in a way that she wouldn't have to invoke [these criteria]. And at the same time she was aghast that she was not able to.
>
> (Berger 1989: 153)

This scene, far from constituting a radical experiment, was a re-enactment of the modernist legend connecting blindness to the origin of representation, as if Morris had tried to find his own Dibutade and recreate the origin of drawing in a woman whom he believed had no concept of visual representation. Like Dibutade, A.A. could not record her own work, but relied on the intercession of the male authority figure for her claim to a place in art history. Whereas Paul Strand had used blindness as a weapon, Morris went one further and used the blind woman as a form of tool. He denied her the chance to formulate her own concepts of art practice and refused to let her establish any rules in her work. In 1856, Théophile Gautier had made this distinction central to his 'programme of the modern school' of art for arts sake:

> The artist must search for his alphabet in the visible world, which supplies him with conventional signs . . .; but if the idea of the beautiful pre-exists within us, would it pre-exist in a man born blind, for example? What image of the beautiful in art could a pensioner of the Quinze Vingts make for himself?
>
> (Gautier 1856: 157)

The relativistic notions of perception which had so fascinated Enlightenment critics no longer applied. Sight was essential not just for art, as might seem obvious, but for the very notions of art and beauty. The very initials

A.A. by which the blind woman is known are indicative of Morris's sense that she was at the origin of art and could have no rules. Soon becoming dissatisfied with her work, Morris discontinued the project, finding it '[s]parer and less controlled than the artist's own blind drawings, they are more about her impressions and feelings' (Fry 1986: 34). Morris withdrew all 52 works created in the *Blind Time II* series from circulation. Modernism had so far abstracted blindness and gender from the body that Morris's encounter with an actual blind woman was bound to end in failure.

When he resumed *Blind Time* in 1985, Morris undertook the works himself. In this version of the project, he added philosophical commentaries on the images produced and the ideas that lay behind them. For example, in one 1985 piece, Morris set about constructing a grid in a seven-minute experiment. As Rosalind Krauss has argued, the grid has been one of the defining motifs of modernism and Morris attached considerable weight to the procedure in his inscription: 'Searching for a metaphor for the occupation of that moment between lapsed time and the possibilities spent on the one hand and an imagined but unoccupiable future on the other, both of which issue from that tightly woven nexus of language, tradition and culture which constructs our narrative of time' (Fry 1986: 37). Although *Blind Time III* makes considerable reference to contemporary physics, citing such figures as Einstein, Bohr and Feynman, this passage seems closer to Marcel Proust and his search for lost time. These literary and philosophical comments could hardly be further removed from the excerpts of conversation between the artist and A.A., which accompanied the previous version of the series. The male artist feels able to explore the metaphorical dimensions and wider implications of his 'blindness', precisely the avenues he had blocked for the anonymous blind woman. Morris's modernism denied the blind any possibility of participating in visual representation. While this exclusion might seem natural, it did not seem so to early modern blind sculptors or indeed to A.A. Within this metaphorical framework, blindness-as-lack-of-sight affects only women, whereas blindness-as-insight is a peculiarly male phenomenon. The radical feminist art collective, the Guerilla Girls, would no doubt wish to note that in Derrida's exhibition at the Louvre, for which he was given access to their entire collection of prints and drawings, the philosopher selected no women artists.[8]

Blindness – or more exactly, the interplay between the insightful artist and the blind woman – is only one metaphor for modernism and is not equivalent to it. But the nexus of race, gender and disability created by the triumph of the Dibutade myth of the origin of painting in the mid-eighteenth century forms a crucial point of investigation for the modern representation of the body, which was caught between two difficult alternatives. The Dibutade myth was itself determined by a wider revision of European intellectual history which excluded African and Semitic influences in favour of a pure Aryan model of ancient Greek history. However, the alternative modernist reading of the body, which privileges the fragmentary and dispersed body and argues that culture oscillates between the poles of blindness and insight, is constructed around a notion of originary gender difference. Both readings of the body thus depend upon essential differences of race or gender, which are both necessarily exclusive and ahistorical. It would be equally disingenuous simply to call for an end to the metaphorization of the body, still more so for an end to the representation of the body – even a Minimalist sculpture can be read as a denial of the body. For it is not enough to reveal yet again that cultural products are social constructions, as Michael Taussig has recently argued: 'What do we do with this old insight? If life is constructed, how come it appears so immutable? How come culture appears so natural?' (Taussig 1993a: xvi). Rather than concluding by producing the white rabbit of cultural construction from the intellectual's top hat, it is my point of departure that these contradictions produce a necessary and productive dis-ease concerning the bodyscape.

However, this constructed understanding of the modern body does not make it any less real, nor does it allow the modern subject to bypass the limits of body in a quest for identity. The body cannot be known or understood without visual representation, yet both the body itself and its image seem inevitably flawed. An indication of this problem is that there is no way to describe the body as imperfect (disabled, incomplete, virtual, etc.) which does not logically and linguistically imply the existence of a perfect body. In order to extend our understanding, it is therefore necessary to examine the persistence and cultural function of notions of the perfect body, the task of the next two chapters.

NOTES

1 In the *ancien régime*, terms such as 'deaf', 'deaf-mute' and 'mute' were synonyms, for it was assumed that the two sensory disfunctions were causally related.
2 This reading revealed more of his older Marxist credentials than Fuller cared to remember, for Theodore Adorno and Max Horkheimer, the leading theoreti-

cians of the Marxist Frankfurt School, yielded to no one in their contempt for popular culture.

3 In Britain, by contrast, the pit was held to be the most important venue for determining public opinion in the theatre.

4 See Anon, *Belisarius and Zariana: A Dialogue* (London, 1709) and the play *Belisarius* by William Philips (London, T. Woodward, 1724), dedicated to General Webb, reprinted in 1758.

5 Plays included: *Belisarius* ascribed to John Phillip Kemble (1778) and *Belisarius* by Hugh Downman (Exeter, 1786); a scene concerning Belisarius was published in *The Oracle* (17 October 1795). Many thanks to Kathleen Wilson for these references.

6 Thomas Crow has suggested that the exile referred to was the minister Turgot, an identification made all the more likely by the English parallel.

7 The polysemicity of blindness in the modern period does not undermine Derrida's interpretation, but rather reinforces it. Derrida has often emphasized that the keywords in his readings, such as deconstruction, glyph, hymen, différance, *pharmakon*, and so on, are not to be individually privileged as the key to the Western metaphysic, but are different points of entry to that discourse.

8 In fact, when Derrida discusses sexuality it is male sexuality that is in question, via an examination of representations of the blinding of Samson, read as castration.

2

THE BODY POLITIC

The representation of the body of the French king and the later Republican State will be considered in this chapter as paradigmatic of the perfect body presumed by artistic theory. Focusing on the transition between the personalized body politic of the monarchy and the allegorical figure of the Republic proposed by the 1789 Revolution, I shall explore the vicissitudes of the body politic in this crucial formative period. The abolition of the monarchy in 1793 inevitably entailed a transformation in the representation of the state, which was now depicted by an allegorical figure. This figure was sometimes male and sometimes female, as recent studies have shown (Hunt 1984; Agulhon 1979). However, it has also been argued that the gender and sexuality of these allegorical figures is beside the point and that they are simply to be considered as neutral, non-sexualized representations of the state. In fact, the body politic during and after the Revolution invoked sexual reproduction as the key to its signification in the new era. Radical forces in the French Revolution believed that the regeneration of the body politic had to be accompanied by a regeneration of the individual body. The politics of fraternity envisaged this regeneration as a reinvigoration of the 'normal' family after the sexual excesses of the *ancien régime* and expected to see a restoration of population growth as a consequence. Central to this dissemination of meaning was the incorporation of the audience in radical constructions of the state as participants in the body politic, rather than as passive spectators. Throughout the modern era, state monuments have required only the passivity of fetishism, whereas radical notions of participatory democracy have demanded engagement. Just as the French Revolution found it difficult to detach the new notion of the body politic from the individual body of the king, which returned when Napoleon declared himself emperor in 1805, so later reformers have found this gendered construction hard to escape. In an epilogue to this chapter, I examine this problem in relation to the Nazi sculpture of Arno

Breker, to body building, and to the Vietnam Veterans Memorial in Washington DC.

THE KING'S TWO BODIES

In medieval and early modern Europe, there was ample evidence of the frailties and imperfections of the human body. The monarchies and princedoms of the period none the less relied upon a stable continuity of powerful and imposing individuals to sustain the autocratic political structures of feudalism. In order to compensate for the weaknesses of individual kings, political theorists developed the notion that the king had two bodies. One was his personal frame, the 'too, too solid flesh' of the human being. The other was a mystical notion of the king who never dies, held to be eternal and beyond the reach of mortal weakness and failings. This quasi-divine Body politic was symbolized by the ritual anointing of the monarch during the coronation ceremony, which separated the king from all other lay persons. Alone of all people, the king wielded divine and secular power in his own right.

Ernst Kantorowicz's important study, *The King's Two Bodies*, explored the medieval origins of this theory, later to be redeployed by the absolutist monarchies of early modern Europe. He demonstrated that the thesis outlived even the absolute monarchies and was used as late as 1887 in English law (Kantorowicz 1953: 4). The principle upon which the Victorians acted was identical to that proposed in the sixteenth century:

> The King has in him two Bodies, viz., a Body natural, and a Body politic. His Body natural (if it be considered in itself) is a Body mortal, subject to all Infirmities that come by Nature or Accident, to the Imbecility of Infancy or old Age, and to the like Defects that happen to the natural Bodies of other People. But his Body politic is a Body that cannot be seen or handled, consisting of Policy and Government, and constituted for the Direction of the People and the Management of the public weal, and this Body is utterly void of Infancy, and old Age, and other natural Defects and Imbecilities, which the Body natural is subject to, and for this Cause, what the King does in his Body politic, cannot be invalidated or frustrated by any Disability in his natural Body.
>
> (Kantorowicz 1953: 7)

This principle accepts that the body in itself is naturally imperfect and of necessity incomplete but avoids the weaknesses implicit in such dependence on the physical body of the king by creating a mystical Body politic that never dies nor weakens (the upper-case will be used to signify such usage). During the English Revolution (1642–9), the rebel Parliamentarians were thus able to claim that they were loyal to the Body politic of the king, rebelling only against the natural body of Charles I. Louis Marin has summarized the transformation entailed by the creation of the king's two bodies: 'The king (with a small k, the real individual with knees swollen by gout – the organic body) is changed entirely into his "image" and becomes "representation" – the King (capital K, dignity, Majesty and the political body)' (Marin 1988 : 222). In its denial of the natural body, the Body politic became entirely dependent upon visual representation.

Central to the question of the body politic is the justification and rationalization of violence. Any offence against the absolute monarch's body was a capital crime, punished with spectacular violence against the perpetrator's own body. The famous opening to Michel Foucault's history of the prison, *Discipline and Punish*, tells the story of the execution of one Damiens in 1757 for the attempted assassination of the French king Louis XV. The sentence was terrible:

> On a scaffold . . . the flesh will be torn from his breasts, arms, thighs and calves with red-hot pincers, his right hand, holding the knife with which he committed the said parricide, burnt with sulphur and, on those places where the flesh will be torn away, poured molten lead, boiling oil, burning resin, wax and sulphur melted together and then his body drawn and quartered by four horses and his limbs and body consumed by fire, reduced to ashes and his ashes thrown to the winds.
>
> (Foucault 1977: 3)

The perfection of the Body politic justified and compelled violence against other bodies. Such was the case for all crimes committed in the king's jurisdiction, as Foucault has explained: 'Beside its immediate victim, the crime attacks the sovereign: it attacks him personally, since the law represents the will of the sovereign; it attacks him physically, since the force of the law is the force of the prince' (Foucault 1977: 47). The body of the king was damaged by the crime, which entailed that the body of the criminal must both confess and be punished for the offence in order to restore the Body politic to perfection.

In Edmund Burke's eighteenth-century writings on beauty, this perfection became a category of the aesthetic: 'I know nothing sublime which is not some modification of power.' The sublime, a central aesthetic category for both Enlightenment and postmodern theorists, depends on aesthetic pleasure being derived from the depiction of something which would in itself be ugly or even terrifying. The standard example of the sublime was a shipwreck, which would be terrifying to experience, but could make a pleasurable subject in representation. A more sophisticated example is offered by the exercise of state power derived from the body of the king. The violence of war or royal authority was the most sublime exercise of power in practice and thus amongst the most aesthetically pleasing in representation. The anthropologist Michael Taussig has argued that modern societies are still organized around the fetishism of the state:

> By State fetishism I mean a certain aura of might as figured by the Leviathan or, in a quite different mode, by Hegel's intricately argued vision of the State as not merely the embodiment of reason, of the Idea, but also as an impressively organic unity, something much greater than the sum of its parts.
>
> (Taussig 1993b: 218)

The State, like the Body politic, thus remains an organic body even when it is not encapsulated by the body of the monarch and can be the object of fetishism.

Taussig's work implies a question as to what this organism might be, once it is no longer the construct of the King's Two Bodies offered by absolutism. His investigation begins with Max Weber's sociological definition of the state as the organization within society which has a monopoly on legal violence, without further exploring the organic quality of the state. If the state is figured organically, its corporal representation is central to maintaining the central illusion of modern state fetishism, that the state is a really existing and palpable body. How can this body be imagined without using the medium of the king's body? In Benedict Anderson's influential description, the modern nation state is envisaged as an 'imagined community', existing only within the imaginations of its citizens and rulers. Unlike the hierarchical relations of the absolutist state, 'the nation is always conceived as a deep, horizontal comradeship. Ultimately, it is this fraternity that makes it possible over the last two centuries, for so many people, not so much to kill, as to willingly die for such limited imaginings' (Anderson 1983: 16). Anderson's insight raises two important lines of inquiry. In the transformation of the body politic from the absolute king to the nation state, the question of violence has become reversed. Whereas the king's body was both the rationale for state violence and its guarantor, the modern state demands each individual citizen to risk their own well-being in exchange for nothing other than the continued existence of that state. In the *ancien régime*, Damiens himself decided to commit the violent act which had such terrible consequences for him. He was punished for that act and not for being a French citizen of a certain age at a time when the state perceived itself to be threatened. Later generations of conscripts did not have that luxury but, despite certain moments of resistance, they have on the whole consented to being placed in danger. The new visual embodiments of the nineteenth- and twentieth-century state need to be considered in the light of this shift in emphasis. Secondly, Anderson indicates that state violence was closely connected to the ideal of fraternity, that elusive third leg of the French Revolutionary tripod. Just as fraternity gendered equality as masculine, so did war and the identity of the state become masculine, despite the obvious involvement of women in both ventures. How, then, does the representation of the state address all its citizens?

THE STONE KING: REPRESENTING LOUIS XIV

The transformation of Louis XIV (1648–1715) from a weak monarch into the all-powerful *roi soleil* is perhaps the most striking example of the power of the Body politic. France had endured over a century of civil and religious wars upon Louis' accession as a minor in 1648. There then followed five years of civil war, known as the *Fronde*, during which Louis was forced to abandon Paris, and the traditional monarchical system was almost overthrown. Louis never forgot this experience and, as soon as he became king in his own right in 1660, he set about eradicating any possibility that such a revolt could ever occur again. Louis was still preoccupied with the issue in 1687 and compelled the city of Paris to apologize formally for its errors during the *Fronde*. Louis curtailed the powers of the nobility by diverting their attention from military conflict to the power struggles at his new court of Versailles. Twenty miles outside Paris, this palace was carefully fabricated to construct the illusion of Louis' power. Courtiers competed against each other for precedence in twin pyramids of ascendancy, one noble and one bourgeois. They were as concerned to prevent the success of one of their rivals as to promote their own cause and Versailles thus served not only to domesticate the French elite, but to control them. By 1691, one Jurieu complained that: 'The King has taken the place of the State, the King is everything, the State is no longer anything. He is an idol to which are sacrificed the provinces, the towns, finance, the great, the small, everything!' (Elias 1974: 117).

This transformation of man into Majesty was the ultimate *trompe l'œil* of the baroque, displayed in a panoply of painting, sculpture, coins, medals, theatre, gardens and architecture. These representations were not hollow images of the king, but in certain important senses they *were* the king. Unlike his natural body, the portrait of the king never slept, fell ill, or aged.

The representation of the king was co-extensive with his natural body, according to the *savant* Lazare Meysonnier: 'If someone among us disrespectfully destroys a piece of paper on which is written the name of our Most Christian King LOUIS DE BOURBON, or tramples it beneath his feet with insolent words, the King will know it, will feel offended in his person and will punish this criminal' (Meysonnier 1669: 67). For, in the remarkable expression of the seventeenth-century logicians of Port-Royal, 'the Portrait of Caesar *is* Caesar'. To damage or assault a representation of the king was to attack the Body politic itself, the most essential element of the absolutist monarchy.

The status of the king's portrait was theorized by André Félibien, Permanent Secretary of the newly established Academy of Painting and Sculpture in his essay *Le Portrait du Roy* (1671). Félibien argued that French painters had particular good fortune as Louis XIV was not simply a king but 'the perfect model of a great King' (87). While this was true for any king: 'Today there is room to say with the greatest degree of truth that in your Person and in your Portrait, we have two Kings, who are both incomparable' (110). Félibien was well aware of the usual difficulties confronting the portrait artist:

> If one is not entirely deceived into taking these figures for real people, nor as surprised as if this action was really happening, it is the failing of the eyes and not that of the Work; because Art has gone as far as it can in deceiving the gaze. But as two rays come out of the eyes which seek to embrace the bodies, wishing to know them, one must not be surprised if bodies which are only painted on a flat surface do not have the same sensation for the gaze as bodies in relief.
>
> (77)

This combination of the modern science of optics with the traditional notion of the King's Two Bodies was typical of absolutist politics, which revived and modernized the traditional powers of the monarchy. Félibien recalled that even the fabled painter Zeuxis had to assemble all the most beautiful women in the town of Crotona in order to select the most beautiful part from each one to create his portrait of Helen of Troy. By contrast 'how much happier is the excellent painter of today in finding in the sole Person of Your Majesty that with which to make the Painting of the King, which will be in future the model for all other Kings' (111). Even the greatest painters of antiquity could not compose a model from many bodies to compare with that presented by the perfection of Louis XIV's Body politic. Absolutism had dramatically reinvested the traditional doctrine of the King's Two Bodies with a new authority, centred around the visual image, which would henceforth set a new standard for both artists and monarchs.

Louis himself recognized the newly dual nature of state power. His saying 'L'Etat, c'est moi' (I am the State) incarnates the personal nature of absolute monarchy. When, however, he saw his own portrait by Charles Le Brun, he remarked 'C'est Louis le Grand' (It is Louis the Great), rather than any simpler recognition that it was a likeness of himself. For the portrait of the king was not a representation of Louis de Bourbon, fourteenth king of that name, but the depiction of the Body politic which never died. It was therefore appropriate for Louis to hail and name the portrait as such. The famous portrait (1701) of Louis by Hyacinthe Rigaud, which showed all the pomp and panoply of majesty, took the king's place in the throne room at Versailles during his absence and it was as much of an offence to turn one's back on the portrait as it was to do so to the king himself.

By the end of his long reign in 1715, no less than 700 statues and paintings had been made of Louis XIV. For the general population, who had no access to the king's cabinet of paintings, the campaign in stone was the most visible manifestation of the absolute monarch. Sculpture was held to be of particular importance in the period and was considered a more accomplished art than painting for, as Lamoignon de Basville reminded his fellow Academicians in 1678, sculpture was 'a profession which drew its origin from God himself' (Lamoignon de Basville 1678: 32). For the Bible tells how God made Adam out of clay, and this distinguished origin had encouraged other notables to pursue the art, including – it was said – Socrates, the Roman Emperor Hadrian and François I of France. In 1685–6 alone, close to twenty major statues of the king were erected in public squares around France. Many of these statues were placed in towns which had displayed signs of political unrest or independence, and the presence of the Stone King seems to have been intended as a reminder of royal authority and majesty. These statues were as close to the king as most French people were likely to get, and each statue was inaugurated with pomp and circumstance. In the Place des Victoires in Paris, a 13 foot-high statue of Louis by Martin Desjardins was erected, showing the king in a *contraposto* stance, wearing his coronation robes. When it was unveiled, the celebrations included speeches, parades, fireworks and music (Burke 1992: 92–6).

The culmination of the statue campaign was the unveiling of François Girardon's colossal equestrian statue in the Place Louis-le-Grand, Paris, in August 1699. The statue was so vast that twenty men had lunch inside it while it was being installed (Burke 1992: 16). Complementing the majestic scope of the work, Girardon had depicted Louis as a Roman emperor, deriving his composition from the equestrian statue of the Emperor Augustus. The colossal size of the piece reinforced the message emanating from Louis' Academies that the present reign was the first to emulate and even surpass the achievements of the Ancients. What Charles Perrault declaimed in the elegant language of the Academy, Girardon made available for all to see. The Paris municipality reinforced the lesson of this sermon in stone with a grand opening ceremony, including traditional representations of the king such as Julius Caesar, Alexander the Great, Clovis and Charlemagne, as well as legendary heroes such as Jason, Hercules and Theseus, and finally the popular French king Henri IV. The message was clear: Louis XIV represented in his one person the greatest of the French monarchy and Classical antiquity, together with the strength and capacity of the demigods of legend.

The imperfections of the king's natural body were, then, amply compensated by its Other, the king's Body politic. Louis recognized the radical distinction between his portrait and himself, as can be seen from the 'audiences' held by Rigaud's portrait while the king himself was elsewhere. This was not a straightforward, binary opposition but was only made possible by the intercession of the sign, that is to say, the physical object of the painting or sculpture. Only the visual sign enabled the transition between imperfect natural body and perfect Body politic. The king's portrait, whether painted or sculpted, contained within it multiple points of analogy and comparison with figures of French history, Classical history and antique legend. While the Body politic formed a distinct and palpable entity, it was not an individual body, but an entity whose superiority was derived precisely from its capacity for multiple and unending representation. In the period, to 'represent' could also mean to carry out one's duties as a public person and, while Louis represented the king, his portrait represented monarchy itself (Burke 1992).

ENGENDERING THE CLASSICAL

Louis XIV created the masculine monarch represented in a Classicized statue as the epitome of the Body politic. As the eighteenth century progressed, all the constituent parts of this ensemble underwent radical rethinking and revision. The monarchy itself failed to maintain the austere standards of Louis' court and it was plagued by sexual and moral scandals, ranging from bankruptcy to allegations that Marie-Antoinette had inces-

65

tuous relations with her young son. At the end of the *ancien régime*, revolutionaries and reformers alike agreed that the character of the monarchy had brought the body politic into disrepute. It was partly in response to this changed public mood that art critics in the latter half of the eighteenth century began to demand that artists should concentrate on renewing the preeminence of history painting for, as one critic put it in 1747: 'Henceforth painting must be a school of morals.' Their claims were read by a wide audience as, for the first time, such art criticism was printed, sold and distributed not just in Paris but throughout France as part of the underground network of literature. This public and moralistic agenda for art was envisaged as a return to the ideals of Classical antiquity and has hence become known as Neo-Classicism. The programme was soon endorsed by the monarchy, but ironically attained its finest moments in David's depictions of the French Revolution and Napoleon.

The Neo-Classical body, far from being a monolithic individual, was imagined as being capable of radical change, being substituted for other bodies, and as being able to represent many bodies. In order to demonstrate this thesis, I shall pursue the Classical male statue from its theorization in the Enlightenment to David's use of the heroic figure to represent the Republican body politic. Both sculpture and masculinity were subject to considerable change in status in the period, so that the Classical statue representing the body politic in the nineteenth century had very different resonances from those of Louis XIV's reign. It is often supposed that the instability of gender can best be seen in examining representations of women, but masculine roles in the *ancien régime* and Revolutionary period were equally unstable, as evidenced by the writings of the Marquis de Sade. In his novel *Justine*, M. de Bressac describes the joy of being penetrated:

> If you only knew the charm of this fantasy, if you could only understand what one feels in the pleasant illusion of becoming nothing but a woman! What an incredible sensation! One abhors the sex, and yet one wants to imitate it! . . . How delightful it is to be the strumpet of all who want you . . . to be, one after another in the same day, the mistress of a porter, a marquis, a valet, a monk. . . . No, no, Thérèse, you do not understand what pleasure is for a head constructed as mine is. . . . But morality apart, what if you imagined the physical sensations associated with this divine taste!. . . . Wrapped in his arms, mouths glued to each other, we wish that our whole existence could be incorporated into his. We would like to fuse into a single being.
>
> (Lever 1993: 205)

Eighteenth-century man seems here anything but a perfect individual, content within himself (gender intended). In the period, as Lynn Hunt has argued: 'Whereas incest is the sign of the absence of the father's law, sodomy is the sign of the disintegration of gender boundaries' (Hunt 1992: 145). In keeping with this interpretation, the monarchy had consistently been accused of incestual practices in the latter days of the *ancien régime*, whereas Republican Man was depicted within the context of heterosexual relations, whose 'normal' outcome was reproduction. Outside that context, both gender roles and artistic reproductivity were in doubt.

The statue played an important role in Enlightenment philosophy, science and art. In 1754, the philosopher Condillac imagined the body as a statue in his highly influential work, the *Treatise on Sensations*. He established a metaphor, which was later given different inflections by figures ranging from the Nazi sculptor Arno Brecker to the body builder Arnold Schwarzenegger. Condillac wanted to investigate the role of the senses in establishing human knowledge and self-awareness and thus proceeded to imagine a statue being invested with the various senses one by one. He sought to describe the changes that resulted from each addition to the sensibility of the statue, but first told his readers: 'It is very important to put ourselves exactly in the place of the statue we are going to observe' (Condillac 1754: 9). Condillac thus erased Descartes' conception of the body as being *a priori* different in substance and space from the mind/self. He envisaged a complete and co-extensive implantation of the reader within the body of the statue, although the reader's Self retained its understanding. When the statue was allowed one or other sense by Condillac, he argued that 'this feeling and his self [*son moi*] are consequently only the same thing.' The philosopher pretending to be the statue was at an advantage, for whereas 'we will again suppose that his marble exterior does not permit any use of his senses, we will reserve for ourselves the liberty of opening them at our choice' (Condillac 1754: 11). Thus the philosopher had complete control over the imagined ego of his creation, which he could manipulate at will, a will that his creation did not possess. The statue had a new form of Self: 'As a result, the Self [*Moi*], rather than being concentrated in the soul, ought to extend itself, to spread and in some way repeat itself in all the parts of the body.' Condillac denied the Cartesian dualism between the mind and the body and, in a striking prefiguration of Freud's notion of the ego, replaced it with an overlapping map in which the body was the Self and the Self was the body.

While Condillac's statue was male, like the philosopher, the reader who was invited to join in this production of a new body could potentially be of either gender. As we know from the paintings of Fragonard and Boucher, the female reader was a recognized and important figure in the new print culture of the period. The ambiguities in this reproductive process were soon eliminated by Jean-Jacques Rousseau's dramatization of the myth of Pygmalion. According to legend, Pygmalion was a Greek sculptor who fell in love with his statue Galatea because the sculpture had achieved such a degree of perfection. The gods took pity on him and caused the sculpture to come to life with a predictably happy ending. Rousseau rendered Pygmalion as a tortured artist, hovering on the margins between sanity and madness in his narcissistic desire for his own work. When he finally admits he is in love with the statue, Pygmalion exclaims:

> Ah! wretched Wand'rer! to thyself return;
> Lament thy Folly, thy Distraction mourn.

He finds himself in agonies of delirium and madness:

> Oh! Torment! empty wishes, vain Desires!
> Rage, hopeless, dreadful Love, my spirit fires.

Then it seems to him that the statue is in fact alive and he believes that he has lost his reason:

> Unfortunate! no Comfort then remains;
> Thy Madness now its full ascendant gains.

Of course, he is not insane and Galatea truly lives. The sculptor's creative fire has gone further than any artist might dare to hope and engendered another being. But Rousseau's scene ends leaving the identity of the protagnonists highly confused:

> Galatea (touches herself and says): 'Me' [moi].
> Pygmalion (transported): 'Me'.
> Galatea (still touching herself): 'It's me.' (Taking several steps and touching a marble): 'This is no longer me.'
> (Pygmalion covers her with ardent kisses)
> Galatea: 'Ah! Me again . . . '
>
> (Rousseau 1779)

Pygmalion has reproduced the ultimate (heterosexual) narcissistic object, himself (moi, the self) in female form. In Rousseau's version of the animation of a statue, it is clear that the male artist was the active creator and the resulting female was formed from an inanimate mass awaiting his touch. Galatea identifies marble as what she was, but is no longer, and names both her body and Pygmalion's as her self, the moi which Condillac had put into play. In Condillac, the anonymous reader shared the manipulative power of the writer over the moi but Rousseau limits that power to men. None the less, although Neo-Classicism attributes generative power to men, Pygmalion is far from being the ideal, individualized male, for Galatea is aware of her corporal limits and yet identifies herself as Pygmalion; and vice versa. Indeed, when Sigmund Freud later considered E.T.A. Hoffmann's story, *The Sandman*, in which the student Nathaniel falls in love with an automatic doll named Olympia, he saw the story as revealing Nathaniel's repressed infantile desires: 'Olympia . . . the automatic doll, can be nothing else than a personification of Nathaniel's feminine attitude towards his father in infancy. . . . Olympia is, as it were, a dissociated complex of Nathaniel's which confronts him as a person' (Freud 1946: 385; Chow 1993: 61–3). Rousseau's opposition between active male and passive female was thus closer to the Marquis de Sade's desire to be penetrated than he might have liked, undermining his desire to create a clear split between the active male and passive female.

This attempt to create an absolute opposition between the creative male and the emotional female became a staple of pre-Revolutionary visual culture, epitomized by David's famous canvasses of the 1780s, the *Oath of the Horatii* (1785) and the *Lictors Returning to Brutus the Bodies of His Sons* (1789). The *Horatii* depicted the three sons of Horatius, taking an oath to their father to defend the Roman Republic against the champions of the neighbouring town of Alba. On the right hand side, their sisters were collapsed in mourning both for their brothers and because one of their number was betrothed to one of the Curatii, champions of Alba. As Thomas Crow has pointed out, 'the body politic appears in the form of the sons, its chosen representatives' (Crow 1985: 213). It was appropriate that the three sons signify the body politic, for it could only appear as one body in the person of the king who incarnated the many bodies of the body politic. The defining opposition in the painting is, however, the visualized divide between the moral men, determined to pursue the common good, and the weaker women, who were concerned with personal, family issues.

This opposition was taken to an extreme in the *Brutus*. The Roman consul Brutus was forced to condemn his sons to death for their participation in a plot to restore the Tarquins as monarchs of Rome. David depicted the moment when the corpses of the executed sons were returned to their home. Again, the women mourn while Brutus remains firm in his resolve, seemingly unmoved by the tragedy that has befallen his family. The composition hinges around the empty chair, which should have been taken by one of the dead sons, dividing the masculine world of public affairs from the feminine domestic sphere. The lone figure of Brutus represents the body politic that must live on, while the dead body of his son, and the grieving women, represent the weakness of the natural body. In this sense,

Brutus might be seen as the very image of *homo clausus*, the masculine individual. In Norbert Elias' view, this individualization was the outcome of specific historical processes, culminating

> from about the Renaissance onward, in the notion of the individual 'ego' in its locked case, the self divided by an invisible wall from what happens 'outside'. It is these civilizational self-controls, functioning in part automatically, that are now experienced in individual self-perception as a wall, either between 'subject' and 'object' or between one's own 'self' and other people.
>
> (Elias 1978: 257)

The marker of difference between one self and another was the body. This austere divide has been taken to prefigure the radical divide between men and women that resulted from the most radical phase of the French Revolution (Outram 1989).

There are significant problems with this argument. First, the clampdown on women's rights and activities dates from October 1793. Prior to that time, the Revolution had seen considerable gains for women, including the development of a feminist movement in the clubs and sections, the right to divorce, and legal rights in respect of property. While it is traditional to ascribe to artists some political foresight, it stretches credulity to presume that David could envisage the most radical phase of the Revolution, which, as Robespierre himself often remarked, no one dreamed of in 1789, and at the same time allow him to ignore the gender politics of the first four years of the Revolution. Put another way, an insistence on separate spheres for men and women was a commonplace of eighteenth century politics. The Revolutionary moment initially opened up possibilities to women, rather than restoring the *ancien régime*'s gender politics. In this sense, David's work was exemplary of very traditional hostilities to the involvement of women in politics, which certainly figured as part of the hostility to Louis XVI's court, but were swept aside in the Revolution by such events as the women's march on Versailles in October 1789.

Second, contemporaries were well aware of the extreme nature of Brutus' sensibilities. One contemporary critic found Brutus 'an almost odious hero' (Schnapper 1989: 200), while others were outraged:

> One cannot without offending all the natural proprieties, suppose that Brutus, after having had his sons butchered would have withdrawn to the room where his mother, wife and two daughters were working; that the bodies of the two sons would be carried through this same chamber to give them their burial. One can easily see from this one instance that the subject contains nothing truthful.
>
> (Crow 1985: 253)

Such comments indicate that Brutus was not universally seen as a male role model. Rather the 1789 Salon was the place of a series of artistic experiments in rendering the relationship between the male artist and his female subjects as an absolute divide rather than as an inevitably hybrid psychic process. This culture in crisis was exemplified in François-André Vincent's painting *Zeuxis choisissant pour modèles les plus belles filles de la ville de Crotone* (Paris, Musée du Louvre), also exhibited at the Salon of 1789 (Figure 10). Since the Salon of 1783, Vincent, one of the founders of Neo-Classicism, had been regarded as one of the outstanding artists of the day. He now depicted the great Greek artist according to Pliny's account of his painting of Helen of Troy, in which Zeuxis composed his figure from the most beautiful fragments of women's bodies that he could discover in the town of Crotona, being unable to find one woman beautiful enough to be the model. The lone male figure of the artist is balanced by, and contrasted with, the group of women. The point of their interaction is across the scene of painting itself, the blank canvas on which Zeuxis has been drawing. Vincent highlights gender difference as a state of being different. The drawing of the body is here presented, not as a straightfor-

Figure 10 François-André Vincent, *Zeuxis choissant pour modèles le plus belles filles de la ville de Crotone* (1789), Louvre, Paris.

71

ward opposition of male and female, but as the interaction between one man and many women. Even the perfect body of Helen was an assembly of fragments, drawn from many different sources, in the absence of a perfect model, such as Louis XIV (Rosenblum 1967a: 22–3). Only on the canvas could the severe, linear distinction between masculine and feminine be – literally – drawn.

The fragmented parts of Vincent's composition were driven together by an urge for gender unity and were linked by the spectator's gaze, called and held by Zeuxis' outward look. On the canvas, only the outline of Helen's figure has been drawn in. Zeuxis has taken the stylus from Dibutade and with it, the right to control the sign, even at its origin. The seemingly empty space between Zeuxis and his models is the point where the sign exchanges its natural physical status for the artificial or composed, making it possible for critics to praise the composition of this apparently disjointed work. But now the sign has become gendered so that it required a male prototype to create the composed, civilized, intellectual sign from the natural, simple female. One woman was not enough to construct the plenitude of Rousseau's state of nature. This myth of Zeuxis creating beauty from fragments represented corporal reason at the outbreak of the Revolution, rather than the solitary figure of *homo clausus*. Neither Brutus nor Zeuxis nor Pygmalion were imaginable without the female figure(s) to whom they were opposed, for the women represented a repressed aspect of the male psyche, rather than having autonomous existence in their own right. It was no coincidence, therefore, that Neo-Classical artists concentrated upon legendary or Classical scenes in depicting the body, for an identifiable eighteenth-century woman would have disrupted their intent. Only the king's body could contain such multiple tendencies within itself, for the Body politic was the only male body which could reproduce itself. As the Revolution began, the Neo-Classical body was in tension between the goal of perfection and the necessity of arriving at such perfection by the combination of gendered fragments.

THE KING ALSO DIES

Following the upheavals of 10 August 1792, the French Revolution moved into its most radical phase. One of the first acts of the Revolutionaries was the destruction of the symbols of monarchy, including the monumental statues of Louis XIV discussed earlier. This destruction commenced the elimination of the ruling myth of the King's Two Bodies by disposing of the king's portrait. The seventeenth-century predictions that such offences would result in physical harm to the perpetrators did not come to pass and strengthened radical resolve for more direct action. The transformation of the body politic in representation became an absolute necessity after the execution of the king on January 21 1793. No longer could one sanctified representation of the king contain the multiple meanings of the body politic, and David strove to find new ways of figuring the Republic. Crucially, he re-imagined the Republic as a male figure, replacing the female figure of Liberty, which had predominated in Revolutionary circles until this time.

For the Revolutionary leader and journalist Jean-Paul Marat, the execution of the king was the culmination of the revolutionary discouse of fraternity:

> The head of the tyrant has just fallen under the blade of the law; the same stroke has overturned the foundations of monarchy among us; I believe finally in the republic . . . . One would have said that [the people] had just attended a religious festival; delivered from the burden of oppression that weighed on them for such a long time and pierced by the sentiment of fraternity, all hearts gave themselves over to the hope of a happier future.
>
> (Hunt 1992: 57)

Only the most radical papers carried such accounts, which the official press and government organs ignored. For decades, *ancien régime* authorities had been seeking to control the flow of blood in the streets of Paris, trying to forbid animal slaughter in the city and to remove all trace of such violence from general view. But from its inception in 1789, the Revolution had seen a spectacular revival of popular violence. On July 16 1789 a vast crowd assembled in the Church of Saint-Roch to witness a parade featuring the heads of de Launay, the governor of the Bastille, and that of his deputy de Fleselles, which were displayed on sticks. Throughout the next three years, the most brutal mutilations could be witnessed in the streets of Paris, culminating in the September Massacres of 1792. The Terror of 1793–4 should in part be understood as an attempt by the political elites of the Revolution to regain control of punishment (Corbin 1991: 216 17). This contest reflected a different concept of the relations of body and power in the Revolution. The popular forces acted on the rhetoric of the Revolution, which declared power no longer to reside in the king's body but in the nation. The people thus had the same right to inflict corporal punishment as that formerly enjoyed by the king. The leaders of the Revolution accepted that the Body politic had changed, but strongly believed that this body, like any other, needed to be controlled by its rational head –

73

the elites – rather than be swayed by the passions of the body itself manifested by the people. In other words, the dispute was as to who constituted the Self of the new body politic.

Revolutionaries of all tempers envisaged a regeneration of the body as one of the key tasks of the time, in compensation for the excesses of the *ancien régime*. Both the popular press and the political elite saw a direct parallel between the reform of the body politic and the health of the physical body of French citizens. Mirabeau told the Assembly that: 'You breathed on remains that seemed inanimate. Suddenly a constitution was organized, and already it is giving off an active force. The cadaver that has been touched by liberty has risen and received a new life' (Ozouf 1989: 793). In a doubled interaction, political action could not only heal the body, it was indispensable for the body's health. However, the precise form and nature of this regeneration was the subject of political contestation between the popular forces and the new political elites created by the Revolution.

There is one extraordinary representation of the king's execution from high art circles that expresses some of the popular excitement at the end of the King's Two Bodies and the unleashing of fraternal feeling it occasioned. In the painting competition organized by the Convention in the Year II (on 24 April 1794), a student of David named Pierre-Etienne Le Sueur entered a preparatory drawing of Louis XVI's execution, entitled *L'exécution du tyran, 21 janvier 1793*. He chose to depict the moment immediately after the act of execution, making his subject the popular celebrations rather than the sublime end of majesty. The overall scheme of the composition and the muscular physiques of the men depicted (only one woman is visible on the extreme left, a seemingly allegorical figure) identify Le Sueur's work as typical of Neo-Classicism. What is so unusual is that the work celebrates the destruction of the body politic and the visceral pleasures of popular politics. In the background of his work, the executioner holds up Louis' head, which 'looks' in the direction of the plinth vacated by the statue of Louis XIV. Both the king's body and his portrait, the Body politic, have been annihilated, releasing a torrent of joy and exuberance. A Dionysiac dance takes place in mid-ground, while the foreground is dominated by two men kissing. Despite the obvious homosocial nature of David's studio, and the homoerotic content of many Neo-Classical paintings, this is a rare instance in which men express their emotion towards each other physically. Nor was this simple fantasy on Le Sueur's part, as one contemporary account indicates: '[The spectators] kissed each other with the effusion of the sweetest union and the happiest fraternity; after which they sang hymns to liberty, dancing around the scaffold and all over the Place de la Révolution (Olander

1989: 38). The execution of Louis XVI was a moment of political and cultural liberation in which repressed desires of violence and sexuality could be fulfilled. Le Sueur's drawing allows us to see in the open the repressed homosexual desire within visual representations of gender in the late eighteenth century that perhaps constitutes the real scandal of these works.

Radicals continued to emphasize the importance of this moment of liberation, contrary to government desires to forget what they saw as a necessary evil. But Le Sueur's work indicates that even the cultural elite were affected by the enormity of the king's execution. Neo-Classicism had been forced to confront the possibility that there was another solution to the representation of the body than the calm assemblage of parts symbolized by Zeuxis' portrait of Helen. The death of the 'Father of all the French' liberated his sons to behave in ways which previously had to be concealed or denied. Even the representation of the body in the most elite practice of history painting was affected by this moment, which could not be forgotten or unlearnt. Even though the monarchy could be and was restored, the myth of the King's Two Bodies could never recover from this transgression. The king had been revealed to be only a man.

REPUBLICAN BODY POLITICS

By November 1793, the Revolution had moved into its most radical phase, during which the artisans and workers known as the *sans-culottes* attempted to shift the politics of the Revolution away from a representative democracy of delegates towards those of an all-inclusive participatory democracy. A maximum level of prices had been declared, the queen was guillotined in October, and the move towards de-Christianization had begun (Hunt 1984: 98). Furthermore, the Revolution had now reasserted its masculinity with the outlawing of women's clubs and political activity in October 1793. Throughout the radical government of the Year II, Jacques-Louis David was at the centre of a concerted effort to re-imagine the body politic without the king and yet without conceding the necessity of a fragmented body. The constant calls for unity which permeated the political scene were matched by an artistic effort to resolve the contradictions of the nation into one durable image. David's solution sought to fuse and complete the monument by the participation of the audience, in a metaphor derived from sexual reproduction.

For the late eighteenth century saw a profound shift in the way in which human reproduction was medically conceptualized. The historian Thomas

Laqueur has recently argued that the human species was previously seen as one. The reproductive organs were not specific to either sex: they were exterior on the male and interior on the female, but were essentially the same. Reproductively, women were inverted men who emitted sperm and whose orgasm was necessary to conception. Now however, men and women came to be seen as having entirely different reproductive organs, which Laqueur has called a 'biology of incommensurability'. This shift in medical concepts of the body and philosophical precepts of identity had important consequences for representation. The statues of Louis XIV represented him as the king of all twenty million French people, for, as Laqueur puts it: 'The one sex body, because it was construed as illustrative rather than determinant, could therefore register and absorb any number of shifts in the axes and valuations of difference' (Laqueur 1990: 62). Now the Republicans were faced not only with replacing the unity symbolized by the king's body but with finding a corporal representation which could include both of the newly differentiated sexes.

On 13 July 1793 Marat was assassinated in his bath by the royalist Charlotte Corday. Marat suffered from a skin condition that forced him to spend most of his time in water to obtain relief from the irritation. The scene at once became part of Revolutionary mythology and was represented in numerous plays, engravings, and most famously by David in his portrait *The Death of Marat* (Figure 11). In this work, the dominant male figure seen in David's earlier paintings constitutes the entire subject. Marat lies in his bath, the open wound to his chest and the knife on the floor evidence of the murderous assault. He is seen at work on his newspaper *L'Ami du peuple* with Charlotte Corday's letter in his hand. His body was represented as healthy and muscular, despite his well-known condition. There is no physical sign of the murderess, for David wished his painting to address women. At Marat's funeral, one speaker declaimed: 'Let the blood of Marat become the seed of intrepid Republicans', and numerous women responded by swearing to 'people the earth with as many Marats as they could' (Hunt 1992: 76). In these more controlled Republican festivals, the emphasis was heavily and exclusively heterosexual. In presenting his painting to the Convention, David addressed his work to those defended by Marat's journalism:

> Hasten all mothers, widows, orphans, oppressed soldiers! all of you whom he defended at peril of his life, approach! and contemplate your friend; he who guarded you is no more; his pen, the terror of traitors, his pen escapes his hands. O despair! our indefatigable friend is dead.
>
> (David An IIa: 2)

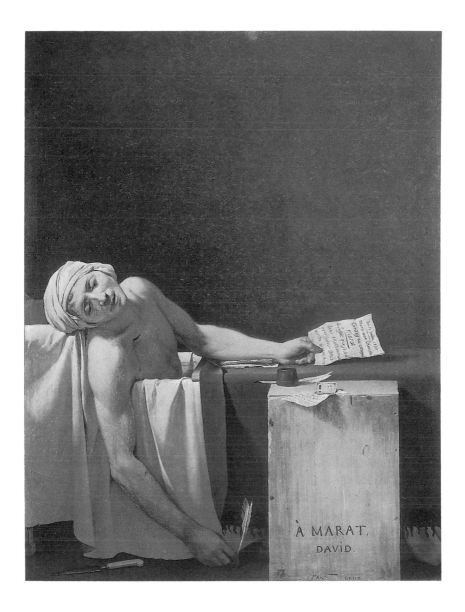

Figure 11 Jacques-Louis David, *The Death of Marat*, Musées Royaux des Beaux-Arts de Belgique, Giraudon/Bridgeman Art Library.

Whereas David's earlier work had addressed the spectator indirectly (see Chapter 1), the *Marat* was constructed with a specific audience in mind. The single revolutionary hero, now male by definition, confronts the audience he himself had helped create even in death. This public of women, mothers, orphans, widows and soldiers was that presumed by *L'Ami du peuple* and continued to be the public for David's painting. By evoking real, if unknown people, the Neo-Classical artist sought to resolve the dilemma of gender ambiguity inherent in visual representations of the body at the period. It was therefore appopriate that the issue of reproduction should be raised, for just as the (presumed male) artist was held to construct his work from feminine Nature, so did Marat conceive of himself shaping the mass of the population into the Revolutionary people. Artists, politicians, and writers had come to find their regenerative and reproductive roles, which had previously been imagined in Classical garb, actually expressed in Revolutionary pratice, and sought to overcome the division between elite and popular conceptions of the body politic by fusing them into one interactive whole.

Three days after offering his *Marat* to the Convention, David took the floor again to announce a competition to create a colossal statue, derived from the figure of Hercules, representing the French Republic (Hunt 1984: 94–116; Wilson 1995). He used the occasion to develop his thoughts on the practice of art under Revolutionary circumstances. Unlike the Neo-Classicism of the *ancien régime*, which had intended the work of art to offer an intelligible moral lesson regardless of potential context or audience, David now envisaged the people as a constituent component of the work of art, who would contribute both to its manufacture and interpretation. This view was consistent with Robespierre's definition of the people as the virtuous check on legislators: 'Before the eyes of so great a number of witnesses, neither corruption, nor intrigue, nor perfidy would dare show its face; only the general will would be consulted, only the voice of reason and public interest would be heard' (Huet 1994: 58). Despite these high-flown sentiments, the notion of the people had also been redefined in keeping with new radical notions of the 'people' as masculine. In these circumstances, a statue representing the people could only be masculine, as Lynn Hunt remarks: 'Hercules represented a higher stage in the development of the Revolution – one characterized by the force and unity of the people, rather than by the sagacity of its representatives' (Hunt 1984: 98). None the less, the audience for this polyvalent Colossus was, like that for the *Marat*, composed of both men and women.

In the competition for and manufacture of the statue, David hoped to create a form of art practice which would be as distinct from artist's work under the monarchy as the piece itself was different from the royal statue:

> Your Committee believes that everything in the proposed monument, both the material and the forms, ought to express in a sensitive and forceful manner the great memories of our revolution and especially to consecrate the victory of the French people over despotism and superstition, its inseparable companion; that the people, trampling underfoot the debris of tyranny, should be represented by a colossal statue in bronze, bearing diverse inscriptions and emblems designed to recall the regenerative principles that we have adopted.
>
> (David An IIb: 3)

David was seeking an image of the regenerated Body politic, which would both remind the people of their past achievements and encourage them to pursue new goals. The base of the statue would be fashioned from the royal statues of Notre Dame to recall the twin triumph over monarchy and religion. It was to be 15m high, located at the west end of what is now the Ile de la Cité. Due to the remarkable revival of sculpture in the period, such an ambitious project seemed feasible. At the Salon of the Year II, 128 sculptures were exhibited, many drawing inspiration from the Revolution, such as Beauvallet's terracotta representation of the Mountain, the term by which the Jacobins were known, and Boichot's bas-relief, *The Natural Rights of Man in Society* (Bianchi 1982: 212). Although the Revolution is remembered for its destruction of statues, this tabula rasa was inseparable from the idea of regeneration, for in the words of one radical leader: 'You must not destroy until you can rebuild' (Bianchi 1982: 157).

David suggested that the very bronze of the statue should terrify the opponents of the Revolution. Therefore, it should be fashioned from cannon captured by the Revolutionary army: 'By this fusion, the statue will be the symbol of unity; I venture to say that it will at the same time be the guarantor and conservation of that unity' (David An IIb: 4). Indeed, the physiology of the period held that the skin was not so much a barrier between the inner self and the outside world as a point of exchange between these different spheres of existence. The skin of the statue was a similar point of exchange between Nation and people. The Colossus was to symbolize popular unity, encapsulated by the decision to place copies of the Declaration of the Rights of Man, the Constitution of 1793, the medal struck to commemorate the events of 10 August 1792, and the decree authorizing the statue itself within the club carried by the figure. These political landmarks enabled the statue to be made and were now to be literally a part of it.

The competition to design the statue sought to move away from the Academic norm by having separate contests for the design and execution of the statue, reasoning that good ideas should not be excluded for want of technique, and vice versa. The entries were to be publicly displayed for two weeks in the Museum before being judged by a jury. The contestants were given broad guidelines for the statue, which 'will carry in one hand the figures of liberty and equality; with the other he will lean on his club. On his forehead, one will read *Light*; on his chest, *Nature, Truth*; on his arms, *Force*, and on his hands, *Work*' (David An IIb: 6). The newly regenerated Body politic, although composed of traditional allegorical forms, sought to signify different ideas to a different audience, which required that they actually be written on the body.

This corporal inscription indicates that the new gender distinctions, resulting from the changed conception of sexual identity, on which the new Republic's imagery in theory depended were in practice far from secure (Wilson 1993). The fallen fathers of the *ancien régime* may have claimed to be regenerated, but they were far less sanguine about being able to communicate these changes visually. Central to the educational effort required to close this legibility gap was the Revolutionary festival. Just before the fall of the Robespierre regime on 27 July 1794, David proposed a festival to celebrate the transfer of two young Republican heroes to the Pantheon. Joseph Bara and Agricol Viola were teenage boys who had died in defence of the Republic, citing the common good over their individual fates in (no doubt apocryphal) last words. In David's view, these examples served to demonstrate the transformation in familial relations under the Republic and an 'entire moral regeneration'. Under the monarchy, the land was untilled, commerce languished and 'its yoke was so heavy that it crushed the desire to be a father and caused women to curse their fecundity'. Now, however, 'mothers have children without sadness or regrets; they bless their fecundity and count their true wealth as the number of their children.' Such renewed enthusiasm was justified by the heroism of Bara and Viola, which was in stark contrast 'to those vile courtesans nourished at court in the heart of luxury, to those effeminate Sybarites whose corrupted souls had not even an idea of virtue' (David An IIc: 2–4). The gender ambiguities of the *ancien régime* would thus yield to the fertile, 'normal' heterosexuality of the Republic. The parade celebrated the 'filial piety' of Bara and Viola. It would proceed in two columns, one of patriotic children, and the other of mothers whose children had died for the Republic. The boys were celebrated as part of the regeneration of both masculinity and femininity, whose consequence was the renewed enthusiasm for parenthood. These Rousseauian views did not presume that masculinity was secure and unchanged, but that both sexes had found their gender roles renewed and reinvigorated by the Revolution. Both the festival and sculpture competition were discarded after the anti-Jacobin coup of 9 Thermidor, Year II.

In 1812, Dubuisson took art as his metaphor for sexual reproduction, rather than vice versa. In his *Tableau de l'amour conjugal*, he argued that human reproduction was a form of artistic practice: 'The semen is to generation what the sculptor is to marble; the male semen is the sculptor who gives shape, the female liquor is the marble or matter, and the sculpture is the fetus or the product of generation' (Huet 1993: 7). If we extend this conceit to the body politic, its creative principle was held to be masculinity, which was impotent without fertile feminine matter to work on. The resulting representation was the product of the intercourse between these two principles, which have proved to be both easily confused and very difficult to dislodge altogether. The Revolutionaries sought to control these variables by including the spectators of the work as more than a passive public, that is, as a participating people. However, it was important that the people retain its masculinity, a quality which could only be ensured by the continued success of the body politic itself, the Revolution.

Given this tortuous logic, it is perhaps not surprising that Napoleon's reconceptualization of the body politic after 1805 as the emperor's body was accepted so readily by artists and the people. David became court painter to Napoleon and in a series of powerful works crafted an image of the emperor that is still effective enough to sell Courvoisier brandy. In *Napoleon in his Study* (1812), for example, David fused elements of the monarchical Body politic with Revolutionary symbolism to create a new version of the old, which might be called the Emperor's Two Bodies (Figure 12). Napoleon's strength and vigour is attested to by the lateness of the hour – 4.10 a.m. by the clock. The burnt-out candles demonstrate that is he is not an early-riser, but has been working all night. His labours are devoted to the Civil Code, Napoleon's reformulation of the law, which, together with his redeployment of local and national governmental apparatus, was to be his lasting legacy. The nearby sword indicates the source of Imperial power, which no longer has to be written on the body. The body itself tells us little, being reduced to the sign 'Napoleon' indicated by the concealed hand and the kiss curl. The emperor's body is surrounded by other signs of empire, such as the 'N' on the chair, which render Napoleon's individual body all but irrelevant. For unlike his royal predecessors, Napoleon could

Figure 12 Jacques-Louis David, *Napoleon in His Study* (1812), Samuel H. Kress
Collection, © 1994 Board of Trustees, National Gallery of Art, Washington.

claim no divine right, or blood link to power, despite his claim to be the Body politic. His power was guaranteed only by his successful exercise of that power, which he no longer owned as a physical property. Despite the changed political context, the body politic remained a seemingly inescapable point of reference. However, the execution of Louis XVI had demonstrated the fiction of the King's Two Bodies, and although it continued to play a role in Western political culture, there was always a certain emptiness to post-Revolutionary representations of the body politic. The physical body of the ruler no longer played a central role in imagining the body politic.

Two important shifts took place in the image of the body politic during the French Revolution. The representation of the state came to be seen as the (re)production of an interaction between the masculine and the feminine, in tune with new notions of biological reproduction. At the same time, the power, or violence, of the state became detached from any one individual's body. Like Napoleon's sword, it could now be attached to a variety of individuals without changing its character. But it is not quite accurate to say that the fetishism of the State with a capital S simply replaced that of the King with a capital K. Certainly, that was and is one possible response to state power, but the radical challenge of Year II had shown the potential for a defiant and participatory alternative, albeit one heavily circumscribed by its gender politics.

DEFYING THE BODY POLITIC

The radical wing of French politics was unable to resolve these contradictions in the nineteenth century, but completed the destruction of the corporal dimension of the body politic during the Paris Commune of 1871. Nineteenth-century French politics were dominated by a fear of a return to the radical days of 1793. In 1830 and February 1848, sections of the middle classes joined with artisans and working-class groups to overthrow reactionary regimes because they feared that their continuation might provoke a worse reaction from what were known in the period as the 'dangerous classes'. The tension between a moderate Republic, symbolized by a female figure known as Marianne, and a radical one depicted by a male figure such as Hercules continued to dominate the iconography of politics (Hunt 1984: 116). Radical politics was kept firmly off centre stage, with the bloody repression of the June Revolution of 1848 serving as a warning of the penalty for attempting to reverse that situation. However, following the collapse of Napoleon III's Second Empire in the Franco-Prussian War of 1870, radical Jacobin politics made one final appearance in French history. After the emperor's surrender, Paris refused to accept the new Versailles government's attempt to disarm the National Guard and conclude peace with the Germans. In a doomed but defiant gesture, Paris declared itself an independent Commune on 18 March 1871.

In its two months of existence before the French army retook the capital, the Commune did not have time to implement its vision of government and society. None the less, the Communards had an acute sense of the historical theatre in which they were engaged and strove to create symbolic moments whose memory would survive them. The destruction of the Vendôme Column on 16 May 1871 was one of the most dramatic and controversial of these acts. The Vendôme Column was initially constructed by Napoleon, forged from the cannon he captured at the battle of Auster-litz. Napoleon thus fulfilled David's idea for the celebration of the Repub-lic to commemorate his own personal rule. His nephew Napoleon III, emperor by plebiscite from 1852 to 1870, had revived memories of his uncle's rule by placing his own statue on the column. For the Commu-nards, this representation of the body politic was both politically and artistically unacceptable, as the journalist Henri Rochefort declared: 'What had made the Place Vendôme famous for so long was always with-out excuse in our eyes, first because it was built in Empire style, the most intolerable of all styles, and secondly because it was erected with the immoral aim of perpetuating the most intolerable of governments' (MO: 17 May).[1] Like David before him, Rochefort realized the importance of both style and content in creating the image of the body politic.

The initial decision to destroy the Column was taken by the Commune on 17 April and the materials of the column were put up for sale a few days later. But the urgent priority was to defend the city and the column remained standing. By 28 April, the Place Vendôme was fortified on all sides, creating inside 'not only a fortress but a permanent camp and a monstrous canteen', using no less than forty ovens (MO: 24 April). It was not until the military situation became hopeless that the Commune pro-ceeded with the destruction of the column, as a symbolic gesture with an eye to the verdict of history. Before the act was even accomplished, the radical paper Le Cri du peuple declared: 'Here's the response of conquered France to victorious Prussia; of Paris, republican and socialist to the partisans of militarism and of monarchy' (CP: 14 May). The column's destruction attracted a huge crowd. The square itself was cleared of all but those engaged in the demolition and spectators packed the side roads, behind the barricades which were breached for the occasion, more sat on the roof of buildings in the Rue de la Paix, and some were even clinging to the chimneys (V: 17 May). The excitement was too much for one Glais-Bizoin, who removed his clothes 'in a movement of juvenile ardour', strikingly reminiscent of the sexualized excitement at the execution of Louis XVI (MO: 18 May). At 3 p.m. military bands played the *Marseillaise* and the *Chant du départ* to mark the commencement of activities. A group of National Guards and regular soldiers gathered at the foot of the column for photographs taken by the deaf photographer Bruno Braquehais, who took one of only two photographic records of the Commune. In his record of the destruction of the Vendôme column, Braquehais sought to create an image of the Commune which might replace that of the emperor. The first scene is relatively disciplined, with a red flag waving overhead, but in the next shot one man blows a trumpet, and others beat drums, while a child rolls on the floor in excitement (Figure 13).

At 3.30 three cables were attached to the column and tightened by capstans, one of which immediately broke. After a long delay to find and attach a new capstan, the pulling began again at 5.15: 'The attention was immense. Everyone held their breath.' Rumours had been circulating that the destruction of the column would bring down the walls of Paris, or at least cause widespread devastation. The body politic retained its mystique even at this juncture. A worker dressed in red placed a *tricolore* on the column so that it would fall with the emperor, destroying the twin symbols of empire. For a quarter of an hour, the ropes were pulled, long enough for Braquehais to photograph the moment. Finally, '[i]t fell at the hour of the *crépuscule*, in front of an enormous crowd come to be present at the execution of this false and odious glory, condemned by history and saluted in its fall by the immense *Vivat* of deliverance issuing from ten thousand throats' (CP: 18 May). From Braquehais' photograph, taken immediately after the fall, we can see that the column missed the earth designed to receive it and broke into fragments. Already a group of Communards had scaled the pedestal with a ladder and raised the red flag (Figure 14).

All the Communard reports revelled in the historic significance of the moment, but some had hoped for 'a little of the symbolism of [17]93, in which a mother would have given the first hammer blow to the column and a child would have burnt its history.' Such a ceremony would have reconstructed the reproductive symbolism of the First Republic, as the bad father would have been brought low by the virtuous mother and the regenerated next generation. Indeed, many felt that 'the Commune has

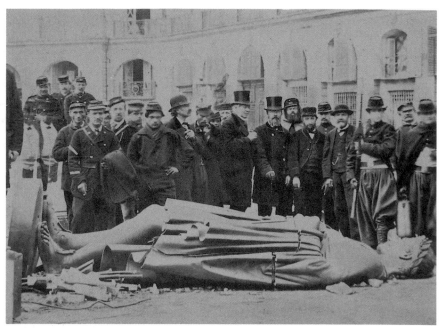

Figure 13 Bruno Braquehais, *The Paris Commune*, Statue of Napoleon III pulled down by Communards, UW-Madison/Art History Department.

Figure 14 Bruno Braquehais, *The Paris Commune*, Vendôme Column after destruction, 1871, UW-Madison/Art History Department.

avenged the First Republic in bringing down the Caesar who had ground it beneath the heel of his boot' (MO: 17 May). The column's destruction was not seen as vandalism but as the inauguration of a new form of history: 'The history of man belongs to the law which he has established on earth. The rest is barbarism' (V: 17 May). Consequently, wrote another journalist, 'history must be remade. Forward the innovators! the Diderots, the Prudhons, the Schillers, the Jacobys! Down with the killers and dissipaters! And when their names appear in historians' writings as a sinister accident, how they will be condemned!' (CP: 14 May). In a famous phrase, Walter Benjamin described how the 'aura' of traditional art was destroyed by the rise of mechanical reproduction. Here the Communards intentionally sought to destroy the aura of the body politic by machines, dragging the Vendôme column into the dust.

The destruction of the Vendôme column was a descendant of the First Republic's political imagery, but it was not exactly the same. The artist Gustave Courbet was famously accused of orchestrating the destruction of the Vendôme column, but whereas David had been central to the iconography of the first Revolution, Courbet's involvement was more marginal. The destruction was genuinely popular. The Commune seemed to offer a wider degree of participation and to be concerned with a broader range of issues. In the final week of the Commune's existence, three thousand men and women attended a public meeting of the Club de la Révolution calling for the expulsion of religious orders from hospitals, indicating an important extension of what was held to be political. In what was to be the final issue of Le Vengeur, an anonymous writer observed: 'I have seen three revolutions in my life, and for the first time, I have seen women getting involved with resolution, women and children. It seems that this revolution is more precisely theirs, and that in defending it, they are defending their own future' (V: 24 May). For the Commune's opponents, the active involvement of women like Louise Michel was one of the greatest scandals of all its heretical deeds. Perhaps during that afternoon on which the Vendôme column fell, it was possible to glimpse or feel what a state which was not a patriarchy might be like. Three weeks after the Commune fell, the railings were restored around the base of the column, guarding the fetish within.

AFTER THE BODY POLITIC?

There is not space here to narrate a full history of the body politic in the nineteenth and twentieth centuries. Nor is there a necessity, for it is the intent of this chapter to demonstrate that the body politic did not evolve in some straightforward fashion from the primitive to the civilized; the open to the closed; the united to the fragmentary, or the absolute to the democratic. Rather, I have sought to show that the body politic was the site of an exchange, whether between the king and the King, or the citizen and the Republic, mediated by the visual sign. In neither case was it a closed or sealed representation, but was always in dialogue with changing ideas of gender and cultural politics. These ideas were not simply reflected in visual culture, but were often worked out and developed in visual imagery. Questions of artistic style were also perceived as questions of political signification, and the monument was always considered in relationship to its audience.

This history has an important bearing on the most emblematic of all representations of the body politic, that of Nazi Germany. It has recently been asserted that the National Socialists made use of a concept of the 'armoured body' in their political art (Foster 1991). Certainly, the monumental Neo-Classical statues of Arno Breker sought to display strength, force and unity. But without comparing these representations to Nazi constructions of the physical body, and the political uses made of such constructions, it is easy to make facile comparisons. The Classicism of Breker had a completely different conception of the body to that of David, and his conservative successors in nineteenth-century France. Superficial formal comparisons are irrelevant in the face of this overwhelming difference. Whereas David sought to make the body a point of exchange and regeneration, the Nazis were at once trying to reconstitute the male body from the fragmentation of military and emotional defeat in the First World War, and seeking to eliminate hidden threats within the German body politic. The attempt to present the Aryan body as a sealed mass was undercut by fear of potential disease and disorder within, which had to be purged.

The sculpture of Arno Breker (1900–91) was central to the Nazi representation of the body politic. Breker was a Classical sculptor whose work was transformed by a visit to Rome in 1933, during which he experienced both what he called the 'street art' of Fascist Italy and the sculpture of Michelangelo (Cone 1992: 159). His conversion to a combination of the Classical form and fascist ideology came at a fortunate juncture, for it was in that same year that the Nazis seized power in Germany. Breker cultivated a friendship with Albert Speer, which paid handsome results. Speer had been an architect for the Nazis since 1931 and he masterminded the design of such monuments as the Nuremberg stadium, as well as overseeing the construction of the concentration camps (Kasher 1992: 55). In 1937, Breker was appointed Official State Sculptor, heading a studio of forty-three practioners, and a second studio employing over one thousand people. In June 1940, Hitler drove around the deserted streets of newly occupied Paris accompanied by Speer and Breker. This imperial tourism around Paris was the public face of Nazism, uniting art, power and ideology.

Breker's monumental sculpture was well suited to the propaganda of the Third Reich. In a documentary of the period, an official commentary hailed his work: 'Force has replaced sensitivity, hardness the fluidity shimmering in the light. . . . The face of the moment has become THE MONU-MENT. . . . The work of the artist has become a political confession' (Adam 1992: 197). Although Breker had already accommodated his work to Nazism before the triumph of the National Socialists, the ideology of the period required constant success over ever-scheming internal dissent. The twin exhibitions of Degenerate Art and The Great German Art Exhibition in 1937 sought to make this dichotomy clear to the German public. For the Expressionist and modern art in the Degenerate Art exhibition was deliberately contrasted with the Classical and Nazi art in the accompanying show. Ironically, far more people attended the Degenerate show than its supposedly healthy twin. From the Nazi point of view, it was clear that a choice constantly had to be made between strength and weakness, and that the source of weakness lay within the German nation itself. Breker worked on sculptures with titles such as *Vengeance*, *The Sacrifice*, *Domination* and *Destruction*, that fully expressed this new aesthetic.

Breker's most characteristic work was the two monumental sculptures he prepared for the Chancellery in Berlin (1933, destroyed). Standing either side of a massive portico, the male figures represented *The Party* (Figure 15) and *The Army*, the twin guarantors of Nazi strength. Both figures were powerful muscular nudes, derived from the Classical model, but with significant departures. Breker used the athlete Gustav Stührk as his model for the figures, in imitation of ancient Greek practice, which may account for the narrowness of the waist in relation to the shoulders. The figure of the Party holds its palm open, while the Army has its fist closed and wears an aggressive frown. While the Party holds a torch of leadership, the Army has a sword. Each statue only gains any sense of expression in relation to the other, for these are not monuments made to be seen, as in the case of David's *Hercules*, but silent sentinels, whose function is fulfilled whether they are witnessed or not. Whereas David knew that his work required participation in order to be complete, Breker simply testified to the existence of power. Robert Musil's perceptive discussion of 1930s sculpture

Figure 15 Arno Breker, *The Party* (1933, destroyed), formerly Berlin, New Reichschancellery, photograph courtesy AKG London.

applies with a vengeance to Breker's work: 'The most striking feature of monuments is that you do not notice them. There is nothing in the world as invisible as monuments. . . . They virtually drive off what they would attract. We cannot say that we do not notice them. We should say that they de-notice us, they withdraw from our senses' (Warner 1985: 21). His figures seek to assert power in as direct and unmediated a fashion as possible, requiring the spectator to 'de-notice' his work. Here the visual sign of the sculpted body had no role to play in the signification of the body politic, and the spectator was not required to testify to its authenticity, but merely had to acquiesce to its power. The contradiction between signifier and signified in this version of the corporal sign was too acute for the sculpted body actually to represent anything concrete.

Breker's work thus fails to convince, even within the impoverished terms of its own discourse. The Nazis were profoundly distrustful of the body as the individual expression and component of the body politic, fearing that it might harbour all manner of weakness and corruption. Many of those who joined the Nazi party were motivated by the defeat in the First World War and an accompanying extreme hostility to women, gays and Jews. However, the disorder was within the Nazi body itself, as Hitler had theorized. Writing in *Mein Kampf* (1925), Hitler described the role of the Jews in German culture as that of a corporal parasite: 'If you cut even cautiously into such an abscess, you found, like a maggot in a rotting body, often dazzled by the sudden light – a kike! . . . This was pestilence, spiritual pestilence, worse than the Black Death of olden times and the people were being infected by it' (Gilman 1991: 101). The Aryan body was therefore contaminated from within and each German had to be purified. This image was sufficiently widespread and literal that medical education films during the Third Reich depicted the white blood cells with little swastikas attacking intruding cells marked with a Star of David. The body politic of Nazi Germany was marked by the fear that the rot was already present, no matter how rigorous the extirpation of those presumed to be the carriers of such contamination. Breker's figures can be characterized in similar terms, as anti-bodies. His anti-bodies express the will of the body politic both to inflict violence on those who contradicted its corporal imperative and to demand sacrifices from even its acceptable citizens.

This ambivalence towards the body undermines Breker's sculpture and accounts for their curious sense of failure and hollowness, despite the fact that in formal and technical terms, his works are superficially similar to many other Classical representations of the body. In his recent study of this subject, Peter Adam has distinguished between Breker's art and that of

Rodin on the grounds of motivation. In his view, Breker was motivated solely by external political considerations and Rodin was moved to express his internal feelings: 'Rodin's aim was to visualise feelings which came from within . . . Breker's statues . . . are merely the messenger of a program imposed on life. Their attributes, like the sword or the torch, are interchangeable. . . . In Rodin each gesture is dictated by an inner necessity' (Adam 1992: 200–1). This seemingly clear distinction relies on the firm boundaries of the individualized body as expressed in the notion of *homo clausus*. However, the Classical body was not, as we have seen, so rigidly defined and in fact its surface was not a boundary but a point of exchange. While the contradiction between inside and outside is indeed the fatal flaw in Breker's work, it does not stem from a lack of properly artistic internal drive to creativity. Indeed, Breker was a passionate admirer of Rodin's work. During the occupation of France in the Second World War, he held an exhibition at the Orangerie in Paris, for which thirty tons of French sculpture had to be melted down to provide sufficient bronze. The Rodin Museum held a welcoming reception for him. The curator, Georges Grappe, later gave a lecture entitled 'From Auguste Rodin to Arno Breker', which recounted the official view of Vichy and Berlin that both the Classicism of the Ecole des Beaux Arts and the work of the Expressionists were equally degenerate (Cone 1992: 163, 23–5). Rodin and Breker were, in this view, far from opposites, but fellow rebels against artistic conformity. Both Rodin and Breker saw themselves as reviving and restoring sculpture to the eminence it had known under the ancient Greeks. Breker deliberately distanced his work from the Neo-Classical tradition, both in its radical origins and the later nineteenth-century orthodoxy. He cannot be described as denying aesthetics, for the most fundamental Nazi ideology was that which Walter Benjamin termed the aestheticization of politics. It is rather Breker's inability to circumvent the Nazi loathing of the body through visual representation of the corporal form that is at the root of his failure. His figures are anti-bodies, full of fear and loathing for the material presence of the body. Even as monuments these works were bankrupt, for they not only deny their audience, but stand for the extermination of considerable sections of that audience.

Just as formal analysis seems to invite a false comparison between Breker's Nazi sculpture and earlier Neo-Classicism, so many writers have been tempted into describing the cult of body building as the 'fascist body'. Again, the facile comparisons of muscular form are belied by the context in which body building operates. The culmination of any body builder's routine is the public display of his or her physique in order to win competitions. Unlike the Nazi monument which sought to be de-noticed, body building is highly narcissistic. Furthermore, stars like Arnold Schwarzenegger are very much aware that a section of their audience is composed of gay men and have no difficulty with that fact, whereas Nazi masculinity rested upon a hysterical denial of any gay or feminine aspects to its composition. Body builders of both sexes have achieved popular success, and the body builder Lisa Lyon often posed for the photographer Robert Mapplethorpe. Finally, while body builders conceive of their work as sculpting, it is in a very different sense to the monumental sculpture of Breker. While Breker's work sought above all to convey a sense of completion, body builders constantly seek further development. Arnold Schwarzenegger speaks of this process in almost mystical terms: 'You don't really see a muscle as part of you, in a way. You look at it as a thing and you say well this thing has to be built a little longer. . . . And you look at it and it doesn't even seem to belong to you. Like a sculpture' (Goldberg 1992: 178). While body building certainly expresses a dis-case with the body, that does not equate it with Nazism. Such confusions highlight the weaknesses of a purely formal analysis even of the Classical form.

IN MEMORIAM

The involvement of the spectator is the key to successful representations of the body politic. The Body politic is after all a myth, which can ultimately be sustained only by consensus. It is perhaps therefore not surprising that only monuments to the excesses of the state seem to carry conviction in the present moment. Governments are no longer building edifices like the equestrian statues of the absolutist monarchies, the Vendôme column, or the Nuremberg stadium. However, there has been a proliferation of memorials to the dead of various wars, especially the civilian victims. Holocaust memorials have become one particular and often emotive variant of this trend. Such memorials at their best call on the spectator to witness the follies and excesses of the state. However, they can also be a meaningless token, serving to illustrate once again the right of the state to control its citizens' bodies.

At the Vietnam Veterans Memorial in Washington DC, examples of both styles exist side by side. Maya Lin's design for the Memorial won the competition while she was still a student at Yale University. Its design is deceptively simple. Along a long angled wall of granite, the name of each American casualty has been inscribed. However, the wall has been built entirely below ground level, so that it cannot be seen as you approach. The names are inscribed chronologically, from the first American casualty in 1959 to the last in 1975. At first, the names are below comfortable reading height but as you walk on, the path descends and the wall rises to tower above your head. There is a physical sense of being overwhelmed by the enormity of the loss represented by the wall, enhanced by the shiny surface of the granite, which enables the visitor to perceive their own reflections on the wall. The formal qualities of the monument thus involve each visitor in the event, allowing us literally to see ourselves as part of the conflict.

However, certain groups were dissatisfied with the Wall and lobbied energetically for a different, figurative monument. Led by the vociferous Texas billionaire Ross Perot, this campaign was successful. It financed a traditional bronze statue group by the sculptor Frederick Hart, depicting three male soldiers. This group demands nothing from the viewer and excludes many who served in Vietnam from being represented, especially women. In 1993, a second campaign by women veterans was similarly successful in installing a monument to their service during the war, entitled the Vietnam Women's Memorial Project. The women who led this campaign said that Hart's sculpture had made the absence of women visible in a way that Lin's memorial had not (Sturken 1991: 131). In Glenna Goodacre's four figure bronze sculpture, it is however noticeable that one of the figures is a man, a wounded soldier being tended to by three nurses. Having these two monuments side by side seems to suggest that the official view is that a woman's place in the army was by the side of a man. In both Hart and Goodacre's statues a conscious effort has been made to represent the diversity of the United States Army by including African-Americans. Unfortunately, the sculptors' desire to make this apparent to the spectator has resulted in virtual caricatures of African-Americans. Although some veterans' groups have welcomed these pieces, they seem to once again celebrate the state's authority and its right to demand physical suffering.

By contrast, the controversy surrounding Lin's Wall has stemmed from what one critic has called its 'antiphallic' quality: 'By "antiphallic" I do not mean to imply that the memorial is somehow a passive or feminine form but rather that it opposes the codes of vertical monuments symbolizing power and honour. The memorial does not stand erect above the landscape; it is continuous with the earth' (Sturken 1991: 123). It is this quality which has led to the memorial becoming a site of remarkable remembrance and participation. It has become the most visited monument in Washington DC and seems to invite its visitors to comment or leave momentoes. These reliquaries are now themselves being collected, as if in echo of the offerings at a Classical temple. Along with the flowers, photographs, personal possessions and mementoes, many have expressed their feelings in writing. One veteran wrote:

> I didn't want a monument, not even one as sober as that vast black wall of broken lives. I didn't want a postage stamp. . . . What I wanted was a simple recognition of the limits of our power as a nation to inflict our will on others. What I wanted was an understanding that the world is neither black-and-white nor ours. What I wanted was an end to monuments.
>
> (Sturken 1991: 135)

Like the French revolutionaries who felt that history required so profound a change that the calendar itself should be started again at zero, this veteran perceived the need for a total revision of the representation of the body politic. Despite the very different means of representation, and the different gender constructions at work, David's participatory representation of the Republic seems to be the forerunner of Maya Lin's work, rather than of the supposedly Classical pieces which confront and seek to negate her work.

Yet even while the Vietnam Veterans Memorial sought to explore new avenues of remembrance and commemoration of the body politic, the very function of such representations has been sharply curtailed. For it has been one of the most salient characteristics of recent times that the nation state, even the superpower, is no longer the final arbiter of the political economy. The globalization of capital through multinational corporations and the exponential growth of capital, currency and equity markets has left the previously all-powerful nation state vulnerable to the decisions of wholly unaccountable financiers. The rise of intra-national nationalism is a response to this debilitating loss of control, seeking to regain the authority of the traditional state within smaller borders. The inevitable disappointments attendant upon such strategies have engendered much of the bitterness and savagery which have accompanied these nationalist manoeuvres. Of course, the nation state remains a central venue for political and cultural activity, especially in the postcolonial nations. None the less, the possibility that the Body politic might at once represent all the citizens of a nation and a sense of new possibilities for the future no longer seems open. The representation of the body politic has been replaced by the logo of the multinational corporation.

The failure of the body politic and the idealized Classical body has, however, left the door open for a re-examination of the Classical heritage in terms other than those of pure celebration. In his epic poem *Omeros*, the Caribbean poet Derek Walcott has appropriated Homer's *Odyssey*, the classic myth of wandering, as a means of understanding his own complex inheritance as a poet of diaspora. The poem alternates between American, Caribbean and British English, Antillean *patois*, and an evocation of the rhythms and cadences of Homer's Greek. Omeros, the title of the poem, is the original Greek name for Homer, but here it refers to a Greek woman living in the United States. Homer also appears as the island poet, Old St Omere, known as Monsieur Seven Seas because of his claim to have travelled the world. This polyvalency and multiplicity of voices creates a remarkable revitalization of the epic tradition, seeming to give the old forms an entirely new life:

> I said 'Omeros',
> And O was the conch shell's invocation, *mer* was
> both mother and sea in our Antillean patois,
> *os*, a grey bone, and the white surf as it crashes
>
> and spreads its sibillant collar on a lace shore.
> Omeros was the crunch of dry leaves, and the washes
> that echoed from a cave mouth when the tide has ebbed.
> (Walcott 1990: 14)

This extraordinary poem, which reads like a novel and a song, explores the polyvalent Classical form for an entirely new audience.

In the visual arts, the Classical has made a series of returns to the contemporary art scene. While exhibitions of ancient Greek sculpture continue to promote the belief that Greek civilization was at the heart of Western culture, certain contemporary artists have returned to the Neo-Classical style in a very mundane example of the appropriations of the postmodern. On the other hand, the American artist Nancy Spero has undertaken a personal and political reassessment of antiquity in a series of works, such as those collected under the title *Rebirth of Venus*. Working on long paper scrolls, Spero designed a new Antiquity using the Mycenean motifs of Knossos – which are also central to Martin Bernal's argument in *Black Athena* – images from the Vietnam war, Classical statues and Pre-Columbian art. The experiences of women are central to this new history painting. In *Let the Priests Tremble* (1984) (Figure 16), Spero's Classical-modern women run across her scroll as a series of figures, some appropriated from Classical art, others composed by Spero in a collage of representations of the female form. The figures are at once powerful and sexual, giving resonance to the phrases stencilled onto the paper: 'Let the priests tremble . . . fall apart on discovering that women aren't men . . . the mother doesn't have one'. Spero reclaims the Classical body from the Body politic and explodes the fetishism of the state by revealing the

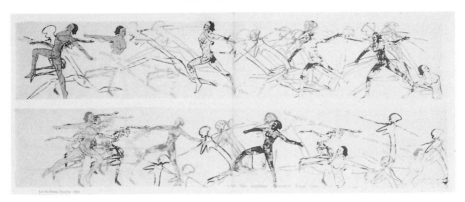

Figure 16 Nancy Spero, *Let the Priest Tremble* (1984), courtesy of the artist.

fetishist's worst nightmare, the woman's lack of a phallus. Spero punningly adds: 'going to show them our sexts'. This revelation of lack does not paralyse the artist or destroy the corporal sign, but opens the possibility of a new form of representation. The French feminist Hélène Cixous has pointed out that: 'Men say that there are two unrepresentable things: death and the feminine sex' (Doane 1987: 118). The Body politic fetishized the state as that which never dies, refusing like all fetishists to accept the sexuality and anatomy of women. In its wake, artists like Walcott and Spero are exploring the possibilities opened by the contemporary crisis in corporal representation, just as the unthinking Classical revival demonstrates how that opportunity might be lost.

NOTE

1 My sources for this history are the following newspapers of the Commune (2 April–24 May 1871): *Le Mot d'Ordre* (MO), *Le Cri du Peuple* (CP) and *Le Vengeur* (V). These abbreviations will be used in the text.

3

LIKE A VIRGIN?

Despite the political importance of the body politic, the depiction of the perfect spiritual body in the form of the Christian gods, saints, and angels was far more common. In this chapter, I shall examine how the Madonna or Virgin Mary, became an important icon in nineteenth-century visual culture, defying the scepticism of the Enlightenment and the de-Christianization of the French Revolution. The Madonna icon and her attendant angels mark a curious trajectory across the history of modern art, connecting popular imagery, official art, photography and avant-garde painting. It was an image that required constant repetition, yet whose definition was always in dispute. The boundaries between the Madonna, the domestic woman and the fallen woman were sufficiently fluid that these categories became confused and overlapped.

The Madonna was the key motif in the work of Jean-Auguste-Dominique Ingres, giving shape and form to his portraiture of society women, Oriental subjects and representations of the body politic. Ingres saw himself as the heir of Raphael and became the prime defender of the French tradition throughout his long life. Later, his paintings derived from Raphael were an inspiration for Pablo Picasso, the pre-eminent twentieth-century avant-garde artist. For both Ingres and Picasso, Raphael's relationship with a baker's daughter became akin to a primal scene of art, which the artist was required to witness, but which he could only approach through the fetish. In this chapter, Sigmund Freud's notion of the fetish as a visual substitute for the female sex is used to explicate the complex psychic structures of nineteenth-century masculinity.

But the Madonna icon was not solely depicted by men, problematizing a reading that emphasizes the Madonna as exclusively a product of the 'male gaze'. Rather, the spectatorshp for these images, especially when presented in Orientalist context, was hybrid and diverse. When the nineteenth-century photographer Julia Margaret Cameron reworked the Madonna series into her work, the contingent and performative nature of this gender identity was made apparent. Needless to say, it has been the singer Madonna who has most fully exploited this interface between religion and sexuality. The controversy that surrounds her work suggests that the Madonna icon retains its ability to move people and, more generally, that the representation of women's bodies has yet to achieve the transformation claimed by postmodern theorists.

POST-REVOLUTIONARY DEPRESSION

In the aftermath of the French Revolution, official art had an almost impossible task to perform: to erase memories of the abolition of the Academy, of the revolutionary goal of virtuous art and of the Napoleonic patronage system. It required desperate acts of denial and some bold leaps of faith for this rewriting even to seem feasible. The icon of the Madonna, the mother of Christ, became central to this endeavour, enabled by the popular revival of the Mary cult in the nineteenth century. Marina Warner has investigated her history with intriguing results: 'It comes as a surprise to believers and non-believers alike that she is rarely mentioned in the Gospels, and is not even always called Mary' (Warner 1983: 335). From a few lines of inconclusive and contradictory evidence in the New Testament and the writings of the church fathers, the Catholic church had constructed a wide-ranging myth concerning the mother of Jesus. Her attributes, such as her virginity, freedom from sin, and perfection, are all later interpretations by theologians or developments in popular religion incorporating elements from other cults, such as that of the Egyptian goddess Isis. At times of crisis, such as the Counter-Reformation of the sixteenth century, the Catholic church has looked to the Madonna as a means of reinvigorating and reviving its fortunes. Consequently, Protestant reformers were especially hostile to the Marian cult (Huet 1992: 27–9). In the wake of Enlightenment scepticism, scientific positivism and political radicalism, the nineteenth-century Catholic church again sought to revive the Madonna icon.

This strategy was successful but it was also a measure of last resort. By way of comparison, the angel was no longer an authentic subject for art or religious believers. In 1530, the scholar Erasmus gave the following advice on bringing up boys:

A well-bred person should always avoid exposing without necessity the parts to which nature has attached modesty. If necessity compels this, it should be done with decency and reserve, even if no witness is present. For angels are always present, and nothing is more welcome to them in a boy than modesty, the companion and guardian of decency.

(Elias 1978 [1939]: 130)

For medieval and Renaissance scholars, angels were simply a fact, whose true nature was much debated. In similar fashion to the rise of Maryology, theologians created a wealth of angelic dogma which departed from scriptural authority. The seventeenth-century English member of Parliament Henry Lawrence compiled a history of angels, which described the composition of an angel's body:

But if they did have any such composition, as may be called a body, it is certainly of the greatest finenesse and subtility a spiritual body, and therefore not like to be of that grossenes that either the aire is, or those heavens that are framed out of the Chaos, but neerer the substance of the highest heavens . . .: To conclude, it will be safe to say that in comparison of God they are bodies, in comparison of us they are pure and might spirits.

(Lawrence 1649: 9)

For Lawrence, Erasmus' strictures still held good:

Even in our bedchambers, the presence of the Angells should hinder us from doing that which it were a shame and a dishonour, to be found doing by men, and should restrain us even to our thoughts and fancies, which they have a great ability to discern and to finde out.

(Lawrence 1649: 50)

This belief in the presence of angels in everyday life came under severe attack from dissident Protestants. Increase Mather, president of Harvard University, agreed that the angels had a specific kind of body that was neither wholly human nor wholly divine: 'Men are not to compare with Angels; but Angels are not to compare with God' (Mather 1696a: 22). However, he argued that with the completion of the scriptures, there was no longer any need for the appearance of angels, and indeed Satan now appeared in the disguise of an angel of light. Although Mather was prepared to accept certain recent appearances of angels as genuine, he was on the whole sceptical. In Peru, a prostitute claimed to see angels who told her that a 'Learned Man' she knew was to become pope and king – he believed her and was burnt: 'Whether his Judges would not have done better to have sent him to Bedlam, and to have administered Hellebore rather than Fire, as a more proper Remedy for his sober distraction, is not my work at present to dispute' (Mather 1696b: n.p.). Angelical apparitions were therefore to be treated with great suspicion, especially given that evil angels could appear exactly like angels of light. Evil angels could even resist the name of Jesus

100

and predict good things, if necessary to their plans. For Mather, only prayer could guard against the angel, more often a sign of madness or the devil than of divine intercession. Such developments fostered the fear of Protestant reformers that the cult of Mary broke the Biblical intercession against graven images and could only lead to other more serious heresies.

Such Protestant scepticism and hostility only enhanced the value placed on the Virgin Mary by the Catholic church, which increasingly asserted her absolute purity. Indeed, it was in 1854 that Pope Pius IX declared that the doctrine of the Immaculate Conception was now an official dogma of the Catholic church. The Catholic church now held not only that Mary had been a virgin, but that she was the only mortal ever born to be entirely free from sin. It was literally impossible for the Virgin to have committed a sin for she was now considered 'the most perfect created being after Jesus Christ' (Warner 1983: 237). All believers had to accept this dogma or leave the church. As Marina Warner has shown, Pius was only recognizing what was already common belief amongst ordinary church-goers, a reversal of standard assumptions concerning elite and popular culture. The beliefs and practices of ordinary church-goers motivated a profound development in the central theology of the Catholic church, just as today's liberation theology has mapped a new path for Catholicism. This manoeuvre placed the nineteenth-century Catholic church firmly in opposition to modern science and rationalism, but also on the side of popular religion. Religion was thus a central political issue for Republicans in nineteenth-century France. The Catholic church was held to have a particularly destructive hold over women, for as the Republican politician Jules Ferry declared 'women must belong to science or they will belong to the Church.' But Ferry's opposition of faith to rationalism ignored the sexualized elements of religious fervour in the period. In a letter of 1859, the novelist Gustave Flaubert was prompted to muse on the subject:

> It's a sad story that you tell me of that young girl, your relative gone mad as a result of religious ideas, but it's a familiar one. You've got to have a robust temperament to ascend the summits of mysticism without losing your head. And then there is in all this (in women especially) questions of temperament that complicate the suffering. Don't you see that all of them are in love with Adonis? He is the eternal husband that they require. Ascetic or libidinous, they dream of love, the great love; and to cure them (at least temporarily), they need not an idea but a fact – a man, a child, a lover.
>
> (Goldstein 1991: 140)

This combination of politics, culture, medicine, sexuality and religion incarnated in the Madonna icon thus allowed the orthodox Ingres to formulate a post-Revolutionary visual ideology that denied the Revolution while being up to date with modern notions of religion and sexuality. In a certain sense, Ingres was a modernist, in the same fashion that the nineteenth-century Catholic resistance to secular ideologies led to the 'modern' declaration of papal infallibility in 1870.

RESTORING ART

It was another pupil of David, Quatremère de Quincy, the perpetual Secretary of the restored Academy of Painting (now a sub-section of the Institut), who sought to redefine the role and function of art under the Restoration (1816–30). In his view, 'the Revolution was a sort of lacuna, a stretch of desert as sterile for the history of art as for the artists of that time' (Bianchi 1982: 187). While his colleagues in the Académie Française were busy removing words which were considered dangerous and superfluous from their 1823 Dictionary, Quatremère similarly scorned all modern schools of art, whether Romantic, Gothic or otherwise, seeking his inspiration in antiquity. He asserted that 'the superiority or perfection which the Greeks achieved [in art] was due to to the fact that the arts were necessary to them' (Quatremère de Quincy 1815: 9). In other words, a combination of race, climate and good fortune created ancient Greek art in circumstances that were almost beyond the control of the Greeks themselves. Their art was a natural emission, a unique overflow of their character and biology, which by definition could not be repeated. The achievements of Greek art were therefore an impossible but necessary goal for nineteenth-century artists. However, the true dilemma for Quatremère lay not in this evocation of the powers of antiquity but in his uneasy awareness that the Neo-Classical artists of the revolutionary period had shared and promoted such ideas. He himself had been a student of David, but despite his new role as the Mark Antony of Neo-Classicism, he had come to bury not honour the work of his youth. In opposition to the Romantics, Quatremère insisted that only the Classical permitted true liberty to the imagination. He now promoted antique subject-matter to the Academy as presenting the most suitable means of distancing the artist from the present: 'A distance from the imitable subject is that which most permits [the artist] to accommodate the fictive representation with the interests of art' (Quatremère 1825: 56). Art could only safely imagine the present by taking refuge in the past. Ingres alone was able to combine the necessary compromises and sustain the inevitable contradictions which were required to perform this feat. After his death, French Classicism evaporated in the face of assaults from without and weaknesses within. The marvel is, as with the *ancien régime* which inspired it, that so feeble a system was sustained for so long.

Ingres' solution to this dilemma of reconciling past failures with present needs was a combination of denial, fetishism, montage and copying. Ingres displaced his biological family in favour of the Neo-Classical studio of David, only later to repudiate his new artistic father in favour of Raphael. Freud described this fantasy as the family romance, an affliction of neurotic or highly gifted boys, in which

> [the] child's imagination becomes engaged in the task of getting free from the parents of whom he now has a low opinion and of replacing them by others who, as a rule, are of higher social standing. He will make use in this connection of any opportune coincidences from his actual experience.
>
> (Freud 1975: 238)

This pattern fits Ingres very well. The son of an artisan from Montauban in southwest France, he possessed artistic talents that were recognized early in life. From these humble beginnings, he journeyed to Paris in 1797, where he joined David's studio, and won the coveted Rome Prize in 1801. While studying in Rome, he was visited by a man in search of a portraitist. Ingres famously dismissed him, saying: 'He who lives here is a history painter' (Rosen and Zerner 1984: 32). Ingres haughtily denied any connection with the artisanal labours of his father and created a new history for himself as part of the elite tradition.

Later he rewrote his history once again: 'Raphael was revealed to me. . . . [M]y impression affected my vocation and filled my life. . . . Ingres is today what the little Ingres was at twelve years' (Rifkin 1983: 161). In this version, Ingres was artistically formed by the appearance of Raphael in his life even before he reached David's studio. His language is strikingly similar to that used by those who have experienced religious visions. He described his work as a vocation, and his body as being filled by Raphael in the same way that others might describe being filled by the grace of the Virgin Mary. Indeed, as has often been remarked, he constructed himself more in the fashion of the 'born' Romantic artist than the master trained in the academy. The family romance was equipped for such radical changes in direction 'for its many-sidedness and its great range of applicability enable it to meet every sort of requirement' (Freud 1975: 240). Even his loyal biographer Delaborde could not help but reveal the peculiarity of Ingres' attachment to Raphael:

> Right up to his last moment were the name of Raphael spoken by him or in his presence, it sufficed to arouse him to an impetuous admiration that was

almost fanatical, to carry him away so suddenly that even his violence imposed respect for a faith so invincible, so quick to manifest itself.

(Rifkin 1983: 157)

This religious intensity is a testament to the overlaid family romance which Ingres had constructed for himself and the force of his need to protect it. It was not for nothing that Baudelaire described Ingres' work as 'belong[ing] to a lower order, an almost sickly order . . . carried away by his almost pathological attention to style' (Baudelaire 1990 [1855]: 225).

In this second enactment of the family romance, Ingres openly fantasized that he would have preferred to live in the sixteenth century: 'I, unhappy enough to regret all my life not having been born in his [Raphael's] century. When I think that, three hundred years earlier, I could really have been his disciple' (Ingres 1947: 45). It was entirely appropriate that he selected Raphael's depiction of the Madonna as the key motif to his own work. Raphael was a role model eminently well suited to the conservative temper of the Academy, having been a loyal servant of princes and a religious painter in a period suitably remote from the dangerous times of the French Revolution. No whiff of controversy attached to his work, which was also of unquestioned artistic excellence. Ingres vigourously immersed himself in this artistic imposture. The Madonna was an especially suitable theme, since it had not been treated by the earlier Neo-Classicists and was undergoing a new lease of religious life. In 1858, a young woman named Bernadette Soubirous saw visions of the Virgin at Lourdes in southwest France. In order to test the truth of her vision, Church officials showed her reproductions of Raphael Madonnas, but she insisted the visions looked more like the statue in her local church. The Church upheld her claims, and Lourdes remains to this day an important place of pilgrimage. For our purposes, the importance lies in the literal deification of Raphael's Madonna, now accepted as the true image of the Mother of Christ, and used as such in contemporary ecclesiastical politics.

Two early Restoration paintings by Ingres were central in establishing the new status of the Madonna icon in the post-Revolutionary era: the *Vow of Louis XIII* (1824) and *Raphael and the Fornarina* (1812). Ingres produced many versions of *Raphael and the Fornarina* in his career, an indication of the centrality of this work to his artistic endeavour (Figure 17). It is a complex image, which directly implicates Ingres' own persona and sets his visual scheme in motion. The painting depicts Raphael seated with the Fornarina on his lap. There is an echo here of David's portrait of the chemist Lavoisier and his wife, in which Mme Lavoisier stands over her husband in a similar pose to that of the Fornarina. The repressed returns,

Figure 17 J.A.D. Ingres, *Raphael and the Fornarina* (1812), courtesy of the Fogg Art Museum, Harvard University Art Museums. Bequest of Grenville L. Winthrop.

105

albeit obliquely. The Fornarina has been painted to resemble her portrait by Raphael (now sometimes attributed to Raphael's student Giulio Romano), which can be seen uncompleted on the easel in Ingres' painting. It is this painting, rather than the 'real' Fornarina, which engages the attention of Raphael. This complication of reality and representation is increased by the presence in the background of Raphael's *Madonna of the Chair* (1510), represented by Ingres in such a way that the Fornarina appears to have been the model for the Madonna as well as for her own portrait. All the women in the painting, from the Madonna to the Fornarina via her portrait, are modelled from the same original. It is ultimately undecidable whether the Madonna or the Fornarina is the original in this series of copies. The Madonna, far from being the polar opposite of the prostitute as Freud assumed, is equated by Ingres with Raphael's mistress. As Baudelaire remarked, Ingres 'unites in a provokingly adulterous way, the calm solidity of Raphael and the affectations of a courtesan' (Baudelaire 1990 [1855]: 241). This interaction was a compelling subject for artists of very different temperaments. The English painter Joseph Turner, who might otherwise be considered a polar opposite to Ingres, also depicted Raphael and the Fornarina in his 1820 painting *Rome Seen from the Vatican; Raphael Accompanied by the Fornarina Preparing Decorations for the Papal Loggia* (London: Tate Gallery). Strikingly, the *Madonna of the Chair* is clearly visible in Turner's work, as are the various paintings with which Raphael was to decorate the Papal loggia. Although he does not show us the Fornarina's face, the prominence of the *Madonna* suggests that she was, as Ingres also believed, the model for the Virgin. Both Turner's Romanticism and Ingres' Classicism can be read as departing from this primal scene of artistic representation.

In Ingres' *Raphael and the Fornarina*, the depicted painter, who represented both Raphael and his surrogate 'son' Ingres, is fascinated by his own drawing of the Fornarina, and yet he holds the 'real' woman tightly. Raphael/Ingres is so placed that he cannot look at the Fornarina and draw at the same time. Indeed, drawing the model from such close proximity would be virtually impossible. If he touches her physically, he cannot see his easel; in order to continue drawing, he must turn away from her and touch her via the displaced touch of the artist on the painting within the painting. As if to signify this relationship between drawing, touch and blindness (see Chapter 1), a maul stick leans against the easel, resembling a blind man's baton.[1] Yet it was Ingres who instructed his students: 'The brushstroke, as accomplished as it may be, should not be visible: otherwise, it prevents the illusion, immoblizes everything. Instead of the object represented, it calls attention to the process: instead of the thought, it betrays the hand' (Rosen and Zerner 1984: 229). The surface of Ingres' paintings was certainly highly finished, with no visible brushstrokes. In the *Raphael*, even the chair knob shines as if catching the light. The picture none the less circulates around the relationship between physical and artistic touch. Ingres was not simply denying the existence of his manual labour, but calling attention to the serial character of his work. His objection was that, in contradiction to the aesthetics of finish, the brushstroke immobilizes the work, for the material quality of the mark distracted the spectator from the flow of serially represented forms as presented in *Raphael and the Fornarina*. The painting becomes meaningless unless each of the iconic forms is observed in relationship to one another.[2]

This complex interaction of gaze, touch and desire in *Raphael and the Fornarina* indicates that Ingres used the representation of woman, circulating around the Madonna icon, as the controlling motif in a heterodox system of visual signification. The *Vow of Louis XIII* made this new superiority of the Madonna icon strikingly clear. It was in effect a pictorial montage, combining a close copy of Raphael's *Sistine Madonna* (1513) with a depiction of the French king Louis XIII, who was later beatified for his dedication of France to the Virgin. Ingres took the body of the king and placed it in subservience to the Madonna, the very subservience to the church that subsequent French monarchs – not to mention the Revolution – were in fact strenuously to resist. In the politics of representation, however, the fallen body of the king was no match for the revived Madonna. The angels at the bottom of Raphael's Madonna have flown down and hold the tablet which records Louis XIII's dedication in 1638 of France to the Virgin of the Assumption. The Madonna herself is clearly no longer to be associated with the earthly sphere and is as superior to the angels as the angels are to humans. By placing her above the portrait of Louis and lowering her eyes, the frank outward look of Raphael's Madonna is transformed into an aristocractic and haughty gaze, enhanced by the low viewpoint of the painting, which effectively places the spectator on the floor. The Madonna, and by extension Raphael, hold sway over the mere vagaries of French history and its populace. Given Ingres' own identification with Raphael, the *Vow of Louis XIII* fully expressed his notorious hauteur and arrogance. One critic complained in 1824 that the Madonna looked too much like those images hawked by blind beggars and Christmas carolers (Rosenblum 1967b: 126). While Ingres would of course have denied the iconographic connection, he sought exactly this kind of populism in his effort to revive the *grand genre* of French painting by his use of the increasingly popular icon of the Madonna. Ingres' denial ran counter to his artistic sources, formation and subject-matter, yet his protestation was found convincing. It was precisely Ingres' ability to sustain such contradictions that made him the only candidate for leadership of official French painting in the post-Revolutionary period. At the heart of the elite culture of the Académie des Beaux-Arts there was, then, a motif whose force derived as much from its connections with popular imagery as with its Raphaelesque origins.

FROM THE MADONNA TO THE HAREM

Throughout the rest of his career, Ingres centred his work around the relay he had created between the prostitute and the Madonna, mediated by the portrait. Only the *Raphael* showed all three types of representation in one mythical historical setting. Otherwise Ingres separated the three categories, representing the sexualized woman as a harem slave, mediated to the Madonna by his carefully selected portraiture. The connectedness of this series was signified to the viewer by a compulsive repetition of visual motifs. Both Raphael's Fornarina, and the Madonna depicted within the painting, wore a turban. This same turban was worn by Ingres' harem figures and by the women in his society portraits. First seen in his *Bathing Woman* (1807), it reappeared in his famous *La Grande Odalisque* (1814), a small, highly finished rendering of a reclining harem nude (Figure 18). The space in which the odalisque was represented was entirely fantastical. Although harems did certainly exist, being the women's quarters of certain Islamic households, the West imagined them as little more than licensed brothels. However, the term *harim* in Arabic means forbidden, and no Western visitor had ever seen the imperial harem in Istanbul, which was at the centre of the sexualized fantasy of the harem. The harem in Western painting was, to quote Ali Behad, 'nothing but a phantasm, a purely fictional construction onto which Europe's own sexual repressions, erotic fantasies, and desire of domination were projected' (Behad 1989: 110). This phantasmic, highly controlled visual space was thus the perfect venue for Ingres to deploy his contradictory, neurotic vision.

The only man authorized to enter the harem, and the only one who had physical access to the women inside, was the sultan himself. For all others, a degree of mutilation was the expected price to be paid for access to the harem. Thus the eunuchs were castrated, and the harem servants were either deaf or dwarfs. Ingres was fully aware of these prohibitions. He

Figure 18 J.A.D. Ingres, *La Grande Odalisque* (1814), Louvre, Paris. Giraudon/ Bridgeman Art Library.

copied into his notebooks the sections of the letters of Lady Mary Wortley Montagu, wife of an eighteenth-century British ambassador to Constantinople, which recorded that all male intruders into the harem other than the Sultan faced the death penalty (Brown 1987: 60). Furthermore, although the harem was a fantasy space, all these categories of servant were well known in European society. For example, the long history of eunuchs in the Christian religion stretched back to the voluntary castrations of the third century but were by the nineteenth century restricted to the *castrati* singers of the papal choir, finally disbanded in 1878.[3] It was, however, the women contained by the harem who were the subject of the most obsessive Western speculation. *La Grande Odalisque* has long been noted both for the extraordinary length of the woman's back, to which Ingres has added three extra vertebrae, and for its general anatomical inaccuracy. The additional vertebrae were the visible manifestation of the necessary physical mutilation required for all members of the harem in the Western imagination. They were also an erotic sign, for the Western gaze 'thematizes as erotic the transgressive crossing of the harem's limits' (Behad 1989: 112). To be able to see the harem woman was an erotic and transgressive act, requiring the mutilating mark of physical difference to make it plain that a harem woman was being depicted.

This sense of power offered the spectator other consolations as well. As Fatima Mernissi has argued, the isolation of the harem was 'based on the assumption that the woman is a powerful and dangerous being. All sexual institutions [in Islam] (polygamy, repudiation, sexual segregation, etc.) can be perceived as a strategy for containing her power' (Mernissi 1975: xvi). While the harem was a space in which woman could be imagined, it also served as a means of containing and controlling the series of women at the centre of Ingres' work, and by extension at the centre of French official painting. As such, it departed from the observation of the actual harem itself. In the eighteenth century, Lady Montagu was able to spend some time with the women of the harem, although not to enter the forbidden space of the *harim* itself. She observed that, for all the restrictions imposed on women in Islam, 'they have in reality more freedom than we do'. In an analogy with the libertine masked balls of London, Lady Montagu noted that the veil itself was not simply restrictive: 'This perpetual masquerade gives them entire liberty of following their inclinations without danger of discovery' (Montagu 1971: 127). The mutilated body of Ingres' *Odalisque* seems designed to prevent such liberty, for as painted this figure cannot be imagined standing. The harem woman could thus be restricted to her proper function in the Western imaginary of awaiting her master. Ingres had achieved what the medicalization of women's bodies in the nineteenth century would later struggle to do, in making the deviancy of women physically visible.

Yet the picture cannot be read as if constructed from the viewpoint of the (male) prince alone. Ingres depicted his subject as seen from behind, but she has turned her head, as if noticing the approach of another into the *harim*, the forbidden space. In Michel Foucault's analysis of Velazquez's seventeenth-century masterpiece *Las Meninas* (1656) (Madrid: Museo del Prado), he described how the spectator of the painting stands at the presumed viewpoint of the king: 'That space where the king and his wife hold sway belongs equally well to the artist and to the spectator.' The viewpoint of Ingres' work cannot be similarly read as an overlap of the painter's gaze with that of the image's spectator and the presumed sultan entering his harem. For Velazquez carefully controlled his viewpoint by depicting a mirror opposite it within his painting, in which only the reflection of the king and queen could be seen. Foucault explains: 'Because they are present within the picture, to the right and to the left, the artist and the visitor cannot be given a place in the mirror: just as the king appears in the looking glass precisely because he does not belong to the picture' (Foucault 1971: 15). Velazquez further controlled the possibilities of spectatorship by including all those who had the right to be present at court within his painting, such as male and female courtiers, the Infanta, the court dwarf and even pets. None of these systems of ordering spectatorship are present in Ingres' picture. The intruder seen by the odalisque may be the authorized presence of the sultan; it may be another woman from within the harem; it may be a eunuch, a deaf attendant or a dwarf; it may even be someone with no official connection to the harem, whether male or female. The ordered spectatorship of the Classical period had given way to a hybrid spectator, who disrupted the painter's gaze from beyond the control of the frame.

The Orient was the appropriate imaginary location for such ambivalent spectatorship. Although Orientalism attempted to construct a system in which the Orient was absolutely Other to the West, in practice the overarching binary opposition of Occident and Orient was not quite effective. The scopic practice of Orientalism involved a gaze that, as we have seen, looks both ways. The ambivalence of the Oriental was heightened by the desire to transgress its boundaries, which had only been reinforced and reinvigorated by the pathologization of the Orient. In the Preface to his *Orientales* of 1828, Victor Hugo mused that 'for empires as well as for literatures, before very long perhaps the East is destined to play a role in the West' (Chambers 1988: 116). The depiction of the harem in European painting of the period expressed varying possibilities for spectatorship and visibility offered by the Orient, as well as making the deviancy of the harem clearly visible. That pathology was made most apparent in the depiction of the various abject bodies depicted within this tightly defined space, who were equal in their subservience to the Western imaginary.

Throughout the nineteenth century, artists continued to be fascinated with Orientalism, culminating with the establishment of the Société des Peintres Orientalistes in 1893, which held its own annual exhibitions in imitation of the official Salon (Rosenthal 1982: 148). In all of this extensive production of imagery, the viewpoint of the image was constantly a subject of experimentation and interest. Jules Clairin (1843–1919) broke Velazquez's convention by explicitly including the sultan in his *Entering the Harem* (Baltimore: Walters Art Gallery, c. 1870) (Figure 19). The sultan has entered the harem through a still open door, and looks beyond a veil held back by a dark-skinned woman to reveal the vast spaces within, which are only fragmentarily shown by Clairin. The eyeline of the picture is very low, as if the spectator is on his or her knees in front of the Sultan, where we are confronted by Clairin's signature in flowing script. Neither the place of the prince nor that of the artist is available to the spectator of this scene, as they are included in the image. By contrast, Jean-Léon Gérôme's (1824– 1904) *The Harem Door* puts all the traditional possibilities into an uncertain play. The painting shows the door to a harem, correctly inscribed in Arabic

Figure 19 Jules Clairin, *Entering the Harem* (*c.* 1870), Baltimore Walters Art Gallery.

'God is Great', with a powerful and impassive African guard standing in front. Anyone may approach this door, but only the prince will gain access. The Orientalist will also gain a certain access by deciphering the Arabic text that will remain a puzzle to the uninitiated. The unanswered question is whether a traveller in disguise might gain unauthorized admittance, as many Western visitors to the East would try to do, often using cross-dressing or other forms of masquerade. Might the gaze itself wear a veil, like the women of Islam?

Finally, let us think of the watercolour by the British artist John Frederick Lewis (1805–1876), entitled *The Hhareem* (London: Victoria & Albert Museum, *c.* 1849), exhibited at the Paris Universal Exhibition in 1855 (Figure 20). The seeming stutter in the title, repeating the 'h' and 'e', signifies that, like Gérôme, Lewis had personal experience of the Orient and was an initiate into the closed world of the East. The critic Edmond About gave a detailed account of Lewis's technique: 'It took many months to execute this large lattice-work room, into which the sun penetrates through a grill and traces little lozenges on the humans and animals. M. Lewis laboured every day on this strange work . . . I think it is difficult to push the fetishism of watercolour painting any further' (Rosenthal 1982:

Figure 20 John Frederick Lewis, *The Hhareem* (*c.* 1849), courtesy of the Board of Trustees, Victoria and Albert Museum, London/Bridgeman Art Library.

113

140). Lewis attempted to render the effects and quality of oil painting in a different medium, watercolour, but it is hard to resist reading this fetishistic attempt at displacement in wider terms. Here Freud's definition of fetishism as a displacement of sexual desire away from the female lack of the penis on to the fetish object may be used with confidence; for, if Freud has a secure subject, it is surely the white, middle-class English male in the nineteenth century. The very term 'fetish' takes its origin from the name *feitiçaria* given by sixteenth-century Portuguese explorers to African figures, so that fetishism was literally unimaginable without the colonial intervention of Europeans into Africa. No more appropriate scene for the fetishist can be imagined than the harem, with its array of eunuchs, fabrics and opportunities for voyeurism. The figures in the watercolour all look to the right, outside the frame, at a scene which we cannot see but may imagine. A woman's clothing can be seen at the extreme right, but she herself cannot be seen, as she is cut off by the frame. The rapt attention of the sultan, intersecting with the cautiously diverted glance of the servant, suggests the possibility that she is about to undress, revealing her 'lack', in a replay of the primal scene of the fetishist, who, according to Freud, adopts as a fetish that which he sees in 'the last moment in which the woman could still be regarded as phallic'. Lewis's transference of that scene was from West to East, from London and Paris to Cairo, where he had himself lived. It was also a transference of spectatorship, given prominence by the attention to light and shade caused by the lattice window, which prevents the inquisitive gaze from outside seeing the forbidden but makes our viewing of the scene not only possible, but rendered in a textured chiaroscuro. That chiaroscuro was given tonal values by the contrast in skin colour between the dark sultan and the pale harem women. In his pioneering studies of hysteria in the 1880s, Jean-Martin Charcot was to identify an *éblouissement de ténèbre* (dazzle of shadow) that disrupted the vision of his patients (Apter 1991: 148). Lewis's meticulously rendered light and shade seems to render visible not just the fetish, but the hysterical gaze which focused upon it. For, as Jan Goldstein has recently shown, hysteria was by no means limited to women, but also afflicted men, such as the Orientalist Flaubert (Goldstein 1991).

Ingres returned this fetishism to French art in his depiction of domestic women. The only trace of identity presented in the *Valpinçon Bather* (1807) is her turban, similar to that later worn by both the Fornarina and the Grande Odalisque (Bryson 1984: 130). Her nudity within a domestic setting connects the exotic alterity of the harem to the Western context. It might be said that Ingres' portraits provide as little sense of individual identity as his bathers, for both the Madonna and the harem are present in these works. In his famous first portrait of *Madame Moitessier* (1856), the features of her face are clearly derived from his vision of Raphael's Madonna, while her headdress recalls the turban in somewhat attenuated form. The curious pose of her fingers was derived from a Roman fresco (Rosenblum 1967b: 164) and the ornate furnishings and costume were typical Second Empire excesses. For all the exaggerated care of execution, Madame Moitessier herself scarcely seems to be represented at all. Curiously, Ingres offers us not one but two views of his subject, for the mirror behind her head presents her shadowy profile. The reflection is wholly incorrect from an optical point of view, but that was the least of Ingres' concerns. This distorted reflection, like the distorted back of the Grande Odalisque, is the visual indication of the inevitable Otherness of women in Ingres' imagination. The luxurious interior is the equivalent of the interiorized space of the harem, an equally mythical domestic sphere in which women dutifully attended to men, just as the harem women attended to the sultan. The artist's studio formed the final element in this series linking the harem and the domestic interior. These settings provided the tightly controlled environments in which Ingres' artistic experiments in corporeal form could unfold. Each was insulated from the effects of politics, but was subject to the threat of the overweening and corrupting influence of women on the male artist, the sultan and the nineteenth-century *pater familias*. This series, connecting the domestic interior to the harem, was widespread in nineteenth-century French culture. In his famous novel satirizing the provincial bourgeoisie, *Madame Bovary* (1857), Gustave Flaubert evoked Ingres at the turning-point of the heroine's affair with the young lawyer Léon: 'She was the beloved mistress of all the novels, the heroine of all the dramas, the vague "she" of all the volumes of verse. On her shoulders, he rediscovered the amber colour of Ingres' *Odalisque*' (Lowe 1991: 1). At the very moment in which Madame Bovary allows herself to fall from domestic grace and enter into an adulterous affair, her lover sees her as a painting by Ingres. Ingres had so successfully reinvented French visual culture by means of the Madonna icon that it was literally impossible to envisage nineteenth-century France in any other way.

Just as Ingres had begun his artistic career with a painting that contained all three possible representations of women, so did he end it with another, the difference being that the women were now all nude. *The Turkish Bath* (1863) contains the three variations of woman that Ingres had derived from his conception of the Madonna. In the foreground, the figure of the

Valpinçon Bather can be seen, this time playing a mandolin. In the right foreground, the Odalisque from Ingres' *Odalisque with a Slave* (1842) makes another appearance. In the left background, we can see the figure of Madame Moitessier, recognizable by her striking gesture with the right hand. In the harem, Madame Moitessier's turban has been restored to full, exotic size and she is otherwise naked. This painting is often dismissed as the erotic ramblings of an old man but it is in fact entirely consistent with Ingres' revision of French painting around the figure of the Madonna, mediated through the portrait and bather to the harem woman. As the Madonna is the one absent figure from this painting, one wonders if Ingres identified the Madonna as himself, or perhaps as his mother, in the manner of Flaubert's famous claim that 'Madame Bovary, c'est moi' (I am Madame Bovary).

Strikingly, Pablo Picasso, who claimed Ingres as an influence, turned back to this same primal scene of painting in his later career. In a series of twenty-four variations on the theme of *Raphael Painting the Fornarina* (1968), Picasso combined Ingres' early sublimated scene of painting with the overt eroticism of the *Turkish Bath*. Picasso transformed the quiet, submissive Raphael of Ingres' painting into a sexually avaricious and almost comically well-endowed monster. Desire is simply figured in Picasso's line drawings as possession of the woman and there is certainly no ambiguity here about who has the signifying phallus: the artistry of the male is equivalent to his anatomy and (hetero)sexuality. Picasso does not simply restate Ingres, but shows how the avant-garde has transformed the Classical lexicon. He pays his dues to the canon of art history, while making it clear that his reproductive powers exceed those of his predecessors. Neither late work should be dismissed as simply reflecting the pathetic desires of two elderly men. For both the *Turkish Bath* and Picasso's *Raphael Painting the Fornarina* contain not simply the desire for lost pleasures, but an artistic restatement and reiteration of the artists' continuing adherence to a visual series, which both claimed male heterosexuality as its dominant motif and was deeply troubled about that sexuality. The carefully controlled environment of the Raphael/Madonna/whore myth speaks more to a fear of unbridled (female) sexuality than it does to an erotic or artistic exuberance. In any system of this kind, what must be denied is the abject, the unthinkable. For Ingres and Picasso, the Madonna of Raphael served as an icon of purity to exclude unclean and unspoken desires and fears. The constant reiteration of female bodies in their work has ultimately less to do with real women – despite the very real consequences for modern women of this phantasmic misreading – than it does with the vulnerabilities of the male ego. For just as Galatea, the speaking statue, could represent the male child's desire for the father, so too could the figure of the Fornarina represent the desire of the artist to adopt what Freud would call the feminine role in relation to the artistic father. In other words, Ingres and Picasso may have wished to play bottom to Raphael's top.

At this point, then, we should pause and consider how the complex nexus of history, art history and biography that has been described circulating around the icon of the Madonna might be brought together. While the notion of the psychoanalyst Jacques Lacan, that the ego is formed in a 'mirror stage', might be evoked in a discussion of *Madame Moitessier*, whose distorted reflection is seen in the mirror behind her, it is less clear how it might be used in describing the Madonna to whom she is clearly linked. Instead, we might do better to do as Freud did and re-examine the problem as an economic one, that is to say, as a question of maintaining a system which is always marked by contradiction. Any such interpretation is necessarily speculative, like that of Freud. It is not, however, a universal nor an ahistorical interpretation, but one which is grounded in – and only applicable to – the specific circumstances of nineteenth-century Western art. Ingres' depiction of women is self-evidently sexualized, yet to generations of observers from the nineteenth century onwards, his work has seemed too cold, too disturbing, even too finished to be straightforwardly erotic. Yet as Freud realized in the latter stages of his career, not every drive leads to pleasure. He was led to rethink his conceptual scheme of the mind by observing his grandson at play. The child threw away a cotton reel, exclaiming 'Fort' (gone) and would then retrieve it to the cry of 'Da' (there). Freud watched the child play this game over and again and came to theorize that the child was mastering his sense of abandonment when left by his mother. The repetition gradually assured the child that being left entailed later being rejoined. Moreover, it became clear to Freud that there was a compulsion to experience both the unpleasure of separation and the pleasure of reunion. In an increasingly complex and speculative essay entitled *Beyond the Pleasure Principle*, Freud famously redefined his description of the drives ('Trieb') to include both the pleasure principle he had earlier elaborated and a death drive. The death drive is inherently conservative and seeks to restore an 'earlier state of things' (Freud 1961: 69). In so redefining his interpretation of the psyche, Freud abandoned a qualitative model, in which two elements were in a binary opposition controlling and modifying each other, in favour of a topographical model (63). The pleasure principle is mediated by the reality principle in its conflict with the death drive. In such a topography, seemingly inconsistent tendencies can be described within an overall structure that is not determined by one dominant principle, but complexly transected by several such drives.

This topography of the psyche permits a far more useful reading of Ingres than another repetition of the mirror stage. Freud remarked at the outset that the visual arts provide evidence that 'even under the dominance of the pleasure principle, there are ways and means of making what is in itself unpleasurable into a subject to be recollected and worked over in the mind' (17). He concluded his essay by observing: 'If it is really the case that seeking to restore an earlier state of things is such a universal characteristic of instincts, we need not be surprised that so many processes take place in mental life independently of the pleasure principle' (75). In Ingres' artistic work, there were several forces at work which cannot be explained solely by reference to desire, and which sought a restoration of past time. He felt compelled to restore the French school to its former glory, erasing the recent transgressions of the French Revolution. At the same time, he wished to maintain the artist's stature as a purely creative figure in the face of the marginalizing processes of modern life, the challenge of mechanical reproduction, and the defiant assertion of manual work by modern painters like Courbet. In seeking this goal, Ingres eliminated his personal history not once but twice and created an impossible parentage for himself from Raphael and the Madonna. His elevating of these twin totems was both personal and political, offering a direction for his own career and for French art in general. Further, the complex of desire within *Raphael and the Fornarina* allowed Ingres an outlet for both his fantasies of domination and those of submission. If we accept with Freud that 'the compulsion to repeat must be ascribed to the conscious repressed' (20), then it is scarcely surprising that the same iconographic figures are revisited time and again by Ingres. All that repression was bound to produce considerable repetition. Within this complex topography, the currents of ego and libido cannot be precisely described. Clearly, Ingres' drive to deny and even deform the female form was intermingled with a fascination with the feminine, not unakin to that of Freud himself.

BUT IS IT ART?

The central role of the Madonna in re-evaluating the functions of high art in the nineteenth century was confirmed in her reappearance in the work of early art photographers Oscar Rejlander and Julia Margaret Cameron.

While Ingres and his successors in academic art such as William Bougereau (1825–1905) sought to use the popularity of the Madonna to revitalize high art, the early art photographers used her image to confirm the status of photography as an art. Critics have continued to debate this question until the present day, but in the mid-nineteenth century it was legally the case that photography could not be considered as art, and therefore did not have the same copyright protections as were enjoyed by fine artists, writers, and makers of prints and engravings. At the same time, the enormous popularity of photography, its inexpensive technical procedures, and its immediate applications for pornographic uses made it seem a less than entirely respectable art. In 1858, the *Stereoscopic Magazine* was established in London to be sold and distributed in reputable book format. For, as the *Liverpool Courier*'s review of the new publication remarked: 'It was obvious to all that something of the kind was needed to develop the real utility of the stereoscope, for already was there such a deluge of ill-selected, crude and unmeaning stereographs, mingled with a few in good taste, that the latter were lost in the crowd' (*Stereoscopic Magazine* 1858: 14). Including stereographic images by Roger Fenton and other leading photographers who aspired to be known as artists, the magazine featured views of plants, cathedrals, museums, country houses, landscapes, statues, and Britain's imperial possessions. The *Stereoscopic Magazine* was a deliberate attempt to render the photographic image in general not only respectable but useful, seeking to inculcate love of country and empire in the nation's youth.

Respectability, utility and morality were similarly the goals of the art photographers who came to create images of the Virgin Mary at this time. In 1856, the Swedish photographer Oscar Rejlander (1813–1875) was work-ing in Wolverhampton, seeking to demonstrate the importance of photo-graphy for artists in general. Working with local children, he produced a series of studies that were hailed by the English photographic press as being as 'beautiful as those of Della Robia, Flamingo, or Raphael' (Jones 1973: 14). However, the art critics did not agree: 'We doubt the propriety of attempting to rival the historical painter. . . . Such pictures as these will have a tendency to lower the appreciation of Art in the eyes of the public, and unfit them for receiving the full impression intended by the artist's production.' In a tone that would not be out of place in the mouths of some contemporary critics, the writer for the *Art Journal* feared that the direct familiarity of photography undermined the potential for a serious audience for art in a manner that was in some sense immoral.

Rejlander disagreed, and set about proving that photography could be as useful, moral and patriotic as painting. In various studies, he demonstrated that the draughtmanship in various classic works of art, such as Titian's *Venus and Adonis* and Rubens' *Peace and War*, was at fault in central matters of anatomy. In an age in which character and respectability were held to be visible in the physiognomy, these mistakes were of no small account. His next effort in this vein was a representation of the angels from Raphael's *Sistine Madonna* (Figure 21). Photography now sought to correct one of the most famous works of the Master of Old Masters. The pose of Rejlander's child models sought to reproduce those of the Italian master but, unsurprisingly, Raphael's puffy angels were able to contort into poses the real children could not manage. Rejlander's typically nineteenth-century concern for observation and experimentation proved Raphael's mistake on one level but ignored the metaphysical quality of angels, as one reviewer of the work noted when it was displayed at the Manchester Art Treasures Exhibition in 1857: 'The best of these [photographs] is that of the cherubs done from the picture of the *Madonna del Siste*; this is done from the life,

Figure 21 Oscar Rejlander, *After Raphael's Sistine Madonna* (c. 1857), Dresden, courtesy of the Gernsheim Collection, University of Texas at Austin.

120

though the angels are rather too much "of the earth, earthy"' (Jones 1973: 18). Displayed alongside photographs of Raphael drawings by Prince Albert, Rejlander's work in this exhibition none the less staked a claim for photography to be considered as art, centring on his famous composition *Two Ways of Life* or *Hope and Repentance*, a moralizing tableau offering a choice between the moral and immoral. There was also a moral lesson in patriotism to be drawn from his angels, for Rejlander entitled the work *Non Angli, sed angeli* (not Angles, but angels), a visual and verbal pun originating in the comment attributed to Saint Augustine on seeing British prisoners in Rome. For in this case, the children were in fact English pretending to be angels. But in the climate of nineteenth-century race science, the title also made less innocent allusions to the supposed superiority of the Anglo-Saxon racial type over all others. By implication, the sober qualities of the Northern artist were required to correct the excesses of the passionate Italian. In 1870, Rejlander wrote that criminals could be identified by the shape of their ears and proposed to create a photographic chart, detailing fifty examples for the use of the police (Jones 1973: 37). This unfulfilled idea antedated the enactment of Alphonse Bertillon's similar procedure in France by nine years and was later to be used by the art connoisseur Morelli in identifying works by Renaissance masters. It was entirely appropriate that Rejlander later supplied illustrations for Charles Darwin's *On the Expression of the Emotions in Man and Animals* (1872), which sought to demonstrate the work of evolution in the expressions. These scientific, moral and patriotic lessons were central to the effort made by British photographers from the 1850s on to rescue their trade from the taint of popular imagery, erotica and craft.

Although Rejlander used Raphael's *Madonna* as part of his campaign to gild photography's image, it was left to Julia Margaret Cameron (1815–1879) to pursue the logical next step, namely photographic images representing the Virgin herself. Cameron's life exemplified the kind of Englishwoman that the art photographers wished to create as their clientele. Herself the daughter of an Imperial civil servant, she married the prominent lawyer Charles Cameron, who helped draft the Indian Law Codes and served on the Council of India from 1843 to 1878. Both in Anglo-Indian society and in England, Julia Margaret Cameron (née Pattle) was a leading society hostess and created a salon frequented by such luminaries as Alfred Tennyson, William Thackeray and Holman Hunt. The Camerons had six children of their own and raised no less than five orphaned relatives.

In 1863, Cameron began her experiments with photography, which were to win her both acclaim and derision. Her work was highly sentimental, concentrating on stylized scenes from poetry and literature, and portraits of her extensive acquaintance. As well as these identified models, Cameron established a local circle of models at her home on the Isle of Wight, pressing her children, friends and servants into service in her *tableaux vivants*. One of her most favoured models was her chambermaid Mary Hillier, who posed repeatedly in her series of religious works. So often did Mary Hillier pose as the Virgin that she became known locally as 'Mary Madonna'. Cameron's devotional scenes make use of her characteristic soft focus and dramatic lighting effects, but they are recognizably set in the Madonna tradition established by Raphael and given new life by Ingres. The 1865 photograph *Divine Love* shows Mary Hillier dressed as the Madonna holding a young child. She is recognizable as the Madonna by her Raphaelesque clothing and headdress, complete with the typical Ingresque hairstyle in which the hair is centrally parted and severely swept back. Mary has downcast eyes and her face is calm, registering no expression. She holds her mouth against the child's forehead, but does not appear to be actually kissing him. The divine love of the title may not be precisely that of the Madonna for the Christ child but a more generalized expression of the charity and love of the Virgin. The child seems to be rather dirty and dishevelled, contrasting with the bright white skin of Mary Hillier's shoulder (Figure 22). In Cameron's 1866 photograph, *Divine Love*, with Mary Hillier again the model, the child is altogether more angelic. He sleeps with his head resting against some support which cannot be seen. Hillier's pose is statuesque, again devoid of expression or movement. Her profile contrasts to the full face of the child and is distinctly less in focus. These devotional subjects were amongst those singled out by the jury at the Berlin International Exhibition of 1865 in awarding Cameron a bronze medal: '[These] are all pictures worthy of close study, and should not be passed by as some people, too easily put off by glaring technical shortcomings, are inclined to do' (Gernsheim 1975: 63).

Indeed, criticism of Cameron's work has centred around the question of technique. For critics of photography maintained that its technical procedures and exactitude of reproduction not only excluded any possible involvement of artistic imagination but relegated the practice to a manual trade. Rejlander denied the charge, claiming that 'the manual part of photographic composition is but wholesale vignetting', a practice which, he averred, was both 'allowed and admired' (Jones 1973: 24). None the less, professional photographers and photographic journals were amongst the severest critics of Cameron's work for its technical incompetence. In the words of one typical review of the Universal Exhibition of 1867: 'Those

Figure 22 Julia Margaret Cameron, *Divine Love* (1865), courtesy of the Gernsheim
Collection, University of Texas at Austin.

large unsharp heads, spotty backgrounds, and deep opaque shadows looked more like bungling pupil's work than masterpieces and for this reason many photographers could hardly restrain their laughter.' However, Cameron refused to master photographic technique as a means of asserting her artistic qualities. Criticized for producing work that was out of focus and had other technical faults, she retorted in 1864:

> I believe in other than mere conventional photography – map-making and skeleton rendering of feature and form without that roundness and fulness of force and feature, that modelling of flesh and limb, which the focus I use only can give, tho' called and condemned as 'out of focus'. What is focus and who has the right to say what focus is the legitimate focus? My aspirations are to enoble photography and to secure for it the character and uses of High Art by combining the real and the ideal and sacrificing nothing of Truth by all possible devotion to Poetry and beauty.
>
> (Gernsheim 1975: 14)

Whereas Ingres insisted on the perfection of technique in order to obscure the manual dimension of art, Cameron deliberately refused to employ conventional photographic technique as an assertion of the artistic nature of her enterprise. Her repeated use of the Madonna as a subject for her work was further evidence of her noble intentions and led to comparisons with Raphael and Leonardo in the non-photographic press.

These photographs were far from being simple essays in art for art's sake. Even though the Madonna had a different cultural role to play in Protestant England from the one she had in Catholic France, these photographs are none the less replete with the cultural assumptions of their time concerning race, class and sexuality. Cameron chose her servant to pose for her religious scenes precisely because, in the eyes of the cultural elite, she was unrecognizable. When Cameron dressed Tennyson as the Dirty Monk, or Millais as Dante, her audience were intended to recognize the sitter, and the photograph depended upon this recognition for its effect. On the other hand, her religious subjects required that her audience should not identify the model, making a servant the perfect choice. Even for those in Cameron's circle who knew Hillier, the choice of a servant to play the Virgin Mary played into the nineteenth century's pious hypocrisy that the poor would find their reward in the next world. Hillier's local nickname, Mary Madonna, suggests that her peers took a less exalted view of her modelling.

For middle-class Victorian men, female servants occupied an ambiguous position. While the rhetoric of separate spheres held men to be utterly indifferent to the female world of the household, Victorian men found the master–servant relationship to be highly sexualized in both fantasy and practice. The anonymous author of *My Secret Life*, a pornographic novel of the period, made much of his extended encounters with female servants, while the unfortunate exploits of Karl Marx with the female servants of his household can stand as a metonym for this common practice. Was the laughter of the male photographers at Cameron's work in part motivated by the apparent incongruity of a domestic servant playing the Virgin Mary, the least appropriate role for such a woman in the male imagination? Even so, Hillier's depiction as the Madonna was entirely consistent with the schema of the Madonna icon outlined above. She was a woman of the domestic interior, who was also to be found in the artist's studio, and therefore would have a role to play in the phantasmic harem. As if in acknowledgement of this series of female roles, Cameron photographed Hillier as Sappho in 1870. Hillier retained her immobile expression from the Madonna series, but her hair flows with abandon. Furthermore, she is now dressed in 'Oriental' fashion, wearing an embroidered blouse with a bold necklace and brooch. The choice of Sappho as a role further complicates the resonances of this image for, as Randolph Trumbach has shown, women who enjoyed same-sex relationships had been known as Sapphists in London since the 1790s (Trumbach 1991: 112–41). Harem women were, as we have seen, also presumed to have same-sex encounters as well as being available for the sultan's heterosexual pleasure.[4] The *Sappho* photograph reveals a further continuity with the Madonna icon. Mary Hillier was posed so that the 'Greek' nature of her profile is clearly visible, with her high straight forehead and straight nose. In this context, it of course makes sense that she should appear Greek, but a similar preoccupation with revealing Hillier's classical profile pervades the Madonna series. No doubt Cameron chose Hillier for such roles because of these anatomical details, which, despite her lower class origins, gave suitably elevated racial characteristics to the Madonna icon.

Cameron's Madonna series is, then, closer in intent to Ingres than might at first appear. Her photographs of Mary Hillier were consistent in race, class and sexuality with the series established by the Neo-Classical painter and, given Cameron's declared intent to win the status of high art for photography, this is perhaps not surprising. But Cameron's series cannot be considered exactly the same as that of Ingres. For, despite Roland Barthes' famous announcement of the death of the author, it does still matter that this series of representations of women was made by a woman, rather than a man. The meanings attached to Cameron's photographs were not entirely determined by her gender, but they are inevitably inflected by this fact. Whereas Ingres' work seems to belong comfortably within the patriarchal culture of the nineteenth century, Cameron's copying of that series calls the naturalness of such gendered roles into question. By copying Ingres' copy of Raphael, Cameron perhaps unwittingly reveals that, as Judith Butler has so forcefully observed, '[g]ender ought not to be construed as a stable identity or locus of agency from which various acts follow; rather gender is an identity tenuously constituted in time, instituted in exterior space through a *stylized repetition of acts*' (Butler 1990: 140). Furthermore, Cameron's repetition of the Madonna series changed its meaning by generating the possibility of same-sex attraction between women, which nineteenth-century discourse found so scandalous. The sexuality of the Madonna was connected by Ingres to the Orientalized fallen woman but was restated by Cameron as being an attraction between women. Despite its intention to repeat the canon of painting in photography, Cameron's work instead threatened to destabilize the gendered structure of official art in the nineteenth century. Her very repetition of the canonical Madonna series demonstrated its wholly contingent and contextual significations, rather than reiterating the revealed truths of art as she no doubt had hoped.

CODA: MADONNAS ON SCREEN

The adoption of the Madonna as an icon for official art led would-be art photographers to use this image to validate their work as art, rather than industrial product. Ironically, their lasting achievement seems to have been the centrality of the Madonna icon in popular visual culture. The Hollywood film industry adopted the multiple characteristics of the Madonna to create screen goddesses, such as Greta Garbo, Marlene Dietrich and Bette Davis. The screen goddess was an amalgam of the three roles constructed in the Madonna series of the nineteenth century, but it has been left to the singer Madonna fully to exploit the sexuality inherent within the motif.

The screen goddess represented a version of femininity which had earlier been delineated in the Madonna series. Greta Garbo was perhaps the leading exponent of this role, leading to her becoming known as the Divine Garbo. Her divinity was, of course, that of the Madonna. Her beauty was also connected to modern art, acknowledged on a 1932 cover of *Vanity Fair*, which depicted her face in the guise of an African mask rendered by Picasso. This recognition of Garbo's face as a mask is central to understanding her importance. In the 1933 film *Queen Christina*, this quality was deliberately enhanced, as Roland Barthes once remarked:

126

the make-up has the snowy thickness of a mask: it is not a painted face, but one set in plaster, protected by the surface of its colour, not by its lineaments. Amidst all this snow at once fragile and compact, the eyes alone, black like strange soft flesh, but not in the least expressive are two tremulous wounds.

(Barthes 1972: 56)

The description might as well be that of the *Grande Odalisque*. Within the pure white Madonna lurks the black interior, with its 'strange soft flesh', so desired and yet so feared. Garbo confused gender roles still further in *Queen Christina* by playing a cross-dressed character for most of the film. She remains recognizably Garbo throughout, but within the terms of the film's own narrative, she successfully passes for a man. The ambiguity of the pure Northern Madonna with a heart of exotic blackness is thus reflected in her ambiguous dress. Barthes sees Garbo's image as an Idea, and so it is – but not that of the Freudian eternal feminine. In a now classic paper published in 1929 at the beginning of the sound motion picture era, the analyst Joan Rivière reformulated the Freudian eternal feminine into her notion of the feminine as masquerade:

The reader may now ask how I define womanliness or where I draw the line between genuine womanliness and the 'masquerade'. My suggestion is not, however, that there is any such difference; whether radical or superficial, they are the same thing.

(Butler 1990: 53)

In this view, there was no essential female to be found lurking behind the mask. Garbo and her contemporaries were afforded such exaggerated respect and adoration in order that this potentially troubling deficiency should not be revealed.

Although Hollywood might have forgotten the origin of the screen goddess, French cinema retained its memory rather better. In Marcel Carné's classic *Les Enfants du Paradis* (1945), the heroine is Garance, played by Arletty. At the denouement of the first act, Garance has secured a role at the Théâtre des Funambules, alongside the mime Debureau, who loves her, although she is indifferent to him at this time. Garance had formerly associated with the criminal mastermind Lacenaire who used her name to rent an apartment as a front for his plan to rob a debt collector. When confronted by the police with her role in the affair, Garance proclaims her innocence, but the detective does not believe her. Under questioning she reveals that her former profession was as an artist's model for the painter Ingres, leading the police to suggest that she must really have been a prostitute. The policeman has not heard of Ingres, but Garance declares that the artist would be 'right up your street'. The quip prompts him to arrest her, forcing Garance to invoke the protection of the Count, who takes her away from the theatre into his jealous custody. It is only late in the second act that we discover that it was at this moment that Garance discovered her love for Baptiste Debureau. We also find that the connection between her posing for Ingres and immorality has now been mediated by her travels in India, so that on her return to Paris, Garance wears an Oriental veil and jewellery. When she learns that Debureau is now married and a father, she tries to avoid him. But the flaw of the Madonna will out, leading to the death of her jealous protector in a Turkish bath and her final break with Baptiste, after they have been surprised by his wife. Garance personifies the serial nature of the Madonna icon in her character, moving from Ingresque Madonna to Oriental temptress via her place in high society.

In similar vein, the success of the pop star Madonna has been due in no small part to her willingness to push these contradictions of the Madonna role as far as possible. In her early songs and videos, such as *Like a Virgin* and *Like a Prayer*, the mixture of overt female sexuality and religious iconography proved explosive and generated a remarkable rise to superstardom (Figure 23). Although Madonna exploited sacrilege as a central motif to her work, her transgressions had distinct limits. When rock star Sinead O'Connor destroyed a photograph of Pope John Paul II on *Saturday Night Live*, Madonna not only publicly rebuked her rival rebel Catholic, but during her own later appearance on the programme, she retaliated by tearing up a photograph of O'Connor. It is as if she unwittingly recognized that any threat to supreme papal authority also undermined the nineteenth-century Madonna icon on which her character is based. Emboldened by this repudiation, Bob Dylan fans booed O'Connor throughout her appearance at his fiftieth birthday concert. The transgressive excitement of sacrilege depends upon the notion of the sacred being in operation in the society in question, as numerous peoples have discovered in attempting to recover their sacred objects from Western museums which consider them as anthropological artifacts.

Being Madonna now implies a constant pushing of frontiers but within certain controlled limits, which negate the subversive potential of her initial impact. Madonna has reinvented herself in a number of different guises but the goal remains the same – to convert the shock caused by her pushing of boundaries into unquestioned supremacy as the leading female performer in the world with corresponding remuneration. Despite the remarkable success of this strategy, it contained the seeds of its own inevitable failure. By her very actions, Madonna transformed what was

Figure 23 Patrick DeMarchellier, *Madonna*, © 1994 Maverick Recording Company.

permissible within the mainstream media. As it became evident that scandal was as much marketing strategy as it was actually a part of Madonna's character, it no longer seemed so remarkable. Madonna responded to the jaded attention spans of her fans by making the first significant mistake of an otherwise skillfully planned rise to the top. Abandoning her favoured ground of the music video, which can successfully seem to promise far more than it actually delivers, Madonna turned to print. Her book of photographs and erotic writing, *Sex* (1992), finally revealed all that which had only been suggested in her videos by repeatedly posing Madonna nude with a variety of partners. The book was, of course, a scandal but it contained the disappointment that Roland Barthes identified in the denouement of the striptease: 'Woman is desexualized at the very moment when she is stripped naked. We may therefore say that we are dealing in a sense with a spectacle based on fear, or rather on the pretence of fear, as if eroticism here went no further than a sort of delicious terror, whose ritual signs have only to be announced to evoke at once the idea of sex and its conjuration' (Barthes 1972: 84). Like the Emperor, the Madonna with no clothes quickly loses her power to fascinate. It is no surprise in this reading that Madonna flirted with the apparatus of sado-masochism in *Sex*. If the striptease was to work, it needed to evoke a certain mild fear in order to finally promote the very Catholic goal of the denial of sex. Indeed, Madonna herself has recently acknowledged the failure of her earlier strategy. On her 1994 single *Take a Bow*, she bids farewell to an alter ego, represented in the video as a matador, but just as likely to be her own Others, the dominatrix Dita and the Virgin Mary. An early shot in the video of a Virgin Mary icon is not repeated, suggesting that Madonna's religious persona epitomized in *Like a Prayer* has also now been abandoned. When Madonna sings 'No more masquerade/You're one lonely star', it seems that she is talking to herself about the end of her domination of the popular music scene. Symptomatically, *Take a Bow* was her first Number 1 in years.

Despite the fascination with Madonna in certain quarters of academia, her influence has peaked and is on the wane. The rise of the waif as the desired physique for supermodels has still further removed Madonna's aerobic body from the centre of the contemporary imagination. The mystique of the Madonna icon has been more successfully exploited by the photographer Cindy Sherman. In her now-famous series of *Untitled Film Stills*, Sherman used herself as the model for an extended series of tableaux recreating the ambience of 1950s B-movies and Hitchcock thrillers. Never overtly erotic, in the sense that Sherman depicts herself clothed and usually alone, her photographs were none the less charged with an uneasy eroticism. Like Ingres' harem women, Sherman's self-portraits seem to be made at the expense of exposing herself to some form of danger. In evoking Hitchcock, Sherman reminds us of the overtly voyeuristic nature of his films and the violence inflicted upon so many of his actresses. As with the earlier photography of Julia Margaret Cameron, the sense of unease in Sherman's work comes from the recreation of masculine viewing pleasure by a woman photographer. In changing the gender of authorship and refusing the traditional distantiation between artist and model, Sherman makes us aware of the constructed nature of the camera's gaze and the power that is inherent in that gaze.

Like Madonna, Sherman has encountered the pressure for change which accompanies fame. In seeking to resist becoming categorized as a photographer known for a certain style, Sherman has changed her subject-matter and areas of representation, while continuing to photograph herself. The intelligence and anger that motivates this later work has enabled Sherman to escape becoming a banal re-enactment of her previous success, without destroying the allure of her basic premise. Sherman continues to intrigue us with her self-portraits precisely because they do not reveal all. If self-portraits were often imagined as the artist representing his or her image in the mirror, Sherman's mirror is a distorting, cracked glass, which does not permit us to see her but to see ourselves looking at her. In 1989, Sherman embarked upon a series of photographs derived from history paintings of the art historical canon. In one especially striking photograph, she recapitulated the pose of Raphael's painting of the Fornarina (Figure 24). The contemporary American woman artist thus put herself into the frame of the Madonna icon, but by so doing disrupts the iconographic series. For now the audience is aware who the Fornarina really is and furthermore that she is responsible for the photograph. Unlike Madonna, Sherman refuses to cater to the voyeurism of her audience. Over her own breasts, Sherman placed a plastic model of large female breasts with especially prominent nipples. The spectator's gaze is both satisfied and denied in an exchange which disrupts the reiteration so essential to the series created by the Madonna icon. Whereas Ingres had denied the spectator the possibility of seeing the artist's hand in order to sustain the mobility of the image, Sherman refuses to reveal her breasts and – to use Lacan's terms – stops the gaze, allowing the eye to reassert itself. In a reversal of *trompe-l'œil* technique, Sherman's use of a prosthesis forces even the most eager viewer to confront the artificiality of her representation and of the Madonna

Figure 24 Cindy Sherman, *Untitled (History Painting #205)* (1989), Metro Pictures, New York.

series derived from Raphael's work. The chain of simulacra leading back to Ingres has now been challenged.

The struggle between the Madonna icon and iconoclasm remains a political issue. Fittingly, one site of that struggle is being played out in Spain, home of the Counter-Reformation. In the sixteenth century, Phillip II built a monastery at El Escorial, which symbolized the connection between Catholic Church and State, still a central issue in twentieth-century Spanish politics. Spain today has 22,000 cults devoted to different images of the Madonna, and over one hundred religious orders devoted to her. As in nineteenth-century France, the Left continues to regard the reduction of this influence as a central task in the modernization of Spain. In El Escorial today, a microcosm of this dispute is being played out between Catholics and Socialists. Since 1981, a cleaning-woman named Amparo Cuevas has being seeing visions of the Madonna. At the site of her first visitation – an ash tree in a local park – believers have rigged a loudspeaker system in order to replay tape-recorded descriptions of her visions to the faithful. Crowds of 1500 people attend from Spain, France and further afield. The Socialist mayor, Mariano Rodriguez, believes the entire operation to be a complicated swindle designed to perpetuate the hold of the Church on the faithful. The council has authority over the park and has consistently removed icons of the Madonna from the ash tree on at least ten occasions, as well as turning off water to the nearby fountain. In post-Franco Spain, these issues are of more than symbolic importance and have attracted national and international attention (*New York Times*: 3/15/ 94). As long as this engagement between icon and iconoclasts persists, the framing of the female body which it implies will remain operative. In the central area of the representation of gender, the old exchange between mass culture and high art continues to be played out around the Madonna icon. Whereas popular imagery of the Madonna served to revitalize the official art of nineteenth-century France and create a subject for early photographers to claim as art, in the contemporary moment it is high art practice (defined as much by audience and reception as medium) that is challenging popular conceptions of the Madonna. Equally, the history of the Madonna icon casts some doubt on received views on the representation of modern women and the presumed emergence of the postmodern body. The continuing reiteration in Western visual culture of the Madonna icon reveals a set of ambiguities and ambivalences in modern gender identity which have yet to be resolved into an entirely new – or postmodern – form.

NOTES

1 My thanks to Richard Shiff for this observation.
2 Here I differ from the interpretation of Norman Bryson in seeing the *Valpinçon Bather* as a part of this series, rather than its controlling origin and emphasizing the political connotations of Ingres' post-Restoration painting (Bryson 1984: 130–47). While I agree with Wendy Leeks that Bryson produces an over-formal interpretation of Ingres, I do not accept that historical distance makes it impossible to discern anything of the artist's intention (Leeks 1986). Rather, like Marilyn R. Brown's investigation of the harem, I seek to place Ingres' work in an exchange with the historical and cultural functions of the Madonna icon in nineteenth-century France (Brown 1987).
3 On the early practice of castration in Christianity, see Brown (1988: 168–70).
4 The photographs of Lady Hawarden, collected in the Victoria & Albert Museum, London, also show a striking preoccupation with relations between women in this period.

4

PHOTOGRAPHY AT THE HEART
OF DARKNESS

The perfect body in Western culture was sustained and made imaginable by the imperfect body of the racial Other. This chapter and the one following examine the impact of racialized thinking on two very different forms of visual practice, colonial photography in the Belgian Congo and graffiti painting in 1980s New York. Whereas the photographer Herbert Lang sought to create an irrefutable visual record of racial difference, Jean-Michel Basquiat tried to imagine being an African-American painter whose work was not marked by the codes of race. These specific case studies have been chosen both in order to resist the generalization that is so characteristic of racialized thought, and because the very contrast between them illustrates the dramatic impact that race has had upon twentieth-century visual culture.

It is becoming increasingly clear that the discourses of race are the most problematic legacy of modernism. For two hundred years, Western scientists, writers and artists have attempted to create a visual taxonomy of race without long-term success. The locus of investigation has changed from the skull and skin to the gene but the mission remains the same. In fact, the recent publication of the scurrilous book, *The Bell Curve* by Charles Murray and Richard J. Herrnstein, even resurrected the old canard of a genetic connection between race and intelligence. Yet, as Henry Louis Gates forcefully reminds us,

> [r]ace as a meaningful criterion within the biological sciences has long been recognized to be a fiction. When we speak of 'the white race' or 'the black race,' or 'the Jewish race' or the 'Aryan race,' we speak in biological misnomers and, more generally, in metaphors.
>
> (Gates 1985: 4)[1]

Although the experience and heritage of ethnicity are certainly of considerable importance, Gates refers here to the search for biological signifiers of essential physical difference, categorized as 'race'. Even prior to the theory of evolution, Europeans who wished to promote theories of absolute racial difference were aware that skin colour alone was insufficient proof. In his vitriolic defence of slavery, the English colonial official Edward Long advanced the belief that Africans closely resembled the physiognomy of the European but were less advanced:

> The supposition then is well-founded, that the brain and intellectual organs so far as they are dependent upon meer [sic] matter, though similar in texture and modification to those of other men, may in some of the Negroe race be so constituted, as *not to result to the same effects*; for we cannot but allow, that the Deity might, if it was his pleasure, diversify his works in this manner, and either withhold the *superior principle* entirely, or in part only, or infuse it into the different classes and races of human creatures, in such portions, as to form the same gradual climax towards perfection in this human system, which is so evidently designed in every other.
>
> (Long 1774: 371)

For Long and generations of racists after him, the divine drive towards perfection was as much marked by the inferiority of the African body as by the perfection of the white. This profound interior difference was necessary to mark the superiority of the white and to convince Europeans that the Other played no part in the Self, that the colonizer was radically different from, and superior to, the colonized.

This taxonomic impulse was above all a search for convincing visual signs of difference. The anthropologist Johannes Fabian describes this impulse as 'visualism', in which 'the ability to visualise a culture or society almost becomes synonymous for understanding it' (Fabian 1983: 106). Race thus could not exist without a visual taxonomy of racial difference. In order to provide and classify such difference, entire archives of visual material came to exist in nineteenth and twentieth century museums, private collections and laboratories. One such archive is that constituted by the mass of photography produced by colonial travellers, scientists and governments in the former colonies of Africa and Asia. These anthropological studies, postcards, views and 'scenes of native life' were quickly designated an embarassment in the era of decolonization, their previous popularity at once forgotten. Works were consigned to a back drawer, an attic or the far corners of a museum basement and left to gather dust. As these photographs are rediscovered, a new series of questions about them must be asked. What do the colonial photographs represent, both for viewers in the period and today? What can be learnt from them about 'the creation of colonial reality', a process which implicated both colonizers and colonized (Taussig 1986: 5)? Can we observe the process by which 'race' is written onto the body, transforming the body from an individual into a specimen?

Two exhibitions in 1993 sought to ask these questions and presented very different answers. In the by now infamous 1993 Whitney Biennial in New York, the representation of the body was a central question for the current generation of American artists. The exhibition was committed, in the words of its director, to examining 'problems of identity and the representation of community' (Whitney 1993: 8). The seriousness of this intent and the intelligence, wit and vision of the art on display were ignored by reviewers in a feeding frenzy of disgust. The *New York Times* critic Michael Kimmelman was so repulsed that he was moved to publish not one but two lengthy condemnations of the show. In the visceral distaste exhibited by these critics, the changing of generations could be observed from the New York painting school that had predominated since the 1950s to a new, looser constellation of artists. These artists were not solely preoccupied with medium, as the critics wished them to be, nor obsessed with message as their detractors claimed. In fact, all the artists exhibited, ranging from established artists like Cindy Sherman and Nancy Spero to that of relative newcomers, found innovative and intriguing means to cast new light on old questions. In short, it is hard to escape the conclusion that the howls of outrage were motivated by the unwelcome return of the repressed to the art world – namely, the body.

Glenn Ligon's installation entitled *Marginal Notes to the Black Book* was exemplary of both the innovative dimensions of this new art and the hostile critical reponse (Figure 25). Ligon interspaced and interpellated a double row of photographs of black men by Robert Mapplethorpe with a series of framed quotations by named critics, models and anonymous spectators. His work provided a unique opportunity for an intertextual discussion between the audience and Mapplethorpe's work, which was made all the more timely by the witchhunt of the latter's work by Senator Jesse Helms and his acolytes. The piece aroused the particular ire of the critics precisely because it negated their function. The spectator was placed in the unusual position of being able to choose between differing views of these photographs in the presence of full scale, quality prints. Of course, Ligon's choice of quotations placed limits on this freedom, but his range was representative of the scholarly views, and showed a wry sense of humour and irony in juxtaposing them with snippets of conversation in very different voices. I was struck by one remark attributed to bell hooks, in which she compared Mapplethorpe's work to her grandmother's refusal to take pictures: 'Isn't it interesting that the photographers always come just when the tribe is dying out? So too with the "celebration" in these Mapplethorpe pictures of black men. Better catch them before they die

Figure 25 Glenn Ligon, *Marginal Notes to the Black Book*, 1991–3, courtesy of
the artist.

out' (hooks 1991: 175). Despite her dismissal of a closer examination of such photographs, hooks' comment has force and insight. Photography was used by anthropologists from its earliest days in their attempts to establish a visual classification of racial, class and sexual difference. In other words, in the colonial photograph, all that can be seen is the colonizer and his or her prejudice. Pictures were selected in order to conform to preconceived ideas of the racial inferiority of Africans and then presented as evidence of those same ideas. In this view, the resurgence of interest in the colonial photograph can be nothing more than imperial nostalgia, masquerading as enlightened concern.

A very different view was presented by the travelling exhibition *African Reflections: Art of North-Eastern Zaire 1909–1915* (catalogue: Schildkrout and Keim, 1992). The show presented the collections of two travellers from the American Museum of Natural History, Herbert Lang and James Chapin, to the north-east of what was then the Congo in 1909–15. Their task was to report on the way of life of the local inhabitants, and to record, collect and identify the local flora and fauna. In the course of a five-year expedition, with over two years being spent in the Mangbetu region,[2] Lang and Chapin also collected a prodigious number of cultural products made by Mangbetu and Azande peoples, which formed the centerpiece of the exhibition. Lang was a dedicated photographer, who took no less than 10,000 plates on his travels, many of which were used to illustrate the show and its catalogue. Enid Schildkrout, one of the curators of *African Reflections*, undertook important and pioneering research into Lang's work as a photographer. From an examination of published works, the forty-volume photographic archive established by Lang at the Museum of Natural History and the contact prints from which he worked, Schildkrout concluded that Lang's work had overcome the barriers of colonial difference. His photographs thus presented a unique view of Mangbetu peoples which 'depict a people who consciously constructed an image of themselves for outsiders that relied on their perception of outsiders' perception of them' (Schildkrout 1991: 71). Unlike hooks, therefore, Schildkrout held that the colonial photograph was not simply a reflection of the colonizer's preconceptions but a place of dialogue between the colonizer and the indigenous people. Rather than pursue the intriguing possibilities of this argument, her essay concludes:

> In some respects, [Lang] always subscribed to ideas of Western superiority and never gave up some stereotypes he brought with him . . . However, in the six years they lived together in northeastern Zaire, he and Chapin developed a deep appreciation for those African cultures and peoples they came to know.

This intimacy is projected in some of Lang's photographs and it transforms them from simple contextual documents for a museum collection into works of art.

(Schildkrout 1991: 85)

In a move all too familiar to art historians, the colonial photograph is transformed by intimacy from a document into art. This transcendent move is designed to shield the work from criticism such as that of bell hooks, and yet ironically has much in common with it. Both positions offer a disinterested view of art as transcending the conditions of artistic production. The difference is that hooks' lack of interest stems from her political refusal that the colonial photograph can ever be anything other than a document of oppression, whereas Schildkrout deploys the Kantian notion of disinterest in order to valorize and aestheticize the photograph. This lack of interest collapses the photograph into a sign, which refers not to the object depicted but has the photographer him or herself as the referent, in contradiction to the conventional notion that the photograph refers to the 'real'. But in using the photograph to determine the essence of the photographer, this reductive semiotics of photography refuses any engagement with the photographs themselves. In these photographs, the subject is overwhelmingly the black body, sometimes named, sometime anonymous, but always preventing a reductive analysis of the photograph. Any reading of photography is dogged by the cultural construction of the photograph as either observed truth or transcendent art. However, any engagement with the colonial photograph which is capable of giving a place to the subjects of those photographs will have to bypass such comforting certainties. Instead, it is necessary to attend to the 'ambivalence and undecidability' that Kobena Mercer has identified in Mapplethorpe's photographs of black men, for both black and white spectators (Mercer 1993: 320).

In the first section of this chapter, I want to use Mercer's insight to examine the possibility of reading colonial photographs as a visual document, conforming to a certain grammar of colonial vision and yet very specific in their individual instances. Without claiming any universal verities, I shall discuss those photographs of the Congo published by Lang as a record of his journey. Lang's work will be treated in the context of the meanings given to the Congo by travel writers, politicians and novelists in the period, in order to perceive both its originality and its conformity to prevalent modes of colonial discourse. Many recent literary readings of colonial literature and travel writing have emphasized the visual dimension to such writing (Pratt 1992). In this view, travel narratives sought to describe the places visited and colonized by Europeans in terms derived from painting and photography, rather than in conventional literary metaphors. It is then simply assumed that the visual imagery of the African colonies has been derived from these literary studies, with notable exceptions (Alloula 1986; Geary 1988). Perhaps the consistent domination of Orientalist studies over 'Africanist' work, noted by Christopher Miller, has contributed to the current situation in which Orientalist painting has been widely commented upon, but European representations of sub-Saharan Africa continue to be ignored (Miller 1985: 14–23). Photography has a unique and important role to play in the construction of such discourse, but it needs to be considered as it was presented, together with its text. Neither stands independently, for just as the photograph visualizes the narrative of the text and makes it explicable, so does the text explain the details of the photograph and render them knowable.[3]

Rather than seek a transcendent interpretation of 'the' colonial photograph, I want to consider how Lang's Congo photographs constructed a cultural geography of colonialism in a specific time and place. Imperialism was never an undifferentiated phenomenon, repeating its manoeuvres regardless of time and place, but was always constructed in regard to local specificities, the domestic agenda of the colonizing nation and with an eye to the other colonial powers (Wilson 1993). For the cultural geography of a place is not quite the same as its physical geography. Here landmarks are not used simply to record a terrain but to designate cultural meaning. It is an imagined geography, which identifies France by the Eiffel Tower and New York by the Statue of Liberty. These metonyms are not simply indexical signs, pointing out the locale represented, but connote the Western sense of place, regardless of the actual travel experience of the spectator. Thus in film and photography, the Eiffel Tower indicates not just Paris, but France as a place of romance and elegance. In the cultural geography of imperialism created by this process, the Congo occupied a specific and important place as the degree zero of the 'primitive' world envisaged by imperialism. Long after its interior had been explored and opened up to colonial exploitation of rubber and ivory, the Congo was considered the very 'heart of darkness', and was immortalized as such by Joseph Conrad in his eponymous novella of 1899.[4]

ENVISAGING THE CONGO

Conrad's construction of the Congo as 'a prehistoric earth' (Conrad 1969: 539) was a well-defined discourse, which was all but impervious to change.

The cultural geography of imperialism and the imperial imaginary depended, and depends, on the Congo as its origin. From Schweinfurth's first published narrative of 1874, entitled *In the Heart of Africa*, subsequent travellers set out to the Congo with the specific aim of encountering the heart of darkness. Lang's first account of his expedition in 1910 was similarly entitled 'In the Heart of Africa', and the title was used yet again for the account of a rival German expedition in the same year. Such conceits have lasted until the present day. The popular novelist Michael Crichton opens his 1980 novel *Congo* in a fashion recognizable to any nineteenth-century travel writer:

> Dawn came to the Congo rain forest. The pale sun burned away the morning mist revealing a gigantic, silent world . . . [t]he basic impression was of a vast, oversized gray-green world – an alien place, inhospitable to man.
>
> (Crichton 1980: 1)

Crichton echoes Marlow's words in *Heart of Darkness*: 'Going up that river was like travelling back to the earliest beginnings of the world, when vegetation rioted on the earth and the big trees were kings. An empty steam, a great silence, an impenetrable forest' (Conrad 1969: 536). The colonial anthropologist, traveller and writer reiterate each other's words in a vain attempt to end the silence of the Other, in defiance of actual conditions in the Congo. For by the time that Lang arrived in the region, Western travellers were far from a novelty. A series of campsites was established for the use of Western itinerants, even in the northeastern region, enabling the British writer Marguerite Roby to cross the Congo from south to north on a bicycle in 1910. The official almanac for the Congo, published by the Belgian government, ran to over 700 pages in 1913, detailing businesses, traders and addresses of Europeans in the Congo. Even when faced with the evidence of such activity, Lang continued to perceive the Congo as the heart of darkness: 'Avakubi is a great rubber station, about twenty tons a month being received from the natives as taxes. . . . Such an isolated spot can hardly exist anywhere in the world' (Dickerson 1910: 161).[5]

Appropriately, Crichton's novel has an epigram from Henry Morton Stanley, the journalist and explorer, who gave shape to the Congo in the late nineteenth and early twentieth century in both cultural and political terms. After his famous feat in finding the missionary David Livingstone, Stanley returned to the Congo as the agent of king Leopold II of Belgium. He secured the colonial rights of the Belgian monarch to the entirety of the Congo basin as a personal fief, rights which were upheld at the Berlin conference of 1885. By the early twentieth century, thanks to the publicity generated by British consul Roger Casement and the journalist E.D. Morel, the Congo had become notorious as the site of the most extreme colonial brutality and oppression. Undoubtedly, the political impact of the reform campaign was reinforced by the European perception that the Congo was a uniquely primitive and dangerous place. Travellers expected to find what Stanley had described, and followed his tracks in order to do so. Both Lang and Adolphus Frederick of Mecklenburg, who led the German expedition of 1908, could find no other way to describe the Congo forest than to quote Stanley:

> Imagine the whole of France and the Iberian peninsula densely covered with trees 6 to 60 metres in height, with smooth trunks, whose leafy tops are so close to one another that they intermingle and obscure the sun and the heavens, each tree over a metre in thickness. The ropes stretching across from one tree to another in the shape of creepers and festoons, or curling round the trunks in thick, heavy coils, like endless anacondas, till they reach the highest point. Imagine them in full bloom, their luxuriant foliage combining with that of the trees to obscure the sunlight, and their hundreds of long festoons covered with slender tendrils hanging down from the highest branches till they touch the ground, interlacing with one another in a complete tangle.
>
> (Mecklenburg 1910: 249; Dickerson 1910: 166)

Both writers charged Stanley with exaggeration, but could not replace his words with their own. Stanley describes the Congo as a place that cannot be described in the traditional fashion, but had to be imagined. The Western heart of darkness had already been written and has yet to be rewritten.

Stanley's passage emphasized the darkness and all but unimaginable magnitude of the forest. Encountering the heart of darkness was thus a visual problem from the outset. It was, in Conrad's phrase, 'the threshold of the invisible' (Conrad 1969: 593). In order to make the darkness visible, three ways of seeing – and not seeing – were possible in the Congo of the period. The first was that of the Emperor Leopold who claimed to own the Congo. Leopold supplied some of the funds for Lang's expedition and gave numerous objects to the American Museum of Natural History, a debt repaid by Lang in a published defence of the Belgian regime in the Museum's *Journal*. Leopold's gaze may be equated with that so well described by Michel Foucault in the Emperor Napoleon I:

> At the moment of its full blossoming, the disciplinary society still assumes with the Emperor the old aspect of the power of spectacle. As a monarch who is at one and the same time a usurper of the ancient throne and the organiser of a new state, he combined into a single, symbolic, ultimate figure the whole

of the long process by which the pomp of sovereignty, the necessarily spectacular manifestations of power, were extinguished one by one in the daily exercise of surveillance.

(Foucault 1977: 217)

Leopold's disciplinary gaze was all-seeing in his possession and exerted its dominion through taxation, legal sanctions and property rights. It was an indifferent gaze, concerned only with the production of rubber and ivory and the maintenance of colonial order. Other events were literally invisible to this colonial gaze.

In opposition to this disciplinary gaze was the modern vision of the Congo reformers. They envisaged a Congo of free producers, whose participation in the market would be all the more effective because of their increased liberty. Casement and Morel, although undoubtedly outraged by the excesses commited in the Congo, sought to bring the colonial administration of the region into twentieth-century terms, rightly perceiving Leopold's system as an embarrasing anachronism. Their vision of the Congo was expressed by Morel:

> Seated in an imaginary airship, which we will fancy perfected and invisible, let us take a bird's eye view of the Congo as it was twenty-five years ago [i.e. before Leopold], not in the spirit of the anthropologist, naturally and rightly on the lookout for strange and repulsive rites; nor in the spirit of the moralist, lamenting the aberrations of primitive man with a zeal inducing unmindfulness of civilization's sores: but in the spirit of the statesman, which presupposes both the student and the man of broad practical sympathies, contemplating this vast new country for the first time . . . The mightiest forest region in the world now unrolls before us its illimitable horizon, the primeval forest whither races of black, brown and copper coloured men have been attracted or driven for untold ages . . . In these fertile villages, man has settled and multiplied. He is well represented almost everywhere on the banks of the rivers except where they are very low lying and habitually flooded. But he has made many thousands of clearings in the forest too, and has cultivated the soil to such good purposes where need was, that we shall be astonished at the number and variety of his plantations. Throughout this enormous forest region . . . we shall note an intelligent, vigorous population, attaining considerable density in certain parts, digging and smelting iron, manufacturing weapons for war and the chase, often of singularly beautiful shape, weaving fibres of sundry plants into tasteful mats and cloths, fabricating a rough pottery, fishing nets, twine baskets.
>
> (Morel 1968: 17, 21)

Power has now attained its modern form in the shape of an invisible airship, which glides above the forest, discovering a society closer to William Morris's *News from Nowhere* than the colonial travel accounts. For Morel, the technology of the all-seeing eye must replace the autocratic body of the King. For Leopold and his supporters, the primitivism of the Congo justified and necessitated traditional forms of colonial power. Neither account represents Truth, but both speak a certain truth of colonial discourse. However, what was truly invisible to Western eyes was not the primeval culture of the region but the obvious changes and upheaval taking place. Seeing the heart of darkness involved and depended upon not seeing both the local cultures and the change they were experiencing due to colonization. Although the colonial gaze fantasized that it was the 'monarch of all I survey' (Pratt 1992: 201), it was in practice impossible for it to achieve this plenitude of vision.

Of course, the indigenous culture was not absolutely invisible, but it could only be seen in certain controlled circumstances and by the use of specific technologies. As Morel suggested, this third way of envisaging the Congo was that of the anthropologist. The anthropologist did not seek to view the region as a whole, nor to judge it. He was there to record it in detail and with precision, for the scientific benefit of Western civilization. Anthropology claimed a remarkably wide scope in the late nineteenth century, which was still in force at time of Lang's expedition. In the words of Paul Broca, one of the founders of the discipline:

> The history of the arts, that of languages, religions, literature, or political societies, that of biology, zoology, palaeontology and geology forms part of the program of anthropology. . . . [A]nthropology can exclude no branch of human knowledge which can furnish any data on the history of man and human society.
>
> (Broca 1868: 227–8)

However, the anthropologist's obsessive recording of detail was above all applied to those countries colonized by the West, and shared much with colonial methods of dealing with tropical conditions. In *Heart of Darkness*, Marlow attributes his survival to this method: 'I had to keep a lookout for the signs of dead wood we could cut up in the night for the next day's steaming. When you have to attend to things of that sort, to the mere incidents of the surface, the reality – the reality, I tell you – fades. The inner truth is hidden luckily, luckily' (Conrad 1969: 537). Marlow concentrated on his job of piloting the steamer up river, rather than trying to understand the Congo. By focusing on the everyday details, the colonialist could thus avoid seeing the truth that was all around him. Herbert Lang opted for this third, anthropological, way of seeing as befitted an expeditionary of the American Museum of Natural History. Even his partner Chapin was astonished by the hysterical energy Lang put into his work, collecting specimens and taking photographs by day, and developing plates by night.

145

ANTHROPOLOGY, EUGENICS AND PHOTOGRAPHY

Photography was no newcomer to the Congo. By 1913, one of the five sections of the Terveruen Musée du Congo Belge was entirely devoted to photography and the Belgian Congo was home to three photography businesses, two cinemas and one self-styled cinematographer (*Annuaire du Congo* 1913: 23, 186–8). Indeed, it was the rule for travel literature from the region to be illustrated with photographs taken by the author. The 1909 German Congo expedition returned with no less than 5,000 photographs (Mecklenburg 1910: x). As such, the photographs served as a guarantee of the authenticity of the writer's account and were extensively captioned in order to explain their subject-matter. These works, often poorly produced and weak in content, were intended to serve as documents, rather than works of art, as Molly Nesbit has argued (Nesbit 1992: 15–17). At the Fifth International Congress of Photography, held in Brussels in 1910 – capital of the Belgian empire – these works were specifically defined:

> A documentary image should be able to be used for studies of diverse kinds, ergo the necessity of including the maximum possible detail. Any image can at any time serve scientific investigation. Nothing is to be disdained: the beauty of the photograph is secondary here, it is enough that the image be very clear, full of detail and carefully treated.

Just as Lang collected animal remains, Mangbetu artifacts and plant specimens, he collected photographs as documents for the use of the American Museum of Natural History.

Lang's photography stemmed from the particular nexus of cultural concerns which caused him to be in the Congo in the first place. In this period, the Museum was increasingly turning its attention to the promotion of the new 'science' of eugenics. Eugenics, in historian George Stocking's view, 'was an attempt to compensate for the failure of natural selection under the conditions of advanced civilisation' (Stocking 1987: 145). These gloomy prophets sought to control the reproduction of the human race under conditions dictated by the laws of statistics, believing that the statistically unusual 'defective' types could be eliminated. Such theories of human breeding control were based on the model of agricultural manipulation of livestock with careful provisos taking account of social factors. Eugenicists sought to eliminate not only disabilities and retardations of all kinds, but social evils, such as alchoholism, pauperism, orphans and the catch-all category of ne'er-do-wells. Far from being confined to a lunatic fringe, these ideas achieved great currency in the early twentieth century and, by the First World War the majority of States in the Union permitted sterilizations of the 'unfit' to take place in prisons, hospitals and asylums. These actions were ruled legal by the Supreme Court of Oliver Wendell Holmes and by 1941 41,000 Americans had been sterilized under these laws. Henry Osborn, who became director of the Museum of Natural History in 1908 and organized the Congo expedition, was excited to stand 'on the threshold of the application of science or knowledge of the laws of Nature as they bear on human morals, welfare and happiness' (Osborn 1910: 63). At the Museum, a new Hall of Public Health was opened and its rationale was described by Osborn as follows: 'It is cruel to bring a child into the world predestined to disease and suffering, hence eugenics. It is cruel to bring into our country the kind of people who will produce children like this, cruel I mean to those already here, hence the survey of immigration' (Osborn 1913: 195). Osborn was further responsible for bringing the second International Congress on Eugenics to New York in 1921. This Museum was an activist institution devoted, in the words of its *Journal*'s masthead, 'to natural history, exploration and the development of public education through the museum'. These goals were linked theoretically to, and motivated by, eugenics.

The Congo expedition was driven by a sense of the imminent disappearance of the indigenous cultures in the face of more 'advanced' Western civilization. The first report from the expedition explained that its goal was

[t]he Upper Congo region, that great, steaming land of equatorial Africa shrouded in jungle . . . .They have seen strange places and stranger primitive peoples, of whom it is time that the world obtain complete scientific record in view of the rapid advance that civilisation must make in the Congo in the immediate future.

(Dickerson 1910: 147)

The disappearance of what the colonizers presumed to have been the formerly widespread practice of cannibalism was proof to the eugenically minded that such transformations were already taking place. Lang claimed that eleven million people had formerly been devoted to anthropophagy from which they had been delivered by the Belgians, with mixed results: '[T]his horrible practice produced some fairly good results in eugenics, as in many tribes weakened people or crippled children helped to nourish their more sturdy brothers' (Lang 1915: 382) (Figure 26). Lang therefore opposed the efforts to reform the administration of the Congo and indeed praised the 'wise decisions of a responsible government' which contrasted unfavorably with the 'impetuosity of the unfortunate campaign of the reformers' (Lang 1915: 380). Lang advocated instead a eugenic solution

Figure 26 Herbert Lang, 'Chief of the Cannibals' (1909/15), the American Museum
of Natural History.

to the climatic, cultural and political problems of the region: 'White man's
impetus must be the motive to progress, whereas the Negro will supply the
activity to bring final order from chaos' (Lang 1919: 698). In other words,
eugenics was to replicate in advanced society that which the cannibal
variation of the survival of the fittest had achieved in the heart of darkness.

No reader of Lang's reports from the Congo in the *Journal* of the
Museum, now titled *Natural History*, could be unaware of the eugenic
ideas which motivated Osborn's Museum. In the edition of December
1919, for example, Lang published an account of his encounter with the
so-called pygmies in the rainforest, the Mbuti people. In order to reach

148

Lang's essay, it was necessary to pass through two lengthy accounts of the intelligence testing performed in the American Army during the First World War. This now notorious exercise in applied eugenics was not officially published until 1921, making the accounts in *Natural History* something of a scoop. The examiners believed that the intelligence tests had revealed important results: '[E]specially startling is the unusually large difference shown here between the distributions for Negroes and the distribution for white men' (Trabue 1919: 681). Plotted on a graph, these results formed a regular curve, with the left side indicating the high percentage of failure by 'Negroes' and the right hand side showing the corresponding degree of success achieved by the whites. According to one psychologist, 'the relationship between color and achievement was quite distinct, those with lighter skins making higher scores' (Trabue 1919: 680). It need hardly be remarked that these 'tests' were administered and conducted precisely in order to achieve such findings and have long been discredited. However, President George B. Cutten of Colgate University used them in the period to cast doubt upon the possibility of sustaining democracy in a country so widely populated with the 'feeble-minded' (Kevles 1985: 84). The diligent reader would thus not have been surprised to read that, in calling for the development of a 'national art' in the United States, Herbert J. Spinden, Assistant Curator in Anthropology at the Museum, did not include Africa in the seven 'type civilisations, upon the products of which must be based any statement of what a national art can and should be' (Spinden 1919: 623). The highest realm of civilization was inevitably the Christian. Spinden ranked other 'culture areas' in descending order with African being last, coming below even Neolithic European cultures.

Only after all of these eugenically inspired pieces does one find Lang's report, entitled 'Nomad Dwarfs and Civilisation'. This context makes it clear that the title was supposed to indicate a contrast rather than a connection. By way of example, Lang described how the Mbuti-Pygmy chief was afraid of the camera, and even when the instrument was disassembled, 'he clung to his belief in the presence of a power for evil, adding that it was evidently harbored in the dark cloth of the bellows and could be destroyed only by fire' (Lang 1919: 708). This incident accorded well with prevailing notions of the primitive, as well as the West's sense that its superiority was manifested in its technology. Indeed, it is so convenient that it seems somewhat suspicious. Twenty years previously, the British missionary Albert Lloyd published a popular account of his experiences in the Congo under the dramatic title *In Dwarf Land and Cannibal Country*.[6]

As one might expect, Lloyd had little sympathy for the indigenous culture, believing that Africa sheltered 'millions of her dusky sons in as gross a state of darkness as they were a thousand years ago' (Lloyd 1899: 12). Lloyd met a group of Mbuti-Pygmies in the Congo and was able to converse with them in Swahili through an interpreter. He at once set up his camera:

> In the morning I tried to photograph my little friends, but it was quite hopeless. It was too dark in the forest itself, and I could not persuade them to come out into a clearing where I might get light enough. I tried time after time, but always failed. I exposed nearly a dozen plates, but with no good results; snapshots were useless, and I could not get them still enough for a time exposure.
>
> (Lloyd 1899: 271)

Nonetheless, Lloyd did later manage to photograph a 'Pygmy lady' and reproduced the image in his book. His account mentions none of the 'primitive' fear of the camera highlighted by Lang, which would have served admirably to bolster his imperial view of the Congo, and indeed the Mbuti seem to have shown considerable patience in sitting through his repeated photographic efforts. It seems highly unlikely, therefore, that the fear of the camera encountered by Lang was a simple reaction of backward primitives to advanced Western technology. If his account is to be believed, it might rather suggest that in the intervening twenty years, Congo peoples had learnt to distrust those bearing cameras. Nor were they wrong to do so, for Lang's eugenic theory held that the 'backward' Pygmies would have to be eliminated in the interests of progress.

Lang's account of his meeting with the Mbuti provides evidence of this resistance to, and accomodation with, colonial authority in the form of mimicry. At one point, he noticed a man doing imitations:

> [T]he little fellow admirably imitated an official, taking especial advantage of the latter's habit of accentuating his instructions with peculiar abrupt gestures. When I asked him to mimic me he grinned happily. During the forenoon I had taken a number of photographs and my tripod camera was still standing in the shade. Without injury to the instrument he mimicked my every movement with just enough exaggeration to make everyone laugh. Finally he indicated that the 'evil eye had seen well' – and now came the climax to the performance. The Pygmy he had pretended to photograph, instead of unconcernedly walking away, dropped to the ground, illustrating the native superstition that the 'big evil eye' of the camera causes death. A block of salt laid on the 'dead' man's stomach instantly resuscitated him and the two entertainers walked off joyously, but only after the clown had received a reward.
>
> (Lang 1919: 712n)

150

The Mbuti mimicker thus connected colonial power, photography and the European belief in African fear of the camera into a satirical narrative of colonial life. Cultural critic Homi Bhabha has identified mimicry 'as one of the most elusive and effective strategies of colonial power and knowledge'. In this view, mimicry 'is the desire for a reformed, recognizable Other as a *subject of difference that is almost the same but not quite*'. This ambivalent process creates an uneasy tension between mimicry and mockery, which may turn into menace. Mimicry was not a simple exercise in colonial authority, creating masks behind which the essence of the colonial subject was concealed, but rather: 'the *menace* of mimicry is its *double* vision which in disclosing the ambivalence of colonial discourse also disrupts its authority' (Bhabha 1987: 321). Bhabha's focus was entirely upon the written text, but his analysis is central to an understanding of the colonial photograph. The mimicry Lang observed was of the colonizer's belief in the power of his practice, which was disrupted by this very imitation. The mimicker parodied both the colonial official and his means of recording the colonial vision. The photographs Lang took, then, are the intersection of the double vision of mimicry, presenting no 'authentic' vision of Africa, nor of colonialism, but a fragmentary glimpse of the interaction between the indigenous peoples and eugenic anthropology. In short, both Europeans and Mbuti had created the Pygmies.

Mimicry was an important constituent of colonial practice in the Congo, but it proved as hard to visualize as the heart of darkness itself. In *Heart of Darkness*, Conrad fictionalized this experience. As Marlow approaches the lost trader Kurtz, he meets first with his Russian deputy:

> I looked at him, lost in astonishment. There he was before me, in motley, as though he had absconded from a troupe of mimes, enthusiastic, fabulous. His very existence was improbable, inexplicable, and altogether bewildering. He was an insoluble problem. It was inconceivable how he had existed, how he had succeeded in getting so far, how he had managed to remain – why he did not instantly disappear.
>
> (Conrad 1969: 568)

Marlow pursues his tactic of not seeing anything beyond the essentials for his expedition and refuses to believe his eyes when confronted with colonial mimicry. He expects that at any moment, the phantom will disappear. The illusion of colonial normality, already all but impossible to sustain in the interior of the Congo, will soon be shattered by the discovery that Kurtz has 'gone native' and turned himself into a god. What Marlow tried so hard not to see was what Conrad famously called 'the horror, the horror'. By the time of Lang's expedition, the situation had changed sufficiently that the local people made great efforts to sustain colonial mimicry, motivated by their experience of the violence meted out by thwarted colonizers. When Lang arrived in Mangbetu, he was disappointed to find that the Great Hall described by Schweinfurth did not exist. Okondo, a chief of the Mangbetu installed by the Belgians, learnt of this disruption to colonial vision and at once set about building the hall desired by Lang. It was dutifully photographed and recorded as an authentic example of Mangbetu culture, but, as Crew and Sims remind us, '[a]uthenticity is not about factuality or reality. Objects have no authority; people do' (Crew and Sims 1991: 163). To be more precise, the objects held no meaning outside the discourse of colonial mimicry. Lang knew what he expected to discover and the Mangbetu hastened to oblige. It was no coincidence therefore that Lang held Mangbetu in great esteem, describing them as: 'the most highly cultured natives of these regions . . . . Their pottery in its best samples reminds one of Ancient Greek work' (Lang 1911: 48).

In describing his meeting with the Mbuti, Lang was principally concerned with the correct identification of their racial type, and specifically 'whether the Pygmies are merely degenerate types of Negroes and therefore of relatively recent origin, or the earliest type from which all taller African races have evolved, or one entirely distinct and as old as any living race' (Lang 1919: 699). The first two theories could easily be accommodated within mainstream eugenics. The third implied a polygenetic view of the human species, that is to say, that several entirely separate varieties of the human race had coexisted for millenia. Lang finessed his own argument by deciding that the Pygmies were indeed the descendants of the first peoples to settle Africa from Asia, then held to be the place of origin of human life. Although the survival of the fittest had driven them out of the rest of Africa, the unique qualities of the heart of darkness allowed them to survive in the rainforest, like the recently discovered okapi. This sweeping assertion was maintained even in the admitted face of failure: 'At present no racial characters setting aside a majority of Pygmies from the tall Negroes can be stated and it is doubtful if physical traits have at any previous period been more uniformly pronounced' (Lang 1919: 703). However, there was no doubt in Lang's mind that these details could be discovered and he set about creating a visual record of these disappearing creatures with his camera.

Lang was careful to follow anthropological and eugenic procedures in his photography. He took ninety sets of head and shoulder shots of local people in his search for the truly typical. Each set consisted of views from the front, side, and three-quarters. The three-quarter view is that traditionally used in Western portraiture and seems therefore more 'sympathetic' to eyes accustomed to reading such portraits. Lang's intention was to avoid all

> personal preference and prejudice . . . . Great is the temptation for a traveler to pick and choose the subjects for his picture gallery with an eye to beauty and interest. But we were anxious that our anthropological series of portraits should not be invalidated. After carefully ascertaining the tribal status of the natives, we lined them up indiscriminately and took every third, fifth, or seventh individual according to the number desired from any crowd.
>
> (Lang 1919: 707–8)

Such elimination of personal preference was a central tenet of scientific practice in the period, which sought to eliminate all trace of the subjectivity of the scientist, leaving judgement and discrimination to the reader (Daston and Galison 1992: 98–110). Despite this care, these portraits failed in their primary purpose: 'It would be too daring to describe as typical these remnants of a race which has not escaped mingling with large neighboring communities' (Lang 1919: 701). The discourse of colonial mimicry invalidated the colonial photograph as a pure scientific document. What was recorded was not the anthropological fantasy of unhindered, pure observation but the cultural product of the interactions between colonizers and colonized. The photographs do not tell us about 'native' life as Lang claimed, but about the ambivalences of colonial culture.

Eugenicists therefore argued for the correlation of word and image. The photograph could not stand on its own as it was an incomplete and atypical document. In his Introduction to a 1910 collection of eugenic studies, the British eugenicist Karl Pearson cautioned that

> [i]t is not always possible to maintain a proper balance between the graphic and the verbal descriptions; but I wish most strongly to insist on the point that neither are to be interpreted *alone*; they are component parts of one whole, and the reader who draws conclusions from the engraved pedigrees without consulting the verbal accounts is certain to be led into error.
>
> (Pearson 1909: ix [orig. emphasis])

In order to signify correctly, the eugenic sign required a correlation of visual representation and critical assessment, in which the latter was dominant over the former. Lang's first published photograph from the Congo showed some buildings at the edge of the forest and carried the following caption: 'The mightiest primeval forest known to man. A cold, gray picture is wholly inadequate to make vivid a tropical country, the splendid color, the sounds, the life – and the heat' (Dickerson 1910: 160)

(Figure 27). The caption directed the viewer's attention away from what was visible – local people and their dwellings – to that which was invisible and beyond the reach of the camera. Lang consistently treated the photograph as a partial notation, rather than the revealer of truth.

In his first article, Lang published a photograph of a Mangbetu woman, wearing a striking rafia headdress. This woman, whom Lang does not name, appears in a number of his photographs, making it reasonable to assume that Lang knew her status in the community (Figure 28). For the headdress was not merely decorative, but a signifier of rank only to be worn by the ruling class (Schildkrout and Keim 1990: 125). Although visitors to *African Reflections* in 1993 were made aware of this point, Lang did not inform his readers of the signification of her headdress. Instead, Lang captioned her photograph: 'A "Parisienne" of the Mangbetu tribe', a notable departure from his usual anthropological objectivity. (Lang 1915: 383). To his American readers, the term 'Parisienne' was a necessarily ambiguous one. It mingled connotations of high fashion with the suspicion that the woman might be a courtesan or fallen woman for, as Molly Nesbit has observed: 'Fascination with her [the Parisienne's] sexuality grew obsessive in the decade just before the First World War' (Nesbit 1992: 133). Lang's readers, unaware of the social position of the woman he had photographed, would certainly have located his Parisienne in this hybrid discourse of fashion and sexuality. Lang was conscious of social distinctions in the region and in the same article, he published photographs of Manziga, an Azande chief (Figure 29), and the 'head wife' of Abiembali, a Mayogo chief. Here, however, amongst Mangbetu whom he otherwise privileged, he described a elite woman as a prostitute. Like many other Europeans, Lang was both fascinated and repelled by the sexuality of the Africans he encountered. He noted privately of Mangbetu men that 'as a rule they behave very arrogant [sic] in the absence of white men and often profit of the charms so easily offered by the Mangbetu women' (Schildkrout and Keim 1990: 63). This remark is self-evidently a fantasy, for Lang could not by definition speak of the ways Mangbetu men acted in the absence of whites. Does Lang's ethnographic slip in identifying the noblewoman as a prostitute indicate that it was in fact he who was tempted by the 'charms' of Mangbetu women? For an anthropologist and eugenicist such desire was unnameable, and yet this one uncharacteristic reference to sexual practice, which is otherwise passed over in silence, suggests that the full story of the American Museum expedition may not have been told.

The supremacy of caption over image is strikingly apparent in Lang's use of the same photograph for entirely different purposes in two publications.

Figure 27 Herbert Lang, 'At the Edge of the Virgin Forest', the American Museum of Natural History.

Figure 28 Herbert Lang, 'A "Parisienne" of the Mangbetu Tribe', the American Museum of Natural History.

Figure 29 Herbert Lang, 'Manziga, a Chief of the Azande', the American Museum of Natural History.

In 1915, Lang published a photograph of a group of Mbuti, posing with bows and arrows pointed at the camera. His caption was simply descriptive: 'Pygmies from Nala, in the Uele district. They live by hunting, and exchange their spoils with the agricultural tribes for vegetables. Two hundred of them visited the expedition and many allowed plaster casts to be made of their faces' (Lang 1915: 384). Four years later in his article on the Mbuti-Pygmies, Lang described how he had won the confidence of the Mbuti chief while being threatened with arrows. An almost identical photograph appeared to bolster the story (Figure 30). It was obviously taken at the same time as the earlier picture, but had been differently cropped, revealing an extra figure at the left, whose arrow points away from the camera, and whose forced expression seems to indicate the posed nature of the scene. Such casual procedure stemmed from a belief that the caption formed the predominant impression in the reader's mind. It states:

> The whir of a Pygmy's arrow is the crowning step in the pursuit of a victim, be it man or beast. In the forest consummate skill does not depend upon shooting at great distances, but on the ability to steal up under the wind, unheard, unseen, and never miss the fleeting chance. Even among Pygmies there are only a few who have the patience, daring, and energy for such accomplishment
>
> (Lang 1919: 705)

In four years, Lang's picture had changed from being evidence of his encounter with a co-operative native people to a testimony of his own

Figure 30 Herbert Lang, 'The whir of a pygmy's arrow is the crowning step in the pursuit of a victim', the American Museum of Natural History.

bravery in confronting such skilled and lethal adversaries. This picture indicates the textual and photographic liberties Lang felt entitled to take despite his avowed desire to achieve an unmediated anthropological truth.

THE POLITICS OF CULTURAL DIFFERENCE

Indeed, the interpretation of photographic representations of the Congo was a politically contested field at this time. Lang and other apologists for the colonial regime in the Congo argued that the entire truth of the region could not be gleaned from photographs alone, whereas the reformers held that the photographs which had emerged from the region told the entire truth of the matter. One of the many intellectuals to become involved in the question of Congo reform was the writer Arthur Conan Doyle. He wrote a Preface to Morel's *Great Britain and the Congo*, which placed this issue at the centre of his argument:

> When we read of the ill-treatment of these poor people, the horrible beatings, the mutilation of limbs, the butt-endings, the starving in hostage-houses – facts which are vouched for by witnesses of several nations and professions, backed by the incorruptible evidence of the Kodak – we may ask again by what right these things are done?

The defenders of the Belgian regime had two answers to such accusations. Firstly, they were dismissed as untrue and, next in the words of Marguerite Roby, the British travel writer:

> As for the 'incorruptible evidence of the Kodak', it is obvious that such evidence is strictly limited in its scope, if honorably employed. I mean to say that from the photograph of a mutilated person you can only deduce the fact that the person in question has suffered according to the picture. *Where* the crime was committed is quite another matter, and unless a very careful record be kept as to where such photographs are taken, it is almost inevitable that mistakes and misunderstandings will arise. Exactly the same remarks apply to the question of *When* was the crime depicted committed? and even the most honourable men may be misled on this score when they have not taken the photographs themselves.
>
> (Roby 1911: 267)

The polemicists of the Congo reform question thus took directly opposed positions on the question of the accuracy of the photograph. Doyle claimed that the photograph spoke for itself, whereas Roby argued that photographs could only be interpreted with the supplement of careful textual notations.

Lang was able both to claim the authorship of his photographs, and to provide the careful documentation Roby required, which he used at length to defend the Belgian administration. Like Roby, he argued that the natives were not oppressed by the colonial government, but rather benefitted from it and needed it:

> None of the natives indulge any longer in cannibalism; yet those most anxious to help them, and many of the professional reformers, speak even now about their 'degraded condition', 'shameless manners', and 'behavior like animals', perhaps just because the warm climate allows them to walk about in just the state that seems, from all accounts, to have been the most satisfactory in Paradise . . . . It is true that they are born and die in the densest superstition, but this latter is their religion, their code of morals, their own very rigid set of laws, which binds them together in spite of all savage feeling in a true democractic spirit . . . . The greatest fallacy in judging natives is the common habit of travelers and many residents of basing their judgment about them upon information received from workmen, servants or half-civilized negroes. Even the most truthful individuals among these natives generally try and speak from the white man's point of view, displaying in this great shrewdness, so that any question asked is answered with the desire of pleasing the inquirer.
>
> (Lang 1915: 386)

This passage is exemplary of Lang's cultural politics of representation. He presents the natives as happy, worthy peoples, who live and die in inevitably primitive conditions. The colonial administration, far from hindering them, has put an end to cannibalism, introduced the principles of commerce and the means for its pursuit in the shape of railways and river steamers. However, Lang was aware that the development of colonial mimicry had made it difficult to ascertain the exact truth as to conditions in the region, and led to the deception of many of his contemporaries.

The apparent acceptance of cultural relativism by the defenders of the Belgian Congo was no more than that – apparent. Lang used his photographs to establish an image of Congo peoples as primitive, superstitious, but happy under the colonial regime. His picture of a group of local children informed the viewer that:

> There are no orphans in the Congo, in the sense of homeless children. Food is plentiful and bringing up children involves little labor or expense; thus an orphan child is always taken into another family. These children lead happy, carefree lives, and, by helping in village and garden, learn without special training the domestic and other arts of their parents.
>
> (Lang 1915)

Any evidence that mitigated this Edenic picture was suppressed. Enid Schildkrout has discovered that both in his published work and the archival albums at the American Museum, Lang 'omitted many of the images that show Western influence' (Schildkrout 1991: 84). These include a shot of the Mangbetu chief Okondo waving good-bye to the expedition, dressed in a Western uniform. This suppression was made not just in the interest of ethnographic 'authenticity' but to preserve the colonial case that the primitive nature of Congo peoples mandated an imperial presence in the region. Lang sought to establish not cultural relativism but an unbridgeable cultural difference between the 'civilized' and the 'primitive', which eugenicists held to be different ranks of humanity. Lang took pains to publish pictures showing the local acceptance of the regime. His picture entitled *Danga, a Prominent Mangbetu Chief* was captioned as follows: 'Beside him stand two female body servants and behind are some of his people. The large medal hanging from his neck is the official sign of his rank as recognized by the Belgian administration. Of this he is very proud.' Similarly, his portrait of *Manziga, a Chief of the Azande* was captioned: 'He is unusually intelligent and exhibits much tact and diplomacy in dealings with the colonial administration' (Lang 1915) (Figure 29). Manziga was portrayed in traditional dress, with the caption also referring to the Azande belief that they would be reincarnated as lions. Manziga is indeed 'almost the same but not quite' (Bhabha 1987: 318). It is that difference, that not quite, to which Lang devoted his attention. Photography sought to discover the difference that the heart of darkness made all but invisible, which is to say, it seemed so apparent, so obvious, and yet resisted the taxonomic efforts of the anthropologist.

The primary motivation behind these colonial photographs was to produce an effect of cultural difference in the eyes of the Western audience. The photographic sign is not purely arbitrary, in the way attributed to the written word by philosophers since Locke in the seventeenth century. Nor is it wholly natural, revealing only that which is 'really there'. It is rather a *motivated* sign, a sign which is supposed to look like something. In this case, Lang's photographs were supposed to show racial difference marked upon the bodies of his African subjects. According to his training both as a mammologist and a eugenic anthropologist, the difference was, by its very nature, visible. Yet that difference stubbornly failed to reveal itself. Lang saw the Mbuti as 'nomad dwarfs', evidently inferior to the 'tall negro', especially the Mangbetu people, but was unable to produce such definitive categorizations. The discourse of colonial mimicry frustrated any effort to reach the 'truth' of Africa. Instead, as Bhabha notes: 'What emerges between mimesis and mimicry is a *writing*' (Bhabha 1987: 320). Lang could not visualize racial difference and was ultimately reduced, like so many of his eugenicist colleagues, to writing the difference of race on to the African body. His essays and captions seek to use the photographs as evidence, but they resist signification without Lang's direction. Like the fetishist, the colonial photographer cannot believe the evidence of his or her eyes and resorts to a dedicated belief in the averted gaze.

This failure to signify was explained and justified by the designation of Africa in general as the Dark Continent and the Congo in particular as the heart of darkness. In such conditions, the implication ran, how could even Western science be expected to see details clearly? The invisibility and inexplicability of Africa has survived into the present day. On a map of the world as served by major international airlines, it often appears that there is a void between the Mediterranean coast of Africa and the 'Western' cities of South Africa. Similarly, Africa does not yet appear on the global representation of the Internet, the computer network upon which so many utopian dreams have recently been based. Western media continue to report political events in Africa as inexplicable, rather than examining the legacies of colonial power and the neo-colonial enterprises of nations such as France and Britain, and the multinational corporations. Faced with the failure of its interpretive models, Western culture is forced to rely upon what it sees as the 'essential' difference, the visible distinction of race, while having to admit that there are no precise means by which to define how one race is to be distinguished from the next. For all its lack of profundity or interpretive power, race remains written upon our bodies. If there were no race to rely on, the structures of difference upon which much of Western society is based would be radically challenged. In the next chapter, I look at one artist's effort to elide or even erase that difference, the graffiti painting of Jean-Michel Basquiat.

NOTES

1 I will henceforth not strain the patience of the reader by placing every racial or racist term in quotation marks, but will presume that it is understood that these categories are purely discursive, with no reference to actual bodily qualities.

2 The reports in the Museum's journal indicate that Lang and Chapin arrived in Avakubi in October 1910 and had returned there by 1912. By 30 September 1914 they had returned to Stanleyville (modern Kisangani) and sailed for home on 18 November 1914.

3 I have therefore restricted my discussion to those photographs published and commented on by Lang. The daunting task of applying this contextual reading to the entire corpus of Lang's photographic archive is far beyond the scope of this essay. Ironically, the consequence is that I shall discuss very few of the photo-

graphs which were displayed in *African Reflections*, the majority of which were taken from the archives.

4 Although the Congo is not named in *Heart of Darkness*, Conrad detailed the geography, climate and culture of the region in precise fashion, down to the 50lb weight carried by 'native' porters, the brass wire used by the Belgians to 'pay' for ivory, and the navigation conditions of the Congo river.

5 By contrast, another traveller wrote in 1910: 'Avakubi is a beautiful place, quite an ideal station. Fine, lofty buildings constructed of good sun-burnt bricks, and the whole place was most compactly arranged. The Europeans' houses, built four square, with an open quadrangle in the centre, and a high brick wall surrounding the back part, which contained the servants' quarters and outhouses . . . . The gardens at once took my fancy, for here not only was there every kind of European vegetable, but also the most beautiful flowerbeds, arranged with great taste' (Lloyd 1899: 288–9).

6 The posthumous account of the explorer Sir Richard F. Burton concerning the 'Pygmies' was also published in 1899: 'The Akkas: The Pygmies of Africa', *The Humanitarian* (January–February): 15–29; 89–100.

5

PAINTING AT THE HEART OF
WHITENESS

In this chapter, I seek to reverse the theme of colonial imagery by examining the work of an African diaspora artist in contemporary New York. It ought to be possible to write about artists without mentioning their ethnicity but as yet, only white European and American artists truly enjoy that privilege. In this second section, I examine the short but intense life of Jean-Michel Basquiat (1960–1988) as an exemplary case of the complex nexus of race, gender and identity which must be confronted by any contemporary artist who does not fall into this limited category. From this study it will become apparent that the body of the artist is also implicated in the body s/he represents. Basquiat's painting explored, celebrated and diversified what it means to paint the body, above all concerned with the question of encorporated identity, of what it might mean to be an artist or a spectator of art in the hybridity of the 1980s. Basquiat's painting was an investigation into the possibility of being African, American and an artist.

Born in Brooklyn in 1960, Basquiat was the son of Haitian and Puerto Rican parents. His French name and Caribbean dreadlocks marked his difference both from the European community and the African-Americans of New York. In a 1982 photograph by James Van Der Zee, Basquiat presents a striking, hybrid image. His tweed jacket and waistcoat, combined with the Siamese cat and the carved chair, suggest a man of leisure and gentility, contrasting with the paint-stained jeans and his shock of hair. Basquiat appears in the role of a nineteenth-century dandy, the *flâneur* immortalized by the poet and critic Charles Baudelaire. By the time this picture was taken, Basquiat had already made his impact on the contemporary art scene. He began his career as a graffiti artist on the streets of New York, part of the emerging hip-hop scene in the late 1970s. Using the tag SAMO – Same Old Shit – Basquiat attracted a considerable reputation on the street which soon translated into work inside the clubs where he was

162

already known as a stylish dancer. Many of his works were first executed as murals for clubs, especially Manhattan's Mudd Club. Graffiti had crossed over into the art scene as early as 1976 in a show at the Artist's Space, but it was the Times Square Show of 1980 that brought this new art form to wider public attention. Basquiat first exhibited at the *New York, New Wave* show at the influential PS1 gallery in 1981. From this point, his rise was meteoric and he was soon showing in such powerhouse galleries as Larry Gagosian and Mary Boone. This influential backing led to his selection for the major contemporary art shows, such as the Whitney Biennial and Documenta. By 1985, Basquiat was working on collaborations with Andy Warhol and was an unquestioned star. Three years later he was dead. He took his art from the streets to New York to the most elite art galleries only to die in renewed obscurity of a drug overdose. It is hard not to tell this story as a cautionary tale, a narrative of loss that would indict the contemporary art world for its racism and hypocrisy. But in so doing, there would be a risk that once again, the work of a black artist would be reduced to an allegorical symbol and his (in this instance) life would become a morality tale. Basquiat's work was above all concerned with the question of identity, of what it meant to be involved with the art world in the hybrid diaspora of the 1980s, especially if you were not a part of those elite groups who regard art as their exclusive birthright. Basquiat's body and his corporal identity were always at the forefront of his work, problematizing the very notion of incorporated identity. To treat his work only as a cautionary tale would be to lose its specificity and power.

GRAFFITI, HIP-HOP AND THE ART WORLD

Basquiat's success on the art scene came at a time of unparalleled hostility to the phenomenon of graffiti in New York. Graffiti was interpreted by the mainstream media as an assault on society, raising ethical questions as to the state of modern civilization. At the height of New York's bankruptcy crisis, Mayor Koch spent over $6.5 million in removing graffiti, while the subway police devoted enormous time and effort to preventing its occurrence on trains, a major target for the graffiti artists to 'bomb'. This all but hysterical response to what were after all only painted messages on the side of subway cars and buildings suggests that a deep nerve had been touched by the graffiti artists. The travel writer and novelist Paul Theroux described graffiti as 'crazy, semi-literate messages, monkey scratches on the wall'. The self-evident racism of this remark conceals a deeper anxiety that the city was being 'lost' by 'us', that is to say by white European-Americans, and was being taken over by 'them', the African-Americans, Latinos, Chinese and others who were supposed to be neither seen nor heard, except in the appropriate venues. The runaway success of Tom Wolfe's 1986 novel, The Bonfire of the Vanities, was further evidence of this cultural panic. Wolfe warned in the preface to the second edition of his book that the mayors of ten major cities in the United States were non-white, as if this were self-evident proof of the decline of American civilization. One of the marks of success for graffiti artists was to place their tags in the most daring and conspicuous place possible. Basquiat often placed his work next to Soho art galleries on the night before an opening. Graffiti challenged the rigid de facto segregation of American cities by placing the work of outsiders where it could be seen by everyone.

Graffiti was perceived not only as a challenge to public order, but as an assault on the hegemonic values of the art world. In her book Has Modernism Failed?, the critic Suzi Gablik identified graffiti as marking 'the end to modernist self-assurance' (Gablik 1984: 103–13). It may seem surprising that the modern art movement in New York, which had claimed hegemony from Europe after the Second World War, and built an international consensus around the goals of modernism as articulated by Clement Greenberg and his epigones, could be threatened by such a new and uncertain phenomenon as graffiti. But graffiti did indeed challenge some of modernism's most cherished beliefs, as well as its structural basis in the international art scene. Graffiti was by its nature quick and dramatic, undermining the modernist ideal of the long-contemplated masterpiece. For example, here is one typical description of Willem de Kooning:

> For hours he sits there and watches the painting, waiting for the next move to come. When it comes, he approaches the canvas like a hunter stalking, brush in hand, loaded with pigment, triggered for action: in one swift motion he goes into a long, downward stroke, a dizzy shivering scrub, a slap.
>
> (Slivka 1989: 219)

This macho, colonial image is a reminder that the myth of the Romantic artist has yet to be dispelled. Graffiti could scarcely present such emotion recollected in tranquillity, being done at night with spray cans in fear of the police. Furthermore, graffiti did not seem to its white viewers to present evidence of the power of the Imagination, that modernist totem, but rather of illiteracy and primitivism. Graffiti was certainly a coded form of representation. In the words of Fab 5 Freddy, an associate of Basquiat's, 'wild style is totally illegible unless you're initiated'. Graffiti thus constructed a world of insiders, who were able to understand the tags and messages, and an opposed world of outsiders who could not. These groups were the inverse of those normally empowered by the art world, for it was precisely those who were initiated into the reading of abstract expressionism, minimalism and so on who were unable to read graffiti.

This reversal of cultural roles soon provoked a bitter backlash against graffiti in general and Basquiat in particular. For many white critics, who were otherwise identified with the Left, graffiti was disturbingly out of place on the gallery scene. Suzi Gablik worried about the inevitable artistic failure awaiting the graffiti artists once they escaped the 'limits of poverty'. In part, this sentiment arises from the myth of the modern artist starving in the attic, but its broader connotations were soon developed by other commentators. In a discussion at the DIA Center for the Arts in 1986, the art historian Thomas Crow offered these thoughts on the success of graffiti: 'Graffiti got empowered. To what effect? To effects that are thoroughly reactionary – that obstruct thinking . . . about why its images are borrowed, stereotyped, sexist and violent, about why it is such a big hit with the new patron class' (Foster 1987: 27). Whether the success of graffiti was self-evidently reactionary depends very much on your point of view. Is it better that the art scene remain exclusively for whites, or that the moral standards of the cultural Left in New York be maintained? Even the New York Police Department operated according to these standards. According to Andy Warhol, they did not arrest the white graffiti artist Keith Haring, because 'he looks normal', while the African-American graffiti artist Michael Stewart was killed by the police in the course of his work (Warhol 1989: 533).

Graffiti was certainly as implicated in the commodity process as any other phenomenon in the contemporary art world. Gallery owner Mel Neulander became involved with graffiti artists, because, as he said: 'For me, it was a money making proposition.' This bald truth lies behind any commercial gallery's operations. Basquiat indeed profited from his fifteen minutes of fame. But if we accept Crow's criticism of the graffiti artists on these grounds, our censure should logically be extended to include his artistic hero David, who charged spectators a day's wages to see his *Sabine Women* in 1799 and asked 100,000 *livres* for his painting of Napoleon's coronation (see Chapter 2). A racialized double-standard seems to be in operation here. While it is acceptable for any young white artist to claim his or her moment of success, black artists are supposed to live to a higher moral standard, maintaining the liberal fetish of the Heroic Black. Basquiat himself was aware of the unlikelihood that his moment of celebrity would last. In 1982, he remarked: 'I wouldn't be surprised if I died like a boxer, really broke.' He was only too aware of the threat that once the audience tired of the novelty, they would move on to other, newer things. Sadly, his fears were justified. The art world lost interest in his work and Basquiat drifted into drug abuse. He died in obscurity of a heroin overdose in 1988 at the age of twenty-seven. Almost inevitably, his death sparked renewed interest in his work, culminating in a Whitney Museum retrospective in 1992.

In the DIA Center discussion, the video artist Martha Rosler added her thoughts to Crow's remark: 'It is a symbolic representation, on centre stage of the other as tamed entertainer – it's like a minstrel show' (Foster 1987: 28). In other words, outside the minstrel tent, symbolized by the art gallery, the Other is wild and free, an existence that is only possible beyond the (white) mainstream. This belief has a long history in American culture. For example, Jack Kerouac described how

> at lilac evening, I walked along with every muscle aching among the lights of 27th and Welton in the Denver colored section, wishing I were a Negro, feeling that the best the white world had offered me was not enough ecstacy for me, not enough life, joy, kicks, darkness, music, not enough night.
>
> (Ross 1989: 69)

For Kerouac and many others, black was by definition not-white, out there not in here, on the street not in the gallery. Graffiti challenged these assumptions and was found exciting as long as it remained in its proper place on the streets, but once it found its way into the sanctuary of the gallery space, it was dismissed out of hand by established critics. The brief moment of financial success enjoyed by graffiti artists was accompanied by critical rejection.

Such attitudes could be found even at the heart of the art world. In 1983, Basquiat started to associate with members of Andy Warhol's circle, a sure sign of being on the inside of the New York art scene. For a while Basquiat dated Paige Powell, an uptown art dealer and friend of Warhol. The liaison did not meet with the approval of her friends, as Warhol's diaries made clear: 'Paige stayed overnight with Jean-Michel in his dirty, smelly loft downtown. How I know it smells is because Chris was there and said (*laughs*) it was like a nigger's loft, that there were crumpled up hundred dollar bills in the corner and bad b.o. all over and you step on paintings' (Warhol 1989: 519). Warhol had been a supporter of Basquiat's work since his days selling T-shirts in the Village in 1982 and later collaborated with him on a series of paintings, but his *Diaries* clearly show the intense ambivalence of the art world to Basquiat's success. He reported various racist comments, but perhaps most revealingly he noted that Basquiat's dealer disliked his new series of 1985 silk-screen prints , saying 'it ruined his [Basquiat's] "intuitive primitivism"' (Warhol 1989: 610). In the eyes of some of the art world, Basquiat represented a tame primitive, an *idiot savant* whose role was to entertain his superiors and know his place.

In an article published in *Elle* magazine in 1986, the leading New York art critic Peter Scheldajl spelt out the terms of this artistic conundrum, defining 'most work by non-whites in the New York mainstream of styles' as '"wannabe": a diffident emulation of established modes'. He was surprised to learn that Basquiat was black and had such a 'grasp of New York big-painting aesthetics' (Lippard 1990: 166). In other words, the black artist was damned both ways. On the one hand, he or she was written off as a 'wannabe', a hustler with more ambition than talent, who did not make it because they did not deserve to. On the other hand, if success was forthcoming, the artist was then effectively 'white' and could be condemned for abandoning his/her 'roots', or, more exactly, the cultural role alloted to the black artist by the white critic. For artists like Basquiat, who wished to use elements of the European tradition, but also sought to create a space within or perhaps beyond that tradition which could incorporate his sense of identity, Scheldajl offered only one role – that of mimic. The black artist who created work that was accepted as being of suitable quality by the art establishment was at once denied his or her 'true' ethnic identity. Basquiat always sought to refute such essentialist notions of identity and insisted that: 'I grew up in an American vacuum' (Lippard 1990: 165). But in contemporary America, there are no racial vacuums.

For these racialized distinctions are not incidental accidents of casual prejudice, but an integral part of modern art's use of race as a system of cultural difference and signification. At the end of Conrad's *Heart of Darkness*, the narrator Marlowe and his audience look around them in the docks of London: 'The offing was barred by a black bank of clouds, and the tranquil waterway leading to the utmost ends of the earth flowed sombre under an overcast sky – seemed to lead into the heart of an immense darkness' (Conrad 1969: 603). This classic modernist text established the heart of darkness within the modern city, but the entire cultural geography of the city was not occupied by that darkness. Instead, certain areas of the city were designated as dark and others as light. In Conrad's London the distinction was between the dark East End, home of the working class, and the light of the West End. In the modern American city, as Kerouac's remarks make clear, the distinction between light and dark is made on grounds of race rather than class. The art world defines itself as part of the city of light, hence the white city. Here I shall explore

Basquiat's effort to paint in the heart of whiteness, composed of what Diego Cortez has called 'white walls, white people, and minimal white art' (Marshall 1992: 66). For it has been held to be axiomatic that culture originates in the light, even if it derives inspiration in style and content from the dark, a metaphor exemplified in the Museum of Modern Art's now infamous 1984 *Primitivism* exhibition, which placed unidentified 'primitive' art objects alongside modernist masterpieces in order to demonstrate the 'source' of Western art's inspiration. Basquiat intervened in this simplistic binary system which presented the cultures of Africa and the African diaspora as no more than source material for Western art in his attempt to create an art form out of a meaningful interaction between artistic traditions.

Basquiat's brief career and early death make it more than usually difficult to talk about his work as a whole, and to identify its major themes as if it amounted to a completed *oeuvre*, to use the art historical term. This difficulty is exacerbated by the nature of his work, which blended fragments from disparate sources into images whose themes were both divergent and dramatic. Rather than claim a false unity for Basquiat's work, I shall do as he did and sample his images in order to explore two themes of particular interest to me: firstly, his interpellation of the modernist construction of a visual system around racial difference; and secondly, his exploration of an alternative notion of identity through the themes of diaspora and exile. Basquiat developed his work in the context of the emerging new style of dance music, now known as hip-hop. Hip-hop is by its very nature a postmodern phenomenon, which turns borrowing and appropriation into a new art form. The methods of scratching and mixing were as central to Basquiat's art practice as to the music of Grandmaster Flash or the Sugar Hill Gang.

Hip-hop began in New York's South Bronx in the late 1970s at street parties and in underground clubs. It was a new synthesis of previously recorded music into a hybrid created by the DJ (disc jockey). Hip-hop is based on a backing beat or rhythm, known as a breakbeat, usually selected from a previously recorded song. In these early days, the task of the DJ was to identify a suitable break, or unaccompanied instrumental section, which could be repeated over and again to create the backdrop for an entirely new track. Particular favourites for this process were disco hits like Chic's *Le Freak*, classic James Brown tunes such as *Funky Drummer*, and even the obligatory drum solo on hard rock and heavy metal albums. Over this basic backing, the DJ then added a series of samples to enliven the mix. With current computer technology, any item of music or vocals can be sampled, but then it was necessary to find a cappella vocal sections, horn breaks or otherwise clearly identifiable sounds to use as samples. A good sample should be at once recognizable in its general style but unusual in particular. Both samples and back beat had to be created by repeated playing of the same section of a record, requiring considerable dexterity and skill as the DJ switched from one turntable to the next to create the effect of seamless sound. Prior to the development of specialized mixers and turntables, it was not uncommon for large teams of DJs to work together to maximize the effect. The final element in this new construction of sound was scratching. In this instance, the DJ deliberately pulls an element of a record counter-clockwise under the needle of the turntable, producing the distinctive scratching sound that has become one of the hallmarks of hip-hop. Contrary to popular opinion, the selection of music to be scratched will determine the effectiveness of the resulting noise and cannot be achieved with a random choice. Finally, the hip-hop sound was completed by the addition of a spoken rap, a rhyming commentary derived from jail house toasting, reggae toasting, the poetry of the Last Poets and the distinctive vocal style of James Brown. The rap could be the vehicle for social comment, for the promotion of the rapper, or for the simple pleasures of rhyme and rhythm in the spoken word. The fusion of these distinctive elements created a musical form that has now become a staple of both black and white popular culture. In the early 1980s, however, it sounded new, angry and distinctly urban.

The scratch and mix method was at the heart of Basquiat's work. Graffiti artists often worked in hip-hop clubs and venues, creating backdrops and murals, sometimes painting at the same time as the music was playing. This method can be located in the least discussed aspect of Basquiat's work, namely his technique, requiring that his work be analysed for more than the verbal content of his graffiti. Basquiat strove for an effect of immediacy and directness, which often required careful reworking and overpainting, for an artist is never more artful than when striving for artlessness. For example, Basquiat's 1982 work *Charles I* has often been commented upon for its logo: 'MOST YOUNG KINGS GET THIER HEAD CUT OFF' (Figure 31). Certainly this graffito suggests an ironic comment on being a Young Turk in the art world and the inevitable transience of earthly power. But it appears only in the bottom left corner of the piece, obscured by overwriting and overpainting. The work derives more of its impact from its composition into three vertical sections, suggesting a triptych. Each section works in its own right, in tension and oscillation with the others, connected and looped by the blue and yellow colour scheme. The painted

Figure 31 Jean-Michel Basquiat, *Charles I* (1982), courtesy Robert Miller Gallery, New York.

words and designs are both forceful and edgy, seeming to vibrate with nervous energy and intensity. Words and symbols are used only to be crossed out, such as the Marvel Comics © at bottom right and the pun on homepeace/piece at top right. The Young King is alternately represented by the Norse god Thor – also a Marvel Comics character – Superman, the crown symbol and the encircled word 'Cherokee'.

The crown was to become a mark representing Basquiat and his gen-

170

ealogy, which he made clear in his *CPRKR* (1983). The piece is a mock tombstone for the jazz musician Charlie Parker recording the place and time of his death. Below this inscription appears the crown symbol and below that the name Charles I. Both Charles' became martyrs to their vocations at relatively young ages. Basquiat thus placed himself – the crown – between Charlie Parker and Charles I, between black creativity and white absolute authority, in a place of danger. The logo at the bottom left thus reinforces this sense of urgency and lack of time, which is first conveyed by the formal elements of the piece, in the same way that the words of a rap are given force by the groove over which they are laid. In both his paintings and drawings, Basquiat's work shares, and contributes to, the driving energy and force of hip-hop as it was coming into being. Basquiat did in fact produce a rap record early in his career, a now coveted 12-inch single entitled *Beat Bop*, featuring fellow graffiti artist Rammellzee on vocals (Marshall 1992: 242). Although Basquiat has mostly been connected to jazz, which he often referred to in his work, he was one of those who very early on saw the connections between jazz and hip-hop as forms of black cultural expression. As the legendary jazz drummer Max Roach put it: 'Hip-hop lives in the world of sound, not the world of music, and that's why it's so revolutionary. What we as black people have always done is show that the world of sound is bigger than white people think' (Lippard 1990: 165). Appropriately, Basquiat made a portrait of Roach in 1984 (Marshall 1992: 182).

RACE AND MODERN ART

Basquiat was also an intuitive visual sampler. Whereas his friend and collaborator Andy Warhol derived his sources from mass culture and iconography, like the famous Campbell's Soup cans and Marilyn Monroe, Basquiat borrowed his images from the kaleidoscope of visual culture ranging from cartoons and comics to Leonardo da Vinci. I intend to focus on his borrowings from 'high' culture, especially Impressionism and the Italian Renaissance, not because these signs are in some way superior to the others used by Basquiat, but because they serve as suitable samples for my own discourse in this book. In a series of works, Basquiat interpellated the visual system of modernism as depending upon racial difference in order to signify. In the early twentieth century, the linguist Ferdinand de Saussure built upon the work of Locke, Condillac and Taine to argue that if language was an arbitrary system, as his predecessors had maintained, meaning was thus only constituted by difference. Signs have meaning because of their differential relation to other signs, not because of any intrinsic, natural meaning. Thus we routinely speak of an image having correct perspective when all the objects depicted recede in proportion to one another and being incorrect if they do not. Perspective is, of course, only a convention as art from other cultures and time periods makes clear. Perspective works as a system of visual signification in relation to a system of difference which has pertinence only within that system.

Basquiat explored the ways in which Western painting depended upon race as a system of visual difference to give coherence to its arbitrary system of signification, and then attempted to imagine depicting the body without signifying race. He selected Manet's *Olympia* (1865) as the subject for one of his most powerful investigations of the operations of race in modern art (Figure 32). *Olympia* has come to have almost unique importance in the etiology of modern art, and is often regarded as the first modern painting. In his 1982 work, *Three-Quarters of Olympia Without the Servant*, Basquiat recreated Manet's depiction of a nineteenth-century Parisian prostitute, but without the accompanying figure of her black servant (Figure 33). By so doing, he placed himself within a modernist tradition of paying homage to *Olympia*, but departed from it by removing

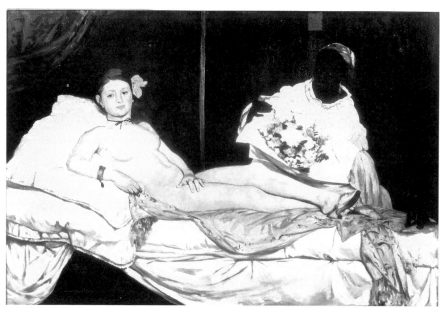

Figure 32 Edouard Manet, *Olympia* (1865), courtesy Giraudon/Bridgeman Art Library.

Figure 33 Jean-Michel Basquiat, *Three-Quarters of Olympia Without the Servant* (1982), © 1982 The Estate of Jean-Michel Basquiat, courtesy Robert Miller Gallery, New York.

the servant. At first sight, the two paintings could not seem more different. Manet's work bears all the hallmarks of his Old Master training and represents the scene with limpidity and clarity. All the elements of his painting are clearly identifiable within realist conventions. Basquiat's work, on the other hand, refuses both the conventions of realistic representation and the signifiers of 'good' technique. The black painted outline, figures and words have been overpainted and even obliterated, especially by the swathes of white paint which seem designed to erase the painting altogether. Although he worked on canvas, Basquiat's painting even refuses the traditional rectilinear frame with its extending sections of the stretcher. In fact, these works have more in common than it seems. Struck by the difficulties encountered by nineteenth-century critics in interpreting Manet's work, T.J. Clark commented: 'There was something about *Olympia* which eluded their normal frame of reference, and writers were almost fond of admitting they had no words for what they saw' (Clark 1985: 92). Despite the apparent formal differences, neither version of *Olympia* lent itself to straightforward interpretation in its own time. Here I will consider the function of race as it intersected with gender and class in creating this problem of reading in the work of Manet, Basquiat and other interpreters of *Olympia*. Furthermore, the complexity of allusion and reference in Basquiat's work shows both the wide-ranging use of 'Western' culture in his art and the sophistication of his engagement with modernism, requiring a detailed explication.

Olympia has been as significant in the writing of art history as it has been for art practice. First hailed as a modernist masterpiece by Emile Zola, the painting has kept this reputation while gaining from the interpretations of new approaches to art history. In feminist art history, *Olympia* has had considerable importance in analyses of the representation of women in nineteenth-century France in particular and modernism in general. The question of gender and spectatorship has been especially important in this regard. It was not until Sander Gilman's ground-breaking 1985 article on *Olympia*, 'Black Bodies, White Bodies: Toward an Iconography of Female Sexuality in Late Nineteenth-Century Art, Medicine and Literature', that the question of racial difference in the work was fully considered. Basing his analysis on the medicalization of sexuality in the nineteenth century, Gilman examined the clinical studies of the so-called Hottentot Venus, Sarah Bartmann, which purported to show that African women were physiologically different to white women. This difference was especially apparent in the labia minora and clitoris, which successive European scientists claimed to find 'overdeveloped' in African women, especially the Hottentots. The propinquity of *Olympia* to the African servant is, then, indicative of more than formal values or the adherence to an iconographic tradition, as Gilman makes clear: 'Black females do not merely represent the sexualized female, they also represent the female as source of corruption and disease. It is the black female as emblem of illness who haunts the background of Manet's *Olympia*' (Gilman 1985: 250). The figure of the servant was an essential signifier of race, corruption and disease without which *Olympia* could not raise the questions of class and gender which have been central to recent interpretations of the picture.

This deployment of race as being inextricably connected to deviant sexuality was an innovation of the mid-nineteenth century. One of the paradoxes of the period is that a century which began full of enthusiasm for the abolition of slavery soon became obsessed with racial classification and stereotypes. This transformation can be observed within French art and would certainly have been known to Manet. In 1819, Théodore Géricault (1791–1824) made an African a heroic figure in his *Raft of the Medusa*, a painting which was in itself motivated by opposition to the slave trade. For the ship *Medusa* which had been wrecked was on its way to Senegal in order to collect a shipment of slaves. After foundering in a storm, the ship did not have enough lifeboats for all the crew, so a raft was constructed to take the others. However, the officers in the lifeboat ordered the raft cut loose from their boat in order to improve their own chances of survival. By chance, the raft was none the less rescued and a political scandal ensued, in which abolitionists argued that the incident showed the inevitable moral corruption associated with slavery (Boime 1990: 12–45). Géricault was working on a painting to be called *The African Slave Trade* at the time of his premature death in 1824. Moral opposition to slavery was thus at the heart of avant-garde French painting in the 1820s.

At the Salon of 1859, however, the sculptor Eugène Frémiet showed his new work *Gorilla Carrying off a Woman*. The gorilla is massive, dominating the pliable European woman with ease and there was no doubt in the mind of Charles Baudelaire as to the subject of the work:

> Here it is not a matter of eating but of rape. Only the ape, the giant ape who is both more and less than a man, sometimes shows a human craving for women. . . . He is dragging her off; will *she* know how to resist? Every woman is bound to wonder about this, with mixed feelings of terror and prurience.
>
> (Baudelaire 1990 [1859]: 389)

In Baudelaire's view, the ape and his supposed close relative the African male had more sexuality and less humanity than his European counterpart. In the nineteenth-century imagination, there was a direct analogy between race and gender which saw a close connection between the white woman and the black man, who were both equally inferior to the white man (Stepan 1986). Women were perceived by race science as a more primitive version of men and thus had connections with Africans, the poor and other degenerated versions of the male. In case viewers were in any doubt as to the racial connotations of his piece, Frémiet made the skull of his gorilla equivalent in shape to that believed to be typical of Africans by race scientists. In the period, skull shape and size was held to be extremely revealing of both personal and racial characteristics. Early anthropologists devoted enormous efforts to collecting and measuring skulls, which were held to reveal certain objective facts as to the superiority of the European race. On the one hand, it allowed scientists to 'prove' that European brains were larger than those of other peoples, a feat which, as Stephen Jay Gould has shown, could only be achieved by manipulation of data, whether deliberate or otherwise (Gould 1981). Second, following the work of the Dutch anatomist Pieter Camper in the 1780s, it was believed that the angle of the forehead to the rest of the skull formed what was termed the cranial angle. The closer this angle was to the perpendicular, the higher the rank of the race. Inevitably, the European race took highest place, but it was signified in caricatures such as that of Grandeville in the 1840s by the head of the Apollo Belvedere, rather than by an actual skull (Callen 1989). Race and artistic representation were thus indissoluble in the nineteenth century. Frémiet's gorilla has an absurdly low cranial angle, as if to make it clear to the least perceptive viewer that the creature, and by analogy Africans, were of a very low standard of evolution. By chance, the sculpture was first exhibited in the same year that Charles Darwin published his *Origin of Species*.

Frémiet's *Gorilla* was so successful that he returned to it on numerous occasions, adding various improvements along the way. For the Salon of 1887, he added coloured wax to the figures in order to make their racial difference definitively apparent. The gorilla has retained its influence in the present century. It is strikingly similar to the gorilla depicted in the film *King Kong* (1933), which famously abducts a white woman, a point of reference of continuing importance in popular culture. The gorilla carries a primitive stone tool in his left hand, and Frémiet no doubt intended this tool to further blur the distinction between the great apes and the 'primitive' Africans, but it has an ironic reference in modern popular literature. In Michael Crichton's 1980 novel *Congo*, the plot concerns a struggle between a multinational mining corporation and a species of talking gorilla deep in the Congo rainforest. The gorillas not only talk but are armed with deadly stone paddles, exactly like that carried by Frémiet's gorilla. Luckily, the Europeans are rescued by a tame gorilla who enjoys smoking and communicates in American Sign Language. From this nightmare of cultural stereotyping it can be seen that, even though nineteenth-century racial science has long been discredited, its cultural forms continue to have an active life.

In his 1983 canvas *Masonic Lodge*, Basquiat addressed and parodied these living fossils. His work is unusually restricted to line and text, with the exception of the eye which stands both as a Masonic symbol and for the eye of the artist. Otherwise, the piece consists of an incomplete cranial diagram, which labels spaces and lines in an uncertain attempt to map the skull. A particular focus is the bulging, prognathous jaw, a symbol of underdevelopment and closeness to the apes. In the top left appears the new classification of degeneracy, 'paranoid schizophrenic'. However, many letters are obliterated so that the label reads 'p-r— sch—phr–'. This elimination gives the work a complex valency. In one sense, the work addresses the failure of diagnosis and the desire to fit observations into a preconceived schema. The blank letters might then be read as spaces to be filled in by more precise measurements. The eye at the heart of the 'skull' speaks to the centrality of visual observation in modern scientific practice, especially in medicine, which trains doctors in the development of a clinical gaze that can perceive the nature and origins of disease, invisible to the untrained eye. By the sketchy and incomplete diagram, the crossed out letters and names, Basquiat further suggests that such diagnosis is in fact a cultural construction, a game of join the dots which has no blueprint from which to operate. At the same time, however, his connection of the terms of race science and psychology draws our attention to the fact that simply revealing social practice to be a cultural construction does not necessarily help transform actual social conditions. The blank space around his outline evokes the difficult work that remains to be done in connecting cultural and political work and in completing any analysis of the means by which that connection might be made.

Basquiat's *Three-Quarters of Olympia* needs to be seen in this context, as an exploration of the longevity of cultural stereotypes of race, and what might occur if they were bypassed. His work is one of a series of re-imaginings of *Olympia* in Western art, but it is the only one to refuse Manet's racial equation. Manet used a number of visual clues to identify *Olympia* as a prostitute – the crumpled bed, the choker and slippers – of which the most important was the black servant. It is furthermore clear that the figure is depicted as if in the presence of a client, as can be seen from the flowers brought by the servant; from Olympia's famous outward gaze; and from the placing of her hand which blocks the gaze of the client from her sex, the object of the forthcoming transaction. The hostility of the black cat on the right hand side indicates that the visitor is not known to the waiting women. The cat and Olympia both look out at the same place, which is occupied by the potential client within the narrative of the painting, but is in fact occupied by the spectator of the painting. This overlap of the spectator with the prostitute's client indicates, as Gilman points out, that

> the 'white man's burden' thus becomes his sexuality and its control, and it is this which is transferred into the need to control the sexuality of the Other, the Other as sexualized female. The colonial mentality which sees 'natives' as needing control is easily transferred to 'woman' – but woman as exemplified by the caste of the prostitute.
>
> (Gilman 1985: 256)

Gilman's attention to the racial dimension in Manet's work thus allows the multiple signifiers of *Olympia* to flow in series. The white woman is identified as a prostitute by a variety of visual clues but predominantly the black woman, whose presence connects deviant sexuality to the physiognomy of the Other and to disease. The black woman ensures that *Olympia* is read as a fallen woman and hence of low class position. Race, gender and class are equally indispensable to reading *Olympia* and it may be regarded as symptomatic of the cultural construction of modernism that it took so long for the dimension of race to be fully included.

The first artist to redraw the subject was Paul Cézanne who created *A Modern Olympia* in 1873. His work addresses the construction of spectatorship in Manet's work and sought to diminish its radical effect by placing the client within the frame. The spectator is therefore not so closely identified with prostitution and is able to adopt the traditional 'disinterested' pose of the aesthete. Cézanne's client is referred to in the top right corner of Basquiat's Olympia, where he appears with a somewhat demonic grin next to the cat. A further reference to the voyeurism implicit in much Impressionist art after Manet comes in the graffito *Woman Dry Her Neck by Edgar©*, a parody of Edgar Degas' bathers series, which centre around the practice of hygiene (Callen 1992). Basquiat's graffito brings out the nineteenth-century connection between the prostitute, hygiene and the security of the bourgeois client seen in Cézanne and Basquiat. The appearance of the word 'absinthe' – a popular but ultimately deadly alcoholic drink – on the extreme right of Basquiat's work indicates that he read *Olympia* as representing all the key social problems of the period. In the nineteenth century, the prostitute was literally imagined as both dirt and a sewer for the channelling away of excess sperm (Corbin 1987: 211). In that imaginary sewer mingled race, sexuality, gender and class connected by the semen itself. I intend 'semen' both in its literal sense, as the product of the male reproductive system, and in the allusive sense suggested by Derrida in which semen is connected to the Greek word for sign *seme*. In this latter allegorical connotation, the female body is the key venue of visual representation in the nineteenth century and *Olympia* is the archetype of that system.

For both Picasso and Gauguin, it was the representation of race as sexuality that remained the dominant motif in this system of visual signification. In Paul Gauguin's *Manao Tupapau* (1891–3), the woman on the bed is rendered as racially Other. Gauguin's work was recognized as deferring to Manet's work by contemporary critics who renamed the painting the 'Olympia of Tahiti' (Pollock 1992: 20). Gauguin imagined his model to represent the Spirit of Death, making explicit the syphilitic threat inherent in the prostitute. In Picasso's 1901 version, the racial Other was retained as *Olympia*, but transferred back to Europe. His drawing shows a fecund African woman with prominent breasts and hips, absolutely passive in the presence of two naked white men. One offers her fruit, in a parody of the original servant's flowers, while the nearer figure reaches out as if to touch her. Unlike Manet's *Olympia*, who was in charge of the forthcoming transaction, Picasso depicts the black *Olympia* as the object of the white men's desire and incapable of independent action. It is not altogether fanciful to see this image of European potency restored by primitive fertility – although not yet physically apparent in Picasso's drawing – as a figure for High Modernism in the Cubist and Abstract Expressionist period. Basquiat's version of *Olympia* refused that connection. Instead, it confronted the (mostly white) New York art public with its own nightmare – Western art without racial difference. Olympia is now seen as a bald, frightening creature, reaching for the spectator with her massive disembodied hand. Rather than dismiss this as a sexist image, the complex allusions within the work make it clear that Basquiat offered the West an image of its own imaginary.

Olympia is one of the high points of the art historical canon in general and that of modernism in particular. Basquiat's reworking suggests that as much was omitted by the modernist vision as was included. One might use the voyage of Conrad's Marlowe up the Congo river in *Heart of Darkness* as a symbol of this modernist vision. Marlowe misses as much as he sees and understands only a fragment of what is transpiring around him. He concentrates on steering the ship up the treacherous river, only too aware that the dense rainforest prevents him from seeing beyond the river, in either literal or metaphorical terms. Yet, as Edward Said observes: 'Whatever is lost or elided or even simply made up in Marlowe's immensely compelling recitation is compensated for in the narrative's sheer historical momentum, the temporal forward movement' (Said 1993: 23). Yet once that momentum is lost, as has now occured, Marlowe's blindness outweighs his insight, his inadequacies overwhelm his sense of mission and our attention shifts to the surrounding continent, away from the narrow, sandy river that was modernism.

DIASPORA, WANDERING AND REPRESENTATION

Basquiat did not limit his work to the critique of modernism, but attempted to create a new imaginary that would find a place for those who did not fit into the overly neat categorizations of disciplinary society. In so doing, he did not take the easy route of adopting an authentic racial identity as the Other, or succumb to the temptation of Afro-centricity. Rather he used his own situation as someone caught in the diaspora of the black Atlantic, lacking a sense of belonging either to the Caribbean or to the United States, to create a new visual vocabulary. In this iconography, the motifs of wandering and exile collide with a disparate collection of mythic ancestors and a sense of the political antecedents of this sensibility. Basquiat should not be mistaken as a redemptive figure, come to save the painterly tradition, but there was none the less a Utopian dimension to this side of his work. Whatever one's impression of the success of his artistic ventures, this bold ambition in such a young artist can only be applauded. Or so you might think. In fact, there has been a continued effort to represent Basquiat as a disturbed borderline psychotic and a fraud. His dealer Mary Boone bizarrely observed after his death that: 'He was too externalized; he didn't have a strong enough internal life' (Marshall 1992: 60). Such characterizations only strengthen the force of his attempt to forge a new mode of representation out of diaspora, for it recalls many other calumnies levelled against blacks, Jews and other diaspora peoples.

The Atlantic was the site of a triangular crossing for European ships in the eighteenth and nineteenth centuries. Ships departed from Europe for the west coast of Africa, where they loaded human cargoes of slaves for the infamous Middle Passage to the Caribbean or North America. Here the slaves were exchanged for goods, such as sugar or cotton, which were then returned for sale in the country of origin at a handsome profit. The ship became a complicated metaphor in Basquiat's work as he explored his notion of diaspora. In one version of his often revised *Undiscovered Genius of the Mississippi Delta* (1983), Basquiat created a diagram of lines and points, labelled as points of the compass (Figure 34). In ironic proximity, he depicted a ship, captioned 'slave ship', and the Statue of Liberty. The diagram is thus revealed to depict the Atlantic crossing, and reminds us

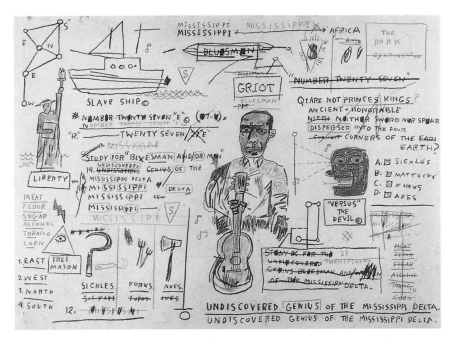

Figure 34 Jean-Michel Basquiat, *Undiscovered Genius of the Mississippi Delta* (1982–3), private collection, © 1983 The Estate of Jean-Michel Basquiat.

exactly why there were blues geniuses awaiting their discovery by ethno-musicologists in the Mississippi Delta. The bluesman is equated with the African figure of the *griot*, or storyteller, a later subject for Basquiat. However, the Statue of Liberty is a reminder that not all Atlantic crossings were made by slave ships. Ships were also the vehicle for such figures of the African diaspora as Frederick Douglass, Alexander Crummell, Marcus Garvey, Langston Hughes and others to travel or escape domestic circum-stances (Gilroy 1993: 13). At the centre of this concatenation of African, European and American imagery and references sits the bluesman himself, who is also a figure for Basquiat, as the reference to the Prince makes clear.

The complexity of the ship as a figure for diaspora can be seen in different contexts in which this representation of a ship recurred in Basquiat's work. In his *Untitled (Quality)* (1983) (Marshall 1992: 173), the ship is the only figurative element in a sea of words (Figure 35). The words are rapidly painted in red and black in varying sizes, obscured with strik-ings out and overwriting, but a pattern emerges if you look closely. The ship sails towards the words 'ghetto' and 'Harlem', closely connected by an arrow to Basquiat's crown symbol. An alternative reading of the ship

181

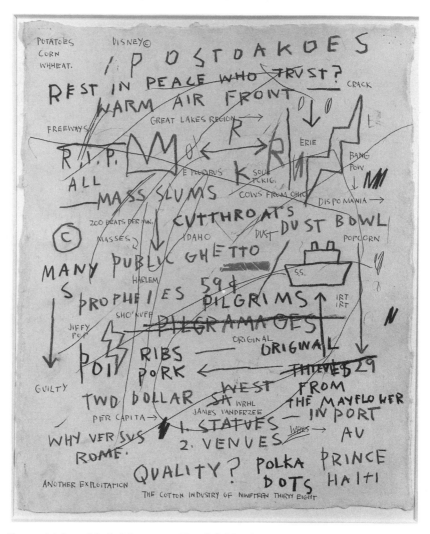

Figure 35 Jean-Michel Basquiat, *Untitled (Quality)* (1983), © 1991 The Estate of Jean-Michel Basquiat, courtesy of the Whitney Museum of Modern Art, New York.

comes from the words on which it might be said to float: 'Pilgrims–Pilgramages'. In the American context, the caption recalls the voyages of the Pilgrim Fathers, whose own diaspora was later to be one cause of the African diaspora. Indeed, an arrow connects these pilgrims to the words 'Thieves from the Mayflower'. A circular connection between religion, exploitation and urban poverty is created with the connection being established by the sea voyages which enabled the process to begin. The role of religion in motivating and causing diaspora was evoked in Basquiat's *50 ¢ Piece* (1982–3) (Marshall 1992: 159), in which the drawing of a ship is labeled as the Ark, complete with its Biblical dimensions of three hundred cubits. Once again, the piece is a mass of words, images and connections, centring on the island of Jamaica. Jamaica is identified as a centre of sugar, banana and rum production, the raw materials of the slave era, as well as a modern nexus of finance and tourism. Disrupting this capitalist evolution is the figure of Marcus Garvey, whose 'Back to Africa' philosophy is reiterated. At the top of the painting, the diagram of naval crossings appears once again, but is now captioned 'Diagram of the Naval Structure'. The sentence is not completed so that the Atlantic ship crossing remains a complex but undecided symbol of persecution and resistance in willing and unwilling diasporas alike. In the same fashion, Paul Gilroy, whose work on diaspora and cultural studies has been so important in recent years, has sought to theorize what he has called the black Atlantic, of which Basquiat's work is a compelling example. Gilroy also uses the Atlantic, that site of so many crossings full of hope and fear, as a figure to conceptualize the 'instability and mutability of identities which are always unfinished, always being remade' (Gilroy 1993: xi). Basquiat's work is a site of this refashioning of diaspora identity, which seeks to escape the biological, religious, and economic determinism of earlier periods but is inevitably inflected by these historical experiences.

At this stage in his career Basquiat treated colonialism directly in his *Native Carrying Some Guns, Bibles, Amorites on Safari* (1982). The painting features a black man carrying a weighty wooden box over his head, next to the outline figure of a colonial hunter, complete with pith helmet and outsize rifle. The tormented but vibrant figure of the African contrasts with the hollow man of colonialism. Basquiat's ironic and angry captions speak for themselves: 'Colonialization: Part Two in a Series, Vol. VI . . . Good Money in Savages'. He creates a flow-chart of association between Good and God, between tusks, skins and dollars, and between the missionaries and pioneer colonizers such as Cortez. Finally, he sardonically writes: 'I won't even mention gold.' The appearance of the crown symbol connects the image to Basquiat and contemporary America. In short, Basquiat highlights the constant complicity between racialized reason and organized terror.

These polemical works can usefully be compared to that of other artists in the African diaspora. Lorna Simpson has attracted considerable attention in recent years for her meditations on being black in America. Her pieces often combine photographic images with attached texts, which allude to the gender and racial stereotypes that often adhere to readings of photography, despite its presumed objectivity. For example, in *Screen 1* (1986), Simpson mounted three photographs of a seated black woman to a folding screen, alluding to the traditional triptych format for religious painting (Wright and Hartman 1992: 30). The pictures show the woman from the waist down, dressed in an anonymous white skirt that suggests a hospital or other institutional setting. This sense of surveillance is reinforced by the fact that the left and centre photographs show the woman in an identical pose, but taken from different sides, as if the photographer has complete control of her subject. In the final panel, the woman is seated in the same pose, except that she now holds a rubber boat, a children's bath toy. This image is both humourous and unsettling for while it obviously incongruous for an adult woman to be holding such a toy, it also reinforces the sense that the setting may be institutional. The red letter text reads 'Marie said she/was from Montreal/although'. The sentence is completed on the reverse of the screen: 'she was from Haiti'. The unease results from this denial of origins and the unstated reasons for such a refusal. Simpson's text suggests that there are degrees within even racial prejudice, so that it is preferable for Marie to be thought of as Canadian rather than Haitian. In the early 1980s, Haiti was thought to be one of the places of origin for AIDS and Haitians were the only ethnic group to be categorized as a high-risk group for infection. Basquiat was himself half-Haitian and could have sympathized with Simpson's work.

Another point of comparison can be found in the work of the black British artist Keith Piper, who has ironically described his formation as an artist: 'Raised and mis-educated in one of Birmingham's many inner city, third world colonies. At the age of nineteen, all else failed, I was sent to Coventry to do a foundation course in Art and Design' (Araeen 1989: 75). In his series *Go West Young Man* (1982), Piper combined this classic injunction with a series of images of the slave trade and personal observations. In this way, he combined the document with his subjective impressions, creating memorable and disturbing images. Alongside a photograph of a black male body, which echoes the pose of Michelangelo's David, Piper comments on the phrase 'Go West Young Man': 'Yes. I heard that joke four hundred years ago. I died laughing.' In the final panel, his handwritten thoughts negotiate his relationship to the stereotypical images of the black body, as created by slavery. Both Piper and Simpson use images of the

black body combined with specific texts to create overtly didactic, con-
sciousness-raising work.

Such directness was, however, unusual in Basquiat's work. More common was a system of allusive references to the mythic experience of
diaspora and an iconography of wandering. In many of Basquiat's paintings, he has graffiti, such as 'aboriginal generative', 'Sun God/Trickster',
and 'Exodus 20 v 15'. This last refers to the Biblical book of Exodus,
specifically the Eighth Commandment, 'Thou shalt not steal.' In the light
of Basquiat's frequent borrowing of visual images, the citation was no
doubt ironically meant. This reference to the Jewish diaspora was
expanded in his other work by the appearance of Egyptian figures, the
word Pharaoh and finally by his *Moses and the Egyptians* (1983) (Marshall
1992: 148). This work was literally shaped to resemble the tablets of the
Ten Commandments, as envisaged by Hollywood. In place of the Biblical
commandments, Basquiat left his red-coloured tablets mostly blank, but
with references to Moses' miracles, such as 'Staff into serpent trick',
suggesting that he had little sympathy for this archetypal patriarch, symbolized by the all-seeing eye in the centre of the composition.

The theme of wandering and exile was developed in his 1983 painting
Pilgrimage. At the centre of this complex work there appears a man on
horseback, wearing what looks like a bishop's mitre. This figure is the
prototype for his 1988 work *Riding with Death*, in which a single figure
rides a curious half-human, half-horse, like the Classical centaur (Marshall
1992: 231). The figure bears considerable resemblance to a Leonardo
drawing entitled *Allegorical Composition*, a suggestive reference, for this
deceptively simple piece contains a range of allusions to the mythologies
of diaspora. For bell hooks, *Riding with Death* 'evok[es] images of obsession, of riding and being ridden in the Haitian *voudoun* sense', that is to say,
the experience of possession by the spirits in the Haitian religion known to
the West as voodoo (hooks 1992: 117).[1] She further interprets Basquiat's
use of bones as an allusion to the art of the Masai peoples of East Africa. In
addition to these images from the African diaspora, *Riding with Death* can
be read as evoking other diasporas, such as the diaspora of the Jews to
which Basquiat had previously referred.

Here I am going to set Basquiat's work alongside that archetype of nine-
teenth- and early twentieth-century-imagination, the Wandering Jew. The
Wandering Jew is an appropriate and suggestive motif for diaspora studies.[2]
Ahasvérus was reputed to have witnessed Christ's last journey with the
cross to Golgotha and urged him to walk faster. In return, Christ condemned the Jew to wander the earth until his Second Coming. As a figure

for diaspora, the Wandering Jew has the advantage that, unlike Gilroy's sailor, or James Clifford's traveller, he has no Romantic connotations and was in fact an anti-semitic stereotype in the later nineteenth century. The legend was not however specific to Jews. In 1869 the Realist critic Champfleury noted in his study of the Wandering Jew that: 'The picture of *Ahasvérus* has been the most popular of all those which have made the presses of Epinal, Metz, and Nancy groan. Since the beginning of the century, the Wandering Jew has consecrated every poor hovel, balanced by a picture of Napoleon. It seems that the common man gave an equal place in his imagination to these two great *marcheurs*' (Champfleury 1869: LV). The story was taken as a measure of the oppression of the little man by the mighty, rather than as a reinforcement of the hatred of the Jews. It was in this sense that the Wandering Jew was the subject for a popular novel by Eugène Sue, *Le Juif errant* (1845), the title of a radical newspaper in the 1848 Revolution, and the source of Gustave Courbet's painting *The Meeting* (1854) (Goldstein 1985: 535). For the Wandering Jew was neither a Jew nor a Christian. Born Jewish, he had been forcibly convinced of the powers of Christ by his punishment and sought to warn others away from a similar fate. Champfleury was much taken with the popular images of the Wandering Jew and, not without a certain condescension, described such imagery as 'original work, which is consequently both naive and popular' (Champfleury 1869: XLVIII). Perhaps the same might be said of Basquiat's work.

The connection between this myth and those of the African diaspora was reinforced by the treatment of the legend at the hands of European intellectuals and scientists in the later nineteenth century. After the establishment of the French Third Republic in 1871, Jean-Martin Charcot became famous for his work on hysteria at the Salpêtrière hospital in Paris. As Michel Foucault has observed, the hysteric was one of the original creations of the nineteenth century. His analysis can be extended into the specific types of hysteric identified by Charcot and his colleagues. It was a cliché of the field that Jews were particularly prone to hysteria for, in the words of one doctor of the period: 'Mental anxiety and worry are the most frequent causes of mental breakdown. They [the Jews] are all excitable and live excitable lives, being constantly under the high pressure of business in town' (Gilman 1991: 63). In 1893, Henry Miège, a colleague of Charcot, sought to explain this high incidence of mental illness amongst Jews by reference to the myth of the Wandering Jew. In his study Miège urged his readers:

> Let us not forget they are Jews, and that it is a characteristic of their race to move with extreme ease. At home nowhere, and at home everywhere, the

Israelites never cease to leave their homes for an important business affair, and particularly if they are ill, to go in search of an effective remedy. Constantly alert for new things, and always quickly informed thanks to their cosmopolitan connections, one sees them coming from all quarters of the earth in order to consult reputable physicians.

(Hasan-Rokem and Dundes 1986 [1893]: 192)

Just as Charcot had interpreted religious painting as evidence for the long history of female hysteria, Miège found the popular imagery of the Wandering Jew to be objective evidence of the long-term existence of the clinical phenomenon of Jewish hysteria. He compared these images, in which the attributes of the Jew were his staff, ragged clothes and lengthy beard, to the physiognomy of his patients. Given these loose parameters, it was not hard for Miège to find parallels, providing that the patients had beards, as any religious Jew does. In other words, Charcot and his colleagues accurately diagnosed that their patients were suffering from being Jewish. As Sander Gilman explains, this was indeed a clinical condition in the late nineteenth and early twentieth century:

> Some views using the model of biological determinism had it that the Jew was at risk simply from inheritance; some views sought after a sociological explanation. But both views, no matter what the etiology, saw a resultant inability of the Jew to deal with the complexities of the modern world, as represented by the Rousseauian city. It is the city . . . which also leads to the pathologization of the psyche. And the source of the madness of the Jews lies in the Jew's sexuality – in the sexual practices of the Jews as well as in the configuration of the Jew's sexual drives. They are as perverse as is the form of his circumcised penis.

(Gilman 1991: 80)

Thus the very outsider quality which made the Wandering Jew a popular hero was the grounds for the medicialization and pathologization of an entire ethnic group. The parallels between such descriptions and the stereotype of blacks in contemporary Western societies are striking. The Jew was characterized as being visibly different from the rest of the population; particular to the city but badly adjusted for life there; hypersexual but ridden with sexually transmitted disease; often homeless; and a disproportionate drag on the health services. This model of the urban outsider, formed between 1885 and 1914 was first applied to Jews and has seemingly been transferred to blacks. The bodies of the Jew and the African alike have been so overwritten by such medicalized discourse as to be invisible in any other way. For according to nineteenth-century race science, the Jews were both literally and metaphorically black. As a race with origins in Africa – the bondage in Egypt – the Jews were an impure race and hence black in comparison to the pure white Aryan. The Jews were also held to be literally black as a side-effect of syphilis, a disease for which Jews were presumed to be the vectors in European society. They therefore suffered from the syphilitic symptom of darkening, that had supposedly affected Jews and Africans alike. In the apogee of such classifications in Nazi Germany, any offspring of mixed race was a *Mischling*, defined as having 'Jewish-Negroid' features (Gilman 1992: 182).

This hatred of miscegenation is at the centre of Western racism and lies at the heart both of Basquiat's difficult search for identity and the strong feelings aroused by his success as an artist. In his 1982 *Self-Portrait as a Heel* Basquiat framed his identity in these terms. The figure is bold, dramatic and outlined in a selfconsciously primitive style. He has given himself a prisoner's number, as if to indicate that any person of colour in the United States is perceived as an actual or potential criminal. Alongside he has portrayed an authentic American icon, the Ace Comb, as if to suggest that it is easier for a product to be American than a dreadlocked young black man. By describing himself as a 'heel', Basquiat used a deliberately anachronistic term, identifying himself with the classic heyday of America in the 1940s and 1950s. In 1983, he made a punning reference to this self-characterization in his *Divine Da Vinci*, which appropriates Leonardo da Vinci's anatomical drawings. At the base of a 'da Vinci' drawing of a leg, Basquiat has inscribed 'Heel' and placed his crown symbol next to the drawn heel. A sombre reading might suggest the black artist trodden underfoot by the European artistic tradition. Alternatively, it could be said that Basquiat was laying claim to that tradition.

However, the critical response to Basquiat's work was dominated not so much by his work as by who he was. The critic Adam Gopnik did not mind the allusions to the Western art tradition, but found his identification with the jazz greats 'unforgivable' (hooks 1992: 74) because Basquiat could not play very well. Ever since its creation, there has been 'a well-documented history of miscegenation in jazz' (Hebdige 1988: 46). Perhaps this miscegenation of styles, which is at the heart of Basquiat's work, is the true source of such anxieties. More worryingly, the characterization of Basquiat often partakes of crude racial stereotypes.[3] Even Andy Warhol constantly referred in his *Diaries* to Basquiat's supposed hypersexuality in a mixture of envy and disgust: 'And now Jean-Michel has this blonde WASP girl that he's fucking. I think he hates all white women' (Warhol 1989: 537). Warhol repeatedly referred to the size of Basquiat's penis and then worried as to whether he would pay the rent on a building he had leased from Warhol. In one revealing anecdote, Warhol writes: 'Jean-Michel is so difficult, you'll never know what kind of a mood he'll be in, what he'll be on. He gets really paranoid and says "You're using me, you're using me", and then he'll get guilty for being paranoid and he'll do everything so nice to try and make up for it' (Warhol 1989: 605). In the space of a few pages, Basquiat is painted as hypersexual, wealthy but mean, and mentally unstable – in short, the classic 'Jewish-Negro'. Basquiat was certainly no saint, but these examples of difficult behaviour sound remarkably typical of a nervous young man in the presence of his established peers. Furthermore, such artistic temperament and personal excess in either alcohol or drugs is practically a prerequisite for success on the art scene and has contributed to the depiction of other artists as heroic outsider figures. Maybe these difficulties were really caused by Basquiat daring to be black, to paint in the heart of whiteness, and to combine these 'pure' categories into a new hybrid?

In the seven years in which he was a professional artist, Jean-Michel Basquiat tried to forge an artistic identity for himself. It was a tripartite process, involving a consideration of what it meant to be in America but not of America; what it meant to be of Haitian and Puerto Rican extraction while growing up in Brooklyn; and finally what it meant to be an artist who was not white. It seems more appropriate to use race in the negative, for exclusion has been among the primary functions of the discursive practice of race in the West. Basquiat tried to imagine a body that was not marked by race, while being constantly reminded of the operations of the racial mark inscribed on his own body by others. Such efforts are central to the contemporary sense that an end to the body as we know it may be at hand. But, as Emily Martin put it, this means 'not the end of the body, but rather the end of one kind of the body and the beginning of another kind of body' (Martin 1992: 123). As Basquiat's work makes clear, a body which is not inscribed by race would also be a body whose identity was not determined by gender, and whose sexuality would be a matter of practice not biological determinism. If these systems of corporal signification are indeed approaching a moment of closure, it is still literally unimaginable what will replace them. The postmodern has created any number of bright new technological dawns, such as virtual reality, cyberspace and the Internet, which have rapidly and without resistance become dedicated to pornography or military applications. In what might be considered a truly postmodern irony, it was Basquiat who came closer with his paints and brushes to presenting a vision of this as yet unpresentable future.

NOTES

1 It might be noted that Basquiat himself always asserted his ignorance of Haitian culture and was much more at ease with his Latino, Puerto Rican side. See Robert Farris Thompson in Marshall, 1992.
2 I am currently working on an extended treatment of the Wandering Jew in nineteenth-century culture.
3 One correspondent to *Art in America* claimed that: 'Collectors and dealers who dealt with [Basquiat] quickly became entangled in a sado-masochistic game, with Jean-Michel in the role of sadist' (*Art in America* [November 1993]: 33). Basquiat's offence appears to have been a desire to promote his work.

EPILOGUE

FROM TERMINATOR TO WITNESS

It should now be clear that the history of the bodyscape is more complex and problematic than any simple evocation of the postmodern transformation of the body might imply. The continuing tenacity of gender and race in marking and defining the body in essentialist terms cannot be denied. Even the refuge in abstraction, which appeared to offer a way out of these dilemmas, has ultimately proved to be a dead end. The squaring of this circle has been the goal of figurative artists since Leonardo's solution in the *Vitruvian Man* with which we began. This book has argued that such tensions are ultimately productive in that they compel a re-examination and reiteration of the human figure. However, in a time in which many of the traditional practices of art have been abandoned, is there any longer a need to draw from the live model, to represent the human body, and to study figurative art whether in traditional form or in new (multi)media? Rather than offer a pat conclusion to what remains an open and developing field of inquiry, I propose to examine whether drawing the body, and observing it in art, can produce anything other than monsters of the imagination, always closely tied to gender and to understanding of the human reproductive system (Huet 1993). As we have seen, this discursive practice can also be extended to the bodyscape. In this epilogue, the drawing of the body is described between two moments: the pregnant moment of Neo-Classicism and the perfect moment of postmodernism. While Neo-Classicism tried to give birth to the ideal form, haunted by the fear of monsters, postmodernism simply aborts its monsters. In order to escape this circle of monsters and the imagination, it will be necessary to make what Walter Benjamin called a 'leap into the open air of history'. Rather than seek a transcendent, eternal body image, we should accept its inevitable incompleteness and testify to our own presence as embodied witnesses.

For the founders of the Royal Academy in eighteenth-century England,

191

there was no doubt that the drawing of the human (read Northern European) body was the pre-eminent task of artists. Joshua Reynolds made it clear to the students of the Academy that drawing the body was not simply a matter of imitating the model to the closest possible extent, but of expressing the ideal potential of that body:

> [The artist's] eye being enabled to distinguish the accidental deficiencies, excrescences, and deformities of things, from their general figures, he makes out an abstract idea of their forms more perfect than any one original; and what may seem a paradox, he learns to design naturally by drawing his figures unlike to any one object.
>
> (Reynolds 1975: 44)

For Reynolds, corporal perfection was a goal that could only be achieved in visual representation. Furthermore, the perfect body could not simply be imagined and then depicted: it must be shown to the greatest possible advantage in the most appropriate setting: 'Perfect beauty in any species must combine all the characters which are beautiful in that species. It cannot consist in any one to the exclusion of the rest: no one, therefore, must be predominant, that no one may be deficient' (Reynolds 1975: 47). In order to fulfill these conditions, artists were enjoined to choose the most dramatic moments from their sources for history paintings, while keeping their dangerous imaginations under control. This moment, which we might call the turning-point, was known to Neo-Classical artists as the 'pregnant moment'. Henry Fuseli explained: 'The power of . . . invention exerts itself chiefly in subjects where the drama, divested of epic or allegoric fiction, meets pure history, and elevates, invigourates, impresses the pregnant moment of a *real* fact, with character and pathos' (Fuseli 1801: 137). The individual body became perfectly expressive in the pregnant moment. Artistic invention had to be restricted to consist 'only in selecting and fixing with dignity, precision, and sentiment, the moment of *reality*' (Fuseli 1801: 142). Any further use of the imagination could lead to that excess which formed monsters. Only a controlled and restrained imagination could successfully achieve 'that union of the two parts of the fact in one moment' (Fuseli 1801: 151), which would engender the ideal form. The Neo-Classical drawing of the body was fraught with danger, sexuality and potential failure, expressed in Goya's famous print *The Sleep of Reason Produces Monsters* (c. 1795). If Reason were to slip for a moment and the dangerous excesses of the imagination allowed free rein, then the cautious construction of a perfect body by the elimination of imperfect detail could break down, releasing the monsters of Unreason.

In recent years, the tension between the perfect and fragmentary body has been expressed in a new form: the fragmentary and transitory glimpse of the perfect body before its inevitable destruction. Slow-motion techniques in television and cinema have allowed audiences to experience the fullness of this perfect moment in far greater detail. The rise of the perfect body/moment has been accompanied by the necessary abortion of the monstrous body, if the pregnant moment should give birth to the monsters of reason. This moment has been especially celebrated in popular cinema. In both *Aliens III* and *Terminator II*, the culminating moments of the films are monstrous abortions. It is significant that both films were sequels, reproductions in themselves. By the final abortive moment, both films sought to deny the possibility of further sequels and thus to claim a terminal originality. *Aliens III* brought the highly successful trilogy of *Alien* films to a close with the final suicide of Ripley, played by Sigourney Weaver. As she leaps into the fire, the alien foetus she has been carrying emerges from her stomach and Ripley's dying act is to clutch her 'child' in her arms, ensuring both its death and the elimination of the species. Ripley's character evolved from the avenging Madonna of the first two films to the penitent Magdelen of the third, symbolized by her brief sexual liaison with the prison doctor and her shaven head. Just as Mary Magdelen suffered for her sins, so was Ripley punished for her sexuality with the monstrous pregnancy of the alien. By her death, normality is restored. The confusing corporal world of the first two films, in which humans may be androids or the cocoon for an alien species, is returned to established (gendered) order within the most Foucauldian of settings – the prison. The docile body produced by the society of control is reasserted and revived but in the briefest possible moment, that between Ripley's leap and her death, albeit slowed down for our appreciation.

Arnold Schwarzenegger's wildly successful character, the Terminator, met an almost identical fate in *Terminator II*. Sent to prevent the birth of the future rebel leader John Connor in the first film, in the sequel the Terminator has again been sent back from the future, but this time by the good guys in order to protect the teenage Connor from an advanced model Terminator. The ruthless killing machine of the first film has become transformed in the second into the best father a boy never had. Schwarzenegger's Terminator triumphs over the advanced model in the most Romantic of fashions, demonstrating once again that true grit and (American) character will be victorious over mere technological supremacy. This was, of course, also the message of Sylvester Stallone's *Rocky* movies, but the Terminator added a new twist. Having destroyed the opposition, the Terminator realizes that he himself must be destroyed in order to complete his mission. As his programming will not permit him to destroy himself, Sarah Connor, John's mother, activates the machinery that slowly lowers the Terminator into molten iron. Given that the film notionally takes place before the Terminator was 'activated', she in effect aborts him. In this moment of selfless abnegation, the Terminator achieves a brief perfection, drawn out by the slow operation of the pulleys, before his inevitable death. With the monster aborted, the unusual coalition of an African-American, a woman, a child and a machine, that sought to make the creation of the Terminators impossible, has been quickly reduced to the stable grouping of mother and child, a renewed Madonna.

Of course, we have learnt to be suspicious of such over-neat moments of closure. These films attest to the bodily dis-ease that permeates contemporary mainstream Western culture, aware that the perfect (straight, white) body is a fiction, but not yet ready to recognize the 'monstrous' births which have put an end to that fiction. It is a striking feature of contemporary culture that as unease over the body grows, so the moment in which it can be shown has shortened. Just as the perfect moment in film can only be realized in slow-motion, so too every moment of importance from the result of a political election to the conclusion of a sports tournament is now displayed in slow motion. By constantly deferring viewing pleasure to these heightened slow-motion clips, contemporary film and television hold out the always disappointed hope of the perfect moment being realized and the perfect body being found. In the United States, this process has become so accelerated that the moment of heroization and demonization are all but co-existent. In a matter of a few weeks, it was possible to buy magazines featuring Hillary Clinton's face montaged onto both the bodies of a dominatrix and of an angel. President Clinton himself has been more widely physically derided – for his thighs, his taste for junk food, his alleged sexual liaisons – than any previous politician, but at the same time polls consistently report very high expectations of the administration. The disappointment of those expectations is played out in abusing the president's body in ways that recall the latter days of the *ancien régime* French monarchy. Whatever the outcome, the body politic is currently dead in the water.

Within the world of the visual arts, 'The Perfect Moment' was the title of the enormously controversial Robert Mapplethorpe exhibition in 1988–9. In the catalogue – printed before the furore broke – curator Janet Kardon explained the logic of the title: 'Mapplethorpe captures the peak of bloom, the apogee of power, the most seductive instant, the ultimate present that stops time and delivers the perfect moment into history' (Kardon 1988:

13). Her essay constantly evokes the heritage of Classical antiquity as the true parallel for Mapplethorpes perfection. Indeed, Mapplethorpe clearly claimed the status of canonical High Art for his work. In his photograph *Thomas in a Circle* (1988), the model Thomas fits his body into a circle in a direct evocation of Leonardo's *Vitruvian Man*. Unlike Leonardo's anonymous figure, with its vague analogy to Jesus, Mapplethorpe depicted a known, African-American man as the Ideal. By posing this challenge to Classical perfection, Mapplethorpe reclaimed the male nude as overtly homoerotic and defied the Western convention that whiteness represents perfection. It was a witty, skillful and brilliantly executed riposte to those same narrow definitions of elite culture that Jean-Michel Basquiat had sought to defy. Mapplethorpe claimed perfection for the African-American gay man and in so doing sought to reverse two centuries of pathologization:

> Perfection means you don't question anything about the photograph. There are certain pictures I've taken in which you really can't move that leaf or that hand. It's where it should be, and you can't say it could have been there. There's nothing to question, as in a great painting. I often have trouble with contemporary art because I find it's not perfect. It doesn't have to be anatomically correct to be perfect either. A Picasso portrait is perfect. It's just not questionable.
>
> (Kardon 1988: 28)

The work was claimed as integrally perfect regardless of its subject-matter, a union of form and moment.

For Mapplethorpe's critics, of course, all that mattered was the identity of the photographer and the content of the small portfolios depicting subjects from the New York gay S/M scene. The idea of a gay photographer was monstrous enough, without that sexuality being the subject of his work, let alone that it should be endorsed by the state. Artist and board member of the National Endowment for the Arts Helen Frankenthaler worried in the *New York Times*, might the United States be 'now beginning to spawn an art monster? Did we lose art along the way, in the guise of encouraging experimentation?' (Bolton 1992: 64). At the obscenity trial provoked by opponents of the exhibition at the Contemporary Arts Center in Cincinnati, a bastion of fundamentalist Christianity, defence witnesses evoked the formal standards of art history against the charge of monstrosity. One critic examined Mapplethorpe's self-portrait, in which the photographer is seen with a bullwhip in his rectum, and demonstrated that it evoked the Classical rule of the Golden Mean. Some later objected that this defence obscured the overt subject matter of the photographs, as if embarrassed by it, but by treating the subject as incidental and insisting on the high formal art quality of his work, the defence were working in a manner much closer to that of Mapplethorpe himself.

At the same time, another critique of Mapplethorpe's work was gaining wide currency in critical circles. In this view, Mapplethorpe used his privilege as a white male to depict African-American men as the epitome of (gay) sexuality, reinforcing stereotypes about both Africans and gay men as being wholly constituted by their monstrous sexual appetites. Amongst the most vocal of these critics was Kobena Mercer, who dismissed Mapplethorpe's work as playing to the worst clichés regarding black sexuality: 'It is as if, according to Mapplethorpe's line of sight, Black + Male = Aesthetic/Erotic object' (Mercer 1993: 310). He later changed his position in the light of Mapplethorpe's condition as a person with AIDS and the transformation of gay culture as a result of the epidemic. Mercer now accepted Mapplethorpe's claim in a late interview that he had in fact been the perfect witness for the gay S/M scene as he was a participant on that scene and not an anonymous observer:

> It was a certain moment and I was in a perfect situation in that most of the people in the photographs were friends of mine and they trusted me. I felt almost an obligation to record those things. It was an obligation for me to do it, to make images that nobody's seen before and to do it in a way that's *aesthetic*.
>
> (Mercer 1993: 322)

There are some important consequences to be drawn from this change in attitude manifested both by Mapplethorpe and his critics. First, the embodiment of the artist is again central to our understanding of the body in visual culture. This is not to say that the physical condition of an individual dictates or limits the corporal representations he or she may make, but that the corporal sign cannot be considered wholly independent of the body which fashions it. The bodyscape does not have a virgin birth but exists in a mediated exchange between the body of the artist, that of the model, and that of the viewer. On occasion, it is the artist's own body that is depicted, as in the work of Cindy Sherman and Jean-Michel Basquiat. At other times, a person depicted by another confronts their own image, as when Louis XIV regarded his own portrait. Again, an artist may construct a work with the viewing public incorporated into the signifying system of that work, such as David's statue of Hercules or Maya Lin's Vietnam Veterans Memorial. The point is that the body in visual culture cannot be wholly perfect, nor entirely fragmented, but is always being renewed and reproduced in an exchange between the sign, the body of the viewer and the body of the artist. If there is now a crisis in the representation of the body, it is because modernism sought to deny and overcome the instability and reiteration of that exchange.

But that exchange ends in each individual case with death. Mapplethorpe's death has been taken as a validation of his controversial photographs of gay men. But rather than revive the Romantic preoccupation with the mortality of the young artist, it seems to me that AIDS should cause us to reject the over-formalized theory that has emerged from the Anglo-American academy in recent years. The hegemony of literary criticism in the humanities, which is now coming to an end, encouraged a formal 'close' reading of individual texts in which the skill of the critic lay in determining the perfect moment for the application of theory. Just as the perfect moment has become ever shorter, the time available for such comforting scholasticism is drawing to a close. The connections between our analytic tools and the material we choose to work upon are never given in advance, but are determined by the exigencies of the present. AIDS demands a response from artists, academics and individuals of all sorts. The purity offered by Leonardo's *Vitruvian Man* cannot be sustained in the face of a messy retrovirus, whose mutations and replications defy the neat schemes of binary categorizations.

Here Mapplethorpe's comment on his photography of the New York gay scene is again important, for he attested to a sense of obligation in this work, a need to testify that I want to call witnessing. Witnessing involves physical participation in an event or moment and the later testimony of what occurred. It is the opposite of the modernist terminology for viewing, whether defined as spectatorship, observing or the pursuit of opticality. This mode of seeing was first defined by Baudelaire's nineteenth-century dandy, who wished to see without being seen, the classic fantasy of the voyeur. Later the pursuit of perfection in abstraction, as exemplified by the work of Frank Stella, was hailed as offering modern opticality in the pure state. In each case a flight from the body was paramount. Seeing became dissociated from the body to such an extent that blindness could be considered a technical term that had no reference to blind people. Witnessing puts the bodies back into art. It does not mean that only figurative art is important, but that the contingency and indeterminacy of the witness's body is an integral part of the way that the artwork itself signifies.

Let me illustrate what I mean with reference to the testimony of one survivor of the Nazi Holocaust, recorded in the Video Archive for Holocaust Testimonies at Yale University. Analyst Dori Laub, the interviewer for this testimony recalls the scene: 'She was relating her memories as an eyewitness of the Auschwitz uprising; a sudden intensity, passion and colour were infused into the narrative. She was fully there. "All of a sudden", she said, "we saw four chimneys going up in flames, exploding. The flames shot into the sky, people were running. It was unbelievable"' (Felman and Laub 1992: 59). The vividness of this memory seems to put hope and defiance back into the most hopeless situation imaginable. Yet there is a problem with this testimony, for as a point of fact only one tower was destroyed in what turned out to be a wholly failed uprising, due to the lack of promised support from the Polish resistance. From the historian's point of view, the Auschwitz Uprising tells us more about Polish anti-semitism and the difficulties of resistance than the optimism recorded by the survivor. Laub's rejoinder to this point of view incarnates what I mean by the power of witnessing:

> The woman was testifying not to the numbers of chimneys blown up, but to something else, more radical, more crucial: the reality of an unimaginable occurrence. One chimney blown up in Auschwitz was as incredible as four. The number mattered less than the fact of the occurrence. The event itself was almost inconceivable. The woman testified to an event that broke the all-compelling frame of Auschwitz, where Jewish armed revolts just did not happen, and had no place. She testified to the breakage of a framework. That was historical truth.
>
> (Felman and Laub 1992: 60)

The truth related by the survivor of Auschwitz is that to which art aspires. Art exists in that space between the memory of the witness and those documentary facts that the historian accepts as 'objective'. It seeks to explore and make visible that indefinable perfect moment, knowable only from instant to instant, in which a person becomes a witness. The choice of Auschwitz as a location for witnessing is not coincidental. The experiences of the late twentieth century make the impartial, rarified distance of the modern observer or spectator an untenable position. There is no optical neutrality to be had from art, and if there were, it would no longer have anything to offer. The modern spectator must give way the postmodern witness. Welcome to the stand.

BIBLIOGRAPHY

Adam, Peter (1992), *Art of the Third Reich*, New York, Abrams.

Adler, Kathleen and Pointon, Marcia (1993), *The Body Imaged: The Human Form and Visual Culture Since the Renaissance*, Cambridge, Cambridge University Press.

Agulhon, Maurice (1979), *Marianne au Combat, l'imagerie et la symbolique républicaines de 1789 à 1880*, Paris, Flammarion.

Alloula, Malek (1992), *The Colonial Harem*, trans. Myrna Godzich and Wlad Godzich, Minneapolis, University of Minnesota Press.

Anderson, Benedict (1983), *Imagined Communities: Reflections on the Origin and Spread of Nationalism*, London, Verso.

Annuaire (1913), *Annuaire du Congo Belge et l'Afrique Occidentale*, Brussels.

Apter, Emily (1991), *Feminizing the Fetish: Psychoanalysis and Narrative Obsession in Turn-of-the-Century France*, Ithaca and London, Cornell University Press.

Araeen, Rasheed (1989), *The Other Story: Afro-Asian Artists in Post-war Britain*, London, Hayward Gallery.

Arnold, Thomas (1894), *The Language of the Senses with Special Reference to the Education of Deaf, Blind, Deaf & Blind*, Margate, England, Keble's Gazette.

Barthes, Roland (1972), *Mythologies*, New York, Hill & Wang.

Baudelaire, Charles (1990), *Curiosités esthéthiques*, Paris, Garnier.

Behad, Ali (1989), 'The Eroticised Orient: Images of the Harem in Montesquieu and His Precursors', *Stanford French Review* 13, 2–3 (Fall).

Bell, Henry (1728) *An Historical Essay on the Original of Painting*, London: J. Worrall.

Benjamin, Walter (1968), *Illuminations*, New York, Schocken.

Berger, John (1972), *Ways of Seeing*, Harmondsworth, Penguin Books.

Berger, Maurice (1989), *Labyrinths: Robert Morris, Minimalism, and the 1960s*, New York, Harper & Row.

Bermingham, Ann (1992), 'The Origin of Painting and the Ends of Art: Wright of Derby's *Corinthian Maid*', in John Barrell (ed.), *Painting and the Politics of Culture: New Essays on British Art 1700–1850*, Oxford, Clarendon Press.

Bernal, Martin (1987), *Black Athena: The Afro-Asiatic Roots of Classical Civilization*, Brunswick NJ, Rutgers University Press.

———— (1991), *Black Athena: The Archaeological and Documentary Evidence*, New Brunswick NJ, Rutgers University Press.

Bhabha, Homi (1987), 'Of Mimicry and Man: The Ambivalence of Colonial Discourse', in Annette Michelson *et al.* (eds), *October: The First Decade*, Cambridge MA, MIT Press.

Bianchi, Serge (1982), *La Révolution culturelle de l'an II: Elites et peuple 1789–1799*, Paris, Aubier.

Boime, Albert (1987), *Art in an Age of Revolution (1750–1800)*, Chicago, Chicago University Press.

———— (1990), *The Art of Exclusion: Representing Blacks in the Nineteenth Century*, Washington, DC, Smithsonian.

Bolton, Richard (1992), *Culture Wars: Documents from the Recent Controversies in the Arts*, New York, New Press.

Bourdon, Sébastien (1740), 'Seventh Conference', in [Anon] 1740, *Seven Conferences Held in the King of France's Cabinet of Paintings*, London, T. Cooper.

Broca, Paul (1868), 'Transactions of the Anthropological Society of Paris during 1865–67', *Anthropological Review* 22 (1868).

Brown, Marilyn R. (1987), 'The Harem DeHistoricized: Ingres' *Turkish Bath*', *Arts Magazine* (Summer): 58–65.

Brown, Peter (1988), *The Body and Society: Men, Women, and Sexual Renunciation in Early Christianity*, New York, Columbia University Press.

Bryson, Norman (1984), *Tradition and Desire: From David to Delacroix*, Cambridge, Cambridge University Press.

Burke, Peter (1992), *The Fabrication of Louis XIV*, New Haven, Yale University Press.

Butler, Judith (1990), *Gender Trouble: Feminism and the Subversion of Identity*, New York, Routledge.

Callen, Anthea (1989), 'Anatomy and Physiognomy: Degas' *Little Dancer of Fourteen Years*', in Richard Kendall (ed.), *Degas' Images of Women*, Liverpool, Tate Gallery.

———— (1992), 'Degas' *Bathers*: Hygiene and Dirt – Gaze and Touch', in Richard Kendall and Griselda Pollock (eds), *Dealing with Degas*, New York, Universe.

Canguilhem, Georges (1991 [1966]), *The Normal and the Pathological*, trans. Caroyn R. Fawcett, New York, Zone.

Chambers, Ross (1988), 'Poetry in the Asiatic Mode: Baudelaire's "Au Lecteur"', *Yale French Studies* 74 : 97–116.

Champfleury (1869), *Histoire de l'imagérie populaire*, Paris, E. Dentu.

Chow, Rey (1993), *Writing Diaspora: Tactics of Intervention in Contemporary Cultural Studies*, Bloomington, Indiana University Press.

Clark, T.J. (1973), *The Image of the People*, London, Thames & Hudson.

———— (1985), *The Painting of Modern Life: Paris in the Art of Manet and his followers*, Princeton, Princeton University Press.

Condillac, Etienne Bonnot de (1754), *Traité des Sensations*, Paris.

Cone, Michèle C. (1992), *Artists Under Vichy: A Case of Prejudice and Persecution*, Princeton, Princeton University Press.

Conrad, Joseph (1969), *Heart of Darkness*, in *The Portable Conrad*, London, Penguin.

Corbin, Alain (1987), 'Commercial Sexuality in Nineteenth Century France: A System of Images and Regulations', in Christine Gallagher and Thomas Laqueur (eds), *The Making of the Modern Body: Sexuality and Society in the Nineteenth Century*, Berkeley, University Of California Press.

———— (1991), *Le Temps, le Désir et l'Horreur*, Paris, Garnier.

———— Couètoux, L. and Hamon de Fougeray (1886), *Manuel pratique des méthodes d'enseignement spéciales aux enfants anormaux (sourds-muets, aveugles, idiots, bègues etc.)*, Paris, Félix Alcan.

Crew, Spencer R. and Sims, James E. (1991), 'Locating Authority', in Ivan Karp and Steven D. Lavine (eds), *Exhibiting Cultures: The Poetics and Politics of Museum Display*, Washington DC, Smithsonian Institution Press, 159–75.

Crow, Thomas E. (1985), *Painters and Public Life in Eighteenth Century Paris*, New Haven, Yale University Press.

D..D..(1725), *Histoire de la peinture anciene par Pline*, London, William Bowyer.

Dagognet, François (1992), *Le Corps multiple et un*, Paris, Les Empêcheurs de Penser en Rond.

Dandrée, Eugène (1806), *Lettres sur le Salon de 1806*, Paris, Brasseur.

Darnton, Robert (1982), *Literary Underground of the Old Regime*, Cambridge MA, Harvard University Press.

Daston, Lorraine and Galison, Peter (1992), 'The Image of Objectivity', *Representations* 40 (Fall): 81–128.

David, Jacques-Louis (An IIa), *Discours prononcé à la Convention Nationale. En lui offrant le tableau représentant Marat assassiné*, Paris, Convention Nationale.

———— (An IIb), *Rapport fait à la Convention Nationale, 27 brumaire an II*, Paris, Convention Nationale.

———— (An IIc), *Rapport sur la fête héroïque pour les honneurs du Panthéon à décerner aux jeunes Barra et Viala*, Paris, Convention Nationale.

De Baeque, Antoine (1989), 'L'Homme nouveau est arrivé: la "régénération du Français"', *XVIIIème Siècle* 20: 193–208.

Deleuze, Gilles (1992), 'Postscript on the Societies of Control', *October* 59 (Winter): 1–8.

De Man, Paul (1983), *Blindness and Insight*, Minneapolis, University of Minnesota Press.

Denis, Théophile (1895), 'Les Artistes sourds-muets au Salon de 1886', in *Etudes variées concernant les sourds-muets. Histoire – Biographie – Beaux-arts*, Paris, Imprimérie de la Revue Française de l'Enseignement des Sourds-muets.

Derrida, Jacques (1993), *Memoirs of the Blind: The Self-Portrait and Other Ruins*, trans. Pascale-Anne Brault and Michael Naas, Chicago, Chicago University Press.

Dickerson, Mary Cynthia (1910), 'In The Heart of Africa', *American Museum Journal* x: 147–68.

Diderot, Denis (1975–), *Œuvres complètes*, 25 vols, Paris, Hermann.

Doane, Mary Ann (1987), *The Desire to Desire: The Woman's Film of the 1940s*, Bloomington, Indiana University Press.

Dryden, John (1695), *De Arte Graphica: The Art of Painting by C.A. du Fresnoy*, London, J. Hcpinstall.

Dubos, Abbé (1748), *Critical Reflexions on Poetry, Painting and Music*, trans. Thomas Nugent, London, J. Nourse.

Elias, Norbert (1978), *The History of Manners: The Civilizing Process*, vol. 1, New York, Pantheon.

———— (1974), *La Société de Cour*, Paris, Flammarion.

Fabian, Johannes (1983), *Time and the Other: How Anthropology Makes Its Object*, New York, Columbia University Press.

Félibien, André (1671), *Le Portrait du Roy*, Paris.

Felman, Shoshana and Laub, Dori (1992), *Testimony: Crises of Witnessing in Literature, Psychoanalysis, and History*, New York, Routledge.

Foster, Hal (ed.) (1987), *Discussions in Contemporary Culture*, Seattle, Bay Press.

———— (1991), 'Armor Fou', *October* 56: 65–98.

Foucault, Michel (1970), *The Order of Things: An Archaeology of the Human Sciences*, New York, Pantheon.

———— (1977), *Discipline and Punish: The Birth of the Prison*, Harmondsworth, Penguin.

———— (1981), *A History of Sexuality*, vol. 1, *An Introduction*, trans. Robert Hurley, Harmondsworth, Penguin.

———— (1983), 'The Subject and Power', in Hubert L. Dreyfus and Paul Rabinow, *Michel Foucault: Beyond Structuralism and Hermeneutics*, Chicago, Chicago University Press.

Fried, Michael (1983), *Absorption and Theatricality*, Chicago, Chicago University Press.

Freud, Sigmund (1946), 'The Uncanny', in *Collected Papers*, vol. 4, London, Hogarth Press.

———— (1959), 'Fetishism', in vol. 5 of *The Standard Edition of the Complete Psychological Works of Sigmund Freud*, trans. James Strachey, New York, Basic Books.

———— (1960), *Beyond the Pleasure Principle*, New York, W.W. Norton.

———— (1961), *Civilization and Its Discontents*, New York, W.W. Norton.

———— (1975), 'Family Romances', in vol. 9 of *The Standard Edition of the Complete Psychological Works of Sigmund Freud*, trans. James Strachey, London, Hogarth Press.

Fry, Edward F. (1986), with Donald P. Kuspit, *Robert Morris: Works of the Eighties*, Chicago, Museum of Contemporary Art.

Fuller, Peter (1988a), *Art and Psychoanalysis*, London, Hogarth Press.

———— (1988b), *Theoria*, London, Chatto & Windus.

Fuseli, Henry (1801), *Lectures on Painting Delivered at the Royal Academy March 1801*, London, J. Johnson.

Gablik, Suzi (1984), *Has Modernism Failed?*, London, Thames & Hudson.

Gates, Henry Louis (1985), 'Writing "race" and the Difference It Makes', in *'Race,' Writing and Difference*, Chicago, University of Chicago Press.

Gautier, Théophile (1856), 'Du Beau dans l'Art' in *L'Art moderne*, Paris, Michel Levy.

Geary, Christraud (1988), *Images of Bamum: German Colonial Photography at the Court of King Nyoja, Cameroon, West Africa 1902–1915*, Washington DC, Smithsonian Institution.

Gernsheim, Helmut (1975), *Julia Margaret Cameron: Her Life and Photographic Work*, New York, Aperture.

Gilman, Sander (1985), 'Black Bodies, White Bodies: Toward an Iconography of Female Sexuality in Late Nineteenth-Century Art, Medicine, and Literature', in Gates (1985), 223–61.

———— (1991), *The Jew's Body*, New York, Routledge.

———— (1992), 'Plague in Germany 1939/89: Cultural Images of Race, Space, and Disease', in Andrew Parker *et al.* (eds), *Nationalisms and Sexualities*, New York, Routledge.

Gilroy, Paul (1993), *The Black Atlantic: Modernity and Double Consciousness*, Cambridge MA, Harvard University Press.

Goldstein, Jan (1985), 'The Wandering Jew and the Problem of Psychiatric Anti-semitism in Fin-de-siècle France', *Journal of Contemporary History*, 20, 521–52.

———— (1991), 'The Uses of Male Hysteria: Medical and Literary Discourse in Nineteenth-Century France', *Representations* 34 (Spring): 134–65.

Gould, Stephen Jay (1981), *The Mismeasure of Man*, New York, Norton.

Grosz, Elizabeth (1992), 'Bodies-Cities', in Beatriz Colomina (ed.), *Sexuality and Space*, New York, Princeton Architectural Press, 241–54.

Guest, Harriet (1992) in John Barrell (ed.), *Painting and the Politics of Culture: New Essays on British Art 1700–1850*, Oxford, Clarendon Press.

Hall, Stuart (1991), 'Cultural Studies and Its Legacies', in Lawrence Grossberg *et al.*, *Cultural Studies*, New York, Routledge.

Hasan-Rokem, Galit and Dundes, Alan (1986), *The Wandering Jew: Essays in the Interpretation of a Christian Legend*, Bloomington, Indiana University Press.

Haworth-Booth, Mark (1987), *Paul Strand*, New York, Aperture.

Hebdidge, Dick (1988), *Subculture: the Meaning of Style*, London, Routledge.

hooks, bell (1991): 'States of Desire: bell hooks and British Filmmaker Isaac Julien on sex, style, and cinema', *Transition: An International Review* 53: 168–84.

———— (1992), *Black Looks: Race and Representation*, Boston, South End Press.

———— (1993), 'Altars of Sacrifice: Re-membering Basquiat', *Art in America* (June): 68–75, 117.

Horkheimer, Max and Adorno, Theodore (1972), *Dialectic of Enlightenment*, New York, Continuum.

Huet, Marie-Hélène (1993), *Monstrous Imagination*, Cambridge MA, Harvard University Press.

———— (1994), 'The Revolutionary Sublime', *Eighteenth Century Studies* 21: 51–64.

Hunt, Lynn (ed.) (1984), *Politics, Culture, and Class in the French Revolution*, Berkeley, University of California Press.

———— (1991), *Eroticism and the Body Politic*, Baltimore, Johns Hopkins University Press.

———— (1992), *The Family Romance of the French Revolution*, Berkeley, University of California Press.

Image World (1990), Marvin Heifferman and Lisa Phillips, *Image World: Art and Media Culture*, New York, Whitney Museum of Art.

Ingres, J.A.D. (1947), *Ecrits sur l'art*, Paris, La Jeune Parque.

Johnson, Dorothy (1989), 'Corporality and Communication: The Gestural Revolution of Diderot, David, and the "Oath of the Horatii"', *Art Bulletin*, lxxi (March): 92–116.

Jones, Edgar Yoxall (1973), *Father of Art Photography O.G. Rejlander 1813–1875*, Greenwich CT, New York Graphic Society.

Josephs, Herbert (1969), *Diderot's Dialogue of Language and Gesture: Le Neveu de Rameau*, Columbus, Ohio State University Press.

Kantorowicz, Ernst (1953), *The King's Two Bodies*, Princeton NJ, Princeton University Press.

Kardon, Janet (1988), *Robert Mapplethorpe: The Perfect Moment*, Philadelphia, Institute of Contemporary Art.

Kasher, Steven (1992), 'The Art of Hitler', *October* 59 (Winter): 49–86.

Kevles, Daniel J. (1985), *In the Name of Eugenics: Genetics and the Uses of Human Heredity*, Berkeley, University of California.

Lacoue-Labarthe, Phillipe (1989), *Typography*, Cambridge MA, Harvard University Press.

Lamoignon de Basville, N. (1678), *Plaidoie pour le Sr Girard Vanopstal*, Paris.

Lang, Herbert (1911), 'Report from the Congo Expedition', *American Museum Journal* xi (1) (January).

———— (1915), 'An Explorer's View of the Congo', *American Museum Journal* xv (December): 379–400.

———— (1919), 'Nomad Dwarfs and Civilization', *Natural History* xix (6) (December).

Laqueur, Thomas (1990), *Making Sex: Body and Gender from the Greeks to Freud*, Cambridge MA, Harvard University Press.

Lawrence, Henry (1649), *An History of angells*, London, William Nealand.

Leeks, Wendy (1986), 'Ingres Other-wise', *Oxford Art Journal* 9: 1: 29–37.

Leonardo da Vinci (1956), *Treatise on Painting*, vol. 1, trans. Philip McMahon, Princeton, Princeton University Press.

Lever, Maurice (1993), *Sade: A Biography*, New York, Farrar, Strauss & Giroux.

Lippard, Lucy R. (1990), *Mixed Blessings: New Art in a Multi-Cultural America*, New York, Pantheon.

Lloyd, Albert (1899), *In Dwarf Land and Cannibal Country*, London.

Long, Edward (1774), *The History of Jamaica, or General Survey of the Antient and Modern State of that Island*, 3 vols, London, T. Lowndes.

La Lumière (1858), vol. 8: 25 (19 June).

Lowe, Lisa (1991), *Critical Terrains: French and British Orientalisms*, Ithaca and London, Cornell University Press.

Marin, Louis (1988), *The Portrait of the King*, Minneapolis, University of Minnesota Press.

Marivaux, Pierre Carlet de Chamblain de (1969), *Journaux et œuvres diverses*, ed. Frédéric Deloffre and Michel Gelot, Paris, Garnier.

Marshall, Richard (ed.) (1992), *Jean-Michel Basquiat*, New York, Whitney Museum of American Art.

Martin, Emily (1992), 'The End of the Body?', *American Ethnologist* 19: 1 (February) : 121–40.

Mather, Increase (1696a), *Angelographia, or a Discourse concerning the Nature and Power of the Holy Angels*, Boston, Samuel Phillips.

———— (1696b), *A Disquisition Concerning Angelical Apparitions*, Boston, Samuel Phillips.

Mecklenburg, Adolf Friedrich, duke of (1910), *In the Heart of Africa*, trans. G. E. Maberly-Oppler, London, Cassell.

Mehlman, Jeffrey (1979), *Cataract: A Study in Diderot*, Middletown CT: Wesleyan University Press.

Mercer, Kobena (1993), 'Reading Racial Fetishism: The Photographs of Robert Mapplethorpe', in Emily Apter and William Peitz (eds), *Fetishism as Cultural Discourse*, Ithaca and London, Cornell University Press, 307–30.

Mernissi, Fatima (1975), *Beyond the Veil: Male–Female Dynamics in a Modern Muslim Society*, New York, Schenkman.

Meysonnier, Lazare (1669), *La Belle Magie*, Lyons.

Miller, Christopher (1985), *Blank Darkness: Africanist Discourse in French*, Chicago, Chicago University Press.

Montagu, Lady Mary Wortley (1971), *Letters from the Levant during the Embassy to Constantinople* (New York, Arno Press & New York Times.

Morel, Edmund D. (1968), *History of the Congo Reform Movement*, ed. Roger Louis and Jean Stengers, Oxford: Oxford University Press.

Nancy, Jean-Luc (1992), *Corpus*, Paris, Fayard.

Nead, Lynda (1988) *Myths of Sexuality: Representations of Women in Victorian Britain*, Oxford, Blackwell.

———— (1992) *The Female Nude: Art, Obscenity and Sexuality*, London, Routledge.

Nesbit, Molly (1992), *Atget's Seven Albums*, New Haven, Yale University Press.

Observations (An II), (Anon) *Observations pour les aveugles de l'Hôpital des Quinze-Vingts sur le projet de décret du comité de secours de la Convention Nationale pour la suppression de cet hôpital*, Paris, J. Grand.

Olander, William (1989), 'French Politics and Painting in 1794: The Great *Concours de l'an II*', in Alan Wintermute (ed.), *1789: French Art During the Revolution*, New York, Colnaghi.

Osborn, Henry (1910), *American Museum Journal* x.

———— (1913) *American Museum Journal* xiii (4) (April).

Outram, Dorinda (1989), *The Body and the French Revolution*, New Haven, Yale University Press.

Ozouf, Mona (1988), 'La Révolution Française et l'idée de l'homme nouveau', in Colin Lucas (ed.), *The Political Culture of the French Revolution*, vol. 2 of *The French Revolution and the Creation of Modern Political Culture*, Oxford, Pergamon.

———— (1989), 'Regeneration', in François Furet and Mona Ozouf (eds), *A Critical Dictionary of the French Revolution*, trans. Arthur Goldhammer, Cambridge MA, Belknap Press.

Paulson, William R. (1987), *Enlightenment, Romanticism and the Blind in France*, Princeton, Princeton University Press.

Pearson, Karl (1909), 'Introduction', in *The Treasury of Human Intelligence*, London, Dulan.

Pellegrin, Nicole (1991), 'L'Uniforme de la Santé: les médécins et la réforme du costume', *XVIIIème Siècle* 23.

Perry, Walter Copland (1882), *Greek and Roman Sculpture*, London, Longman.

Pointon, Marcia (1990), *Naked Authority: The Body in Western Art 1830–1908*, Cambridge, Cambridge University Press.

Pollock, Griselda (1992), *Avant-Garde Gambits 1888–1893: Gender and the Colour of Art History*, London, Thames & Hudson.

Pratt, Mary-Louise (1992), *Imperial Eyes: Travel Writing and Transculturation*, London, Routledge.

Quatremère de Quincy (1815), *Considérations morales sur la destination des ouvrages de l'art*, Paris.

———— (1825), 'De l'Emploi des sujets d'histoire moderne dans la poésie et leur abus dans la peinture', in *Receuil des discours prononcés sur la séance publique de l'Institut Royal de la France*, Paris.

Rey, Roselyne (1993), 'Hygiène et souci de soi dans la pensée des lumières', *Communications* 56, 24–33.

Reynolds, Joshua (1975), *Discourses on Art*, introduction by Robert R. Wark, New Haven, Yale University Press.

Rifkin, Adrian (1983), 'Ingres and the Academic Dictionary: An Essay on Ideology and the Social Stupefaction of the "Artist"', *Art History* 6: 2 (June).

Roby, Marguerite (1911), *My Adventures in the Congo*, London, Edward Arnold.

Rosen, Charles and Zerner, Henri (1984), *Romanticism and Realism: The Mythology of Nineteenth Century Art*, London, Faber & Faber.

Rosenblum, Robert (1967a), *Transformations in Late Eighteenth Century Art*, Princeton, Princeton University Press.

——— (1967b), *Ingres*, New York, Abrams.

Rosenthal, Donald A. (1982), *Orientalism: The Near East in French Painting 1800–1880*, Rochester NY, Memorial Art Gallery.

Ross, Andrew (1989), *No Respect: Intellectuals and Popular Culture*, New York, Routledge.

Rousseau, Jean-Jacques (1779), *Pygmalion*, London, J. Kearby.

Said, Edward (1993), *Culture and Imperialism*, New York, Alfred A. Knopf.

Schildkrout, Enid (1991) 'The Spectacle of Africa Through the Lens of Herbert Lang: Belgian Congo Photographs 1909–15', *African Arts* xxiv: 4.

Schildkrout, Enid and Keim, Curtis A. (1990), *African Reflections: Art from Northeastern Zaire*, New York, American Museum of Natural History.

Schnapper, Antoine (1989), *David*, Paris, Editions des Réunions des Musées Nationaux.

Schweinfurth, Georg (1874), *In the Heart of Africa*, London, S. Low, Marston, Low & Searle.

Shilling, Chris (1993), *The Body and Social Theory*, London, Sage.

Slivka, Rose C.S. (1989), 'Willem de Kooning', *Art Journal*, 48: 3 (Fall): 219–22.

Solomon-Godeau, Abigail (1991), *Photography at the Dock*, Minneapolis, Minnesota University Press.

Spinden, Herbert R. (1919), 'Creating a National Art', *Natural History* xix (6) (December).

Steadman Jones, Gareth (1971), *Outcast London: A Study of the Relationships between Classes in Victorian Society*, Harmondsworth, Penguin.

Stepan, Nancy Leys (1986), 'Race and Gender: The Role of Analogy in Science', *Isis* 77: 261–77.

The Stereoscopic Magazine: A Gallery of Landscape Scenery, Architecture, Antiquities and Natural History, vol. 1, London, Lovell Reeve, 1858.

Stocking, George W. (1987), *Victorian Anthropology*, New York, Free Press.

Sturken, Marita (1991), 'The Wall, the Screen, and the Image: The Vietnam Veterans Memorial', *Representations* 35 (Summer): 118–42.

Taussig, Michael (1986), *Shamanism, Colonialism, and the Wild Man: A Study in Terror and Healing*, Chicago, University of Chicago Press.

——— (1993a), *Mimesis and Alterity: A Particular History of the Senses*, New York, Routledge.

———— (1993b), 'Maleficium: State Fetishism', in Emily Apter and William Pietz (eds), Fetishism as Cultural Discourse, Ithaca and London, Cornell University Press, 217–47.

Trabue, M.R. (1919), 'The Intelligence of Negro Recruits', Natural History xix (6) (December).

Trumbach, Randolph (1991), 'London's Sapphists: From Three Sexes to Four Genders in the Making of Modern Culture', in Julia Epstein and Kristina Straub (eds), Body Guards: The Cultural Politics of Gender Ambiguity, New York, Routledge.

Vigée Lebrun, Elizabeth (1989), Memoirs of Madame Vigée Lebrun, New York, George Braziller.

Walcott, Derek (1990), Omeros, New York, Noonday Press.

Warhol, Andy (1989), The Andy Warhol Diaries, ed. Pat Hackett, New York, Warner.

Warner, Marina (1983), Alone of All Her Sex: The Myth and Cult of the Virgin Mary, New York, Vintage.

———— (1985), Monuments and Maidens: The Allegory of the Female Form, New York, Atheneum.

Whitney (1993), The Whitney Biennial Exhibition Catalogue, New York, Whitney Museum of American Art.

Wilson, Kathleen (1993), 'Empire of Virtue: The Imperial Project and Hanoverian Culture', in Lawrence Stone (ed.), An Imperial Nation at War, New York, Routledge.

———— (1995), The Sense of the People: Politics, Culture, and Imperialism in England, 1715–85, New York, Cambridge University Press.

Wright, Beryl and Hartman, Saidiyn V. (1992), Lorna Simpson: For the Sake of the Viewer, New York, Universe.

INDEX